A CORNER OF THE TAP-ROOM OF THE WADSWORTH INN,
HARTFORD

LITTLE PILGRIMAGES
Among Old New England Inns

BEING AN ACCOUNT OF LITTLE JOURNEYS TO VARIOUS QUAINT INNS AND HOSTELRIES OF COLONIAL NEW ENGLAND

BY

Mary Caroline Crawford

Author of "The Romance of Old New England Rooftrees," "The College Girl of America," etc.

ILLUSTRATED

BOSTON

MDCCCCVII

HERITAGE BOOKS
2013

HERITAGE BOOKS
AN IMPRINT OF HERITAGE BOOKS, INC.

Books, CDs, and more—Worldwide

For our listing of thousands of titles see our website
at
www.HeritageBooks.com

A Facsimile Reprint
Published 2013 by
HERITAGE BOOKS, INC.
Publishing Division
100 Railroad Ave. #104
Westminster, Maryland 21157

Originally published 1907

— Publisher's Notice —

In reprints such as this, it is often not possible to remove blemishes from the original. We feel the contents of this book warrant its reissue despite these blemishes and hope you will agree and read it with pleasure.

We regret the absence of the illustration of Conkey's Tavern, which appeared opposite page 43 in the original edition.

International Standard Book Numbers
Paperbound: 978-0-7884-0873-1
Clothbound: 978-0-7884-6970-1

"I'LL view the manners of the town,
   Peruse the traders, gaze upon the buildings
And then return, and sleep within mine inn."
                              COMEDY OF ERRORS.

"THERE is no private house in which people can enjoy themselves so well as at a capital tavern. . . . At a tavern there is general freedom from anxiety; you are sure you are welcome . . . and the more trouble you give, the more good things you call for, the welcomer you are. . . . No, sir, there is nothing which has yet been contrived by man by which so much happiness is produced as by a good tavern or inn."
                              DR. JOHNSON.

"THE gods who are most interested in the human race preside over the tavern. . . . The tavern will compare favorably with the church. The church is the place where prayers and sermons are delivered, but the tavern is where they are to take effect, and if the former are good the latter cannot be bad."
                              THOREAU.

"WHOE'ER has travell'd life's dull round
   Where'er his stages may have been,
May sigh to think he still has found
   The warmest welcome at an inn."
                              SHENSTONE.
                    Written on a Window of an Inn.

FOREWORD

A BOOK on Old New England Inns needs no elaborate justification. Few of us are so dull of soul that our pulses are not quickened and our imaginations stirred as we pass, at a country four-corners, a deserted house and rambling barn of unmistakable tavern descent. There it stands, in its sombre and often disreputable coat of weather-stained shingles, mournful reminder of a fragrant time that is now no more, mute witness to the truth of the familiar plaint that bygone days were — what these are not. Always one is eager to know the story of such a house and to repeople its empty rooms, in fancy at least, with those who once made merry there. Because I have so often shared that wish I am happy to offer here some slight additions to available truth and tradition concerning these relics of the past, acknowledging, as I do so, deep indebtedness to Mrs. Alice Morse Earle's " Stage Coach and Tavern Days " and to Mr. Edward Field's suggestive book

Foreword

on "The Colonial Tavern." Town histories too numerous to name, Miss Elizabeth Ward's "Old Times in Shrewsbury," Rev. T. Frank Waters's Ipswich volume, Currier's "Ould Newbury," the valuable files of the *New England Magazine* and the carefully compiled works of the late Samuel Adams Drake have also been frequently consulted.

But especially do I feel very deep and real gratitude to the many friends all over New England who have contributed, by their interest and kindliness, to the material for this book; and, in particular, I wish to thank the Rhode Island Historical Society, through whose courtesy half a dozen of the plates published in Field's "Rhode Island at the End of the Century" are here reproduced.

M. C. C.

CHARLESTOWN, MASS., *August*, 1907.

CONTENTS

CHAPTER		PAGE
I.	When the Inn Was a Puritan Ordinary	1
II.	Madam Knight: Traveller and Tavern-keeper	21
III.	The Father of the Turnpike and Some Related Taverns	36
IV.	Gubernatorial and Other Tavern Junkets	54
V.	The Inns of Old Boston	73
VI.	Some Revolutionary Taverns	104
VII.	Some Rhode Island Taverns in Which History Was Made	121
VIII.	The Taverns That Entertained Washington	148
IX.	The Wayside Inn	191
X.	Entertainment for Man and Beast	208
XI.	Tavern Signs — and Wonders	228
XII.	Old Tavern Days in Newbury	241
XIII.	The Inns of Ipswich	274
XIV.	Some Portsmouth Publicans and Their Famous Guests	292
XV.	On the Road	311
XVI.	Some Taverns of Romance	334
XVII.	When Lafayette Came Back	351

LIST OF ILLUSTRATIONS

	PAGE
A Corner of the Tap-room of the Wadsworth Inn, Hartford . . .	*Frontispiece*
Roger Mowry Tavern, Providence . . .	6
Old Ordinary at Duxbury	11
Kimball Tavern, Bradford	24
Bull Dog Tavern, Providence	28
Pease Tavern, Shrewsbury	37
Conkey's Tavern, Pelham	43
Upton Tavern, Fitchburg	45
Boltwood's Tavern (afterwards the Amherst House), Amherst	53
Dwight House, Brookfield. — Frary House, Deerfield	62
Liberty Tree Tavern, Boston	84
The Green Dragon, Boston	96
Hancock Tavern, Boston	102
Golden Ball Tavern, Weston	104
Wright Tavern, Concord. — Cooper's Tavern, Arlington	112
Arnold's Tavern, Weymouth. — Sawtell's Tavern, Shirley	114
Knapp Tavern, Greenwich. — Interior of Knapp Tavern (now Putnam Cottage)	120
Sabin Tavern, Providence	122
David Arnold Tavern, Warwick. — Peleg Arnold Tavern, near Woonsocket .	139

List of Illustrations

	PAGE
Eleazer Arnold Tavern, near Quinsnicket, Lincoln. — Greenville Tavern, Smithfield	142
Ye Olde Tavern, West Brookfield	158
Williams Tavern, Marlborough	160
Abbott Tavern, Andover	182
Wayside Inn, Sudbury	192
Tap-room, Wayside Inn, Sudbury	197
Winn House, Woburn. — Paxton Inn, Paxton	209
Ellery Tavern, Gloucester. — Brigham's Tavern (now the Westborough Hotel), Westborough	224
Sign of the Hancock Tavern, Boston	229
Sign of the Benjamin Wiggin Tavern, Hopkinton. — Sign of the Wolfe Tavern, Newburyport	236
Sign of Boltwood's Tavern, Amherst	239
Coffin House, Newbury	243
Wolfe Tavern, Newburyport	252
Notice of Prince Stetson Regarding His Taking Charge of the Wolfe Tavern	259
Home of Mrs. Harriett Prescott Spofford, Newburyport. — Boynton Tavern, on the Newburyport Road	272
Whipple House, Ipswich. — Caleb Lord House, Ipswich	285
Ross Tavern, Ipswich	291
The Earl of Halifax (Stavers Inn), Portsmouth	296
Rice Tavern, Kittery, opposite Portsmouth	300
Purcell House, Portsmouth	306
Old Concord Coach. — Wadsworth Inn, Hartford	312
Groton Inn, Groton	328
Eagle Tavern, East Poultney	331

List of Illustrations

	PAGE
FOWLER TAVERN, WESTFIELD	334
BERRY TAVERN, DANVERS	342
GOLDEN BALL TAVERN, PROVIDENCE	355
WIGGIN TAVERN, HOPKINTON	366
JAMESON TAVERN, FREEPORT	368
SHEPARD INN, BATH	370

Little Pilgrimages Among Old New England Inns

CHAPTER I

WHEN THE INN WAS A PURITAN ORDINARY

"In the brave days of old," as writers of historical novels are fond of calling our colonial period, every department of public life was bound up with the church. To this rule the "ordinary" or inn of the time presented no exception. Odd as it seems to us public houses were licensed for the express purpose of promoting the worship of God! Usually the ordinary was right next door to the meeting-house; often such proximity was indeed the single condition upon which permits to sell "beare" were granted. Thus we find the records of 1651 granting John Vyall of Boston "Libertie to keep a house of Common entertainment if the Countie Court Con-

Among Old New England Inns

sent, *provided he keepe it near the new meeting house."* The contrast to the present laws which prohibit the sale of liquor within a certain distance of any church is striking.

Yet there was just as good a reason that the ordinary of the seventeenth century should be near the place of public worship as that the "hotel" of the twentieth century should be well removed therefrom. Physical as well as mental discomfort attended the church-going of that far-off time. A fire was never kindled in the colonial meeting-house and it was almost necessary to continued existence that the good people who had come from miles away to worship the Lord should find a cheerful place in which to thaw out between the cold drive and the chilly service. Naturally the ordinary came in for a reciprocal benefit during the noon rest for refreshment. It then had opportunity to sell many a mug of the potent flip, invaluable for raising spirits which had been depressed by dreary discourses on Hell. Occasionally, indeed, pious folk were made so comfortable in the tap-room at noon that they were incapacitated for attendance at the afternoon service, thus bringing scandal upon the inn-keeper concerned.

When the Inn Was a Puritan Ordinary

So close was the relationship between the tavern and the church in Puritan days that religious services were not infrequently held in an inn pending the erection of a suitable meeting-house. Such was the case in Fitchburg, Massachusetts, and in Providence, Rhode Island, where Roger Williams preached for many years.

No tavern with which we shall have to do is richer in traditions than this first hostelry ever established in the Providence settlement. Before its destruction about eight years ago, it was not only the oldest house in that city but it was long distinguished, among other things, as being the only one in the north end of the town that escaped when Providence was burned during King Philip's War. Goodman Mowry, who came to Rhode Island from Salem, was licensed in May 1655 to keep a house of entertainment, and was directed to " sett out a convenient signe at ye most perspicuous place of ye saide house thereby to give notice to strangers that it is a house of entertainment." From this time on Mowry's house was a prominent feature of the town's life. In many ways its uses were typical of hundreds of other ordinaries. Here the people of the settlement assembled

Among Old New England Inns

and discussed the news; here the town council held its meetings, and here was enacted several thrilling scenes of one of those terrible tragedies which now and then darken the pages of early New England history.

Among the young men helped by the noble Roger Williams during his life in Providence was a young Dutch lad named John Clauson, whom he had one day come across in a half-naked and starving condition and taken to his own home for food and shelter. No friends or family turning up to claim the youth, Williams brought him up in his own household, whence, having grown to man's estate, he went forth to serve his townsmen as a carpenter. Ere long he had so prospered that he acquired a tract of land and built himself a good house.

Then, one winter morning in 1660 Clauson was found in a dying condition near a clump of barberry bushes which grew at the roadside a stone's throw from Mowry's tavern. His head had been cut as with a broadaxe, and though he was tenderly cared for at Williams' home near-by, to which he was immediately carried, he soon died, in the presence of a little group of friends, including Williams. But he did not pass away,

When the Inn Was a Puritan Ordinary

difficult as it was for him to speak, without first accusing a neighbour, John Hernton, of being the instigator of his murder and calling down upon this man, his children and his children's children the curse of being "marked with split chins and haunted by barberry bushes."

The horror of the scene can be imagined when it is added that, among the first to reach the side of the wounded youth after he had been carried to the home of his childhood, were the father and mother of the very man he now accused of his death. They had been administering "sack and sugar whilst he lay wounded" says the record!

Great excitement prevailed about the town when the news of Clauson's curse got abroad but, before long, the deed was fastened upon one Waumanitt, an Indian, and he was apprehended and taken to Mowry's tavern where he was locked up and securely guarded. In spite of the accusation of the dying man, John Hernton was not condemned by his townspeople, though the tradition that he inspired the deed probably died hard.

The records are chiefly concerned with the expenses attending the trial of the Indian.

Among Old New England Inns

As Clauson had no kindred, the town treasurer was directed to pay the charges for the prosecution from the sale of the property of the dead Dutchman. We find a bill rendered by Henry Fowler, the town blacksmith, " for irons " to bind the murderer. (This was the first murder in the settlement and none of the paraphernalia of punishment was at hand.) A guard of nine men, including " the man at Moories," charged three shillings a night to watch the prisoner; and Stephen Northup, the town constable, was paid three shillings for " warning the town about the prisoner." Landlord Mowry rendered a bill of four shillings " for houseroom for the prisoner," and at the preliminary hearing Roger Williams and Valentine Whitman, who could speak the Indian tongue, earned twelve shillings as interpreters.

A Puritan ordinary, which was sometimes used as a church, was held, however, to be no proper place in which to confine a redskin murderer, and it was accordingly determined " that the prisoner Waumanitt shall be sent down unto Newport to the Collony prison There to be kept until his tyme of Triall." So, in a boat with two of the townsmen, who had been provided, — still at the dead man's

ROGER MOWRY TAVERN, PROVIDENCE

When the Inn Was a Puritan Ordinary

expense, — with " 1 pint of liquor, and powder and shott to carry along with ye prisoner" the slayer of Clauson passes from further connection with the tavern.

Not only was a tavern sometimes used as a meeting-house, as was the case with Mowry's, but a meeting-house was occasionally turned into a tavern. So it happened at Little Compton, Rhode Island, where, to put an end to the struggle between opposing factions, the place which had served for the worship of God became a house of entertainment for travellers. Our ancestors had no reverence for a meeting-house save as such, and the interchangeable character of these two public institutions, the church and the tavern, gave them no shock. The Great House at Charlestown, Massachusetts, which was the official residence of Governor Winthrop, was in 1663 made a meeting-house, and later became quite easily the Three Cranes, a public house kept for many years by Robert Leary and his descendants. It is interesting to note that under the very roof which afterwards sheltered a tavern tap-room Governor Winthrop thought out the first of all New England temperance pledges, recorded in his diary as follows: " The

Among Old New England Inns

Governor, upon consideration of the inconveniences which have grown in England by drinking one to another, restrained it at his own table and wished others to do the like."

Yet Puritan New England saw very little drunkenness. Landlords were forbidden by the court in 1645 " to suffer anyone to be drunk or drink excessively, or continue tippling above the space of half an hour in any of their said houses under penalty of 5s for every such offence suffered; and every person found drunk in the said houses or elsewhere shall forfeit 10s; and for every excessive drinking he shall forfeit 3s. 4d; for sitting idle and continuing drinking above half an hour, 2s 6d; and it is declared to be excessive drinking of wine when above half a pint of wine is allowed at one time to one person to drink: provided that it shall be lawful for any strangers, or lodgers, or any person or persons, in an orderly way to continue in such houses of common entertainment during meal times or upon lawful business, what time their occasions shall require."

The tithing-man saw to it that " strangers " obeyed the law, too. John Josselyn, an English visitor to Boston in 1663, bears witness

When the Inn Was a Puritan Ordinary

to this fact as follows: " At houses of entertainment into which a stranger went, he was presently followed by one appointed to that office, who would thrust himself into the company uninvited, and if he called for more drink than the officer thought in his judgment he could soberly bear away he would presently countermand it and appoint the proportion beyond which he could not get one drop."

Governor Winthrop, a few years before, had described thus the relation of one Boston constable to a lodger in a Boston ordinary: " There fell out a troublesome business . . . An English sailor happened to be drunk and was carried to his lodging; and the Constable (a Godly man and much zealous against such disorders) hearing of it found him out, being upon his bed asleep; so he awaked him and led him to the stocks, no magistrate being at home. He being left in the stocks, some one of La Tour's French gentlemen visitors in Boston lifted up the stocks and let him out. The Constable, hearing of it, went to the Frenchman (being then gone and quiet) and would needs carry him to the stocks. The Frenchman offered to yield himself to go to prison but the Constable, not understanding his language, pressed him to go to the stocks. The Frenchman resisted and drew his sword. With that company came in and disarmed him, and carried him by force to the stocks; but soon after the Constable took him out and carried him to prison."

When the stocks were not found effective to cure drunkenness, a Scarlet Letter method was employed. Thus we find Robert Coles condemned in 1634 " for drunkenness by him committed at Rocksbury shalbe disfranchizd, Weare about his neck and so to hang upon his outwd garment a D. made of redd cloth & sett upon white: to continyu this for a yeare, & not to have it off any time hee comes among company; . . . also *hee is to wear the D outwards."*

Besides being closely associated with the church, the Puritan ordinary was often the place where the court convened. At such times the public house became the resort of large numbers of people, and the heart of the tavern-keeper rejoiced within him. In what is now York county in Maine, the courts were usually held at the tavern of Samuel Austin, the jurors being allowed " two meals a day at the expense of the county

OLD ORDINARY AT DUXBURY

When the Inn Was a Puritan Ordinary

during the time of their attendance upon the trial." One of the important functionaries at these tavern-trials was the court drummer, who drew two shillings a day for beating a tattoo to attract the populace to the seat of justice. It was before this court at Austin's Tavern in Wells that several good citizens and their wives were brought, in the middle of the seventeenth century, for saying "the Divil a bit;" and it was by order of a decree here made that George Gaylord was in 1661 subjected to thirty-nine lashes "for visiting the widow Hitchcock." Wherein this was considered a crime the records fail to state.

Duxbury had several interesting old ordinaries. In 1660 Mr. Collier, who was eminently distinguished in the public affairs of the colony, was licensed to sell the beverage to his neighbours in Duxbury, and this not at all for gain, but because the magistrates knew him to be a sober and discreet man and one who would not be likely to suffer any transgression of their laws. Constant Southworth, one of the Deputies, was similarly distinguished in 1648. In 1678 Mr. Seabury was permitted "to sell liquors unto such sober minded naighbors, as hee shall thinke meet, soe as hee sell not lesse then the quantie of a gallon att a time to one p^rson, and not in smaller quantities by retaile to the occationing of drunkenes."

The ordinaries of the seventeenth century were far from luxurious in their furnishings as may be seen from almost any of the inventories made up when they changed proprietors. In 1674 John Whipple of Providence, who had come to that town from Dorchester, was granted a license to "keepe a house of Intertainment" and for years thereafter this was a famous place of resort. Yet when Whipple died in 1685 the inventory made it plain that his inn consisted of but two rooms, "ye lower room" and "ye chamber." In the "lower room" there was "an old bedstead and a bed cord," "a cubbard press," "3 old curtains and a valian (valance)," "an old Rotten feather bed about 12 pounds of old feathers in it," "a joynt work chest, 1 joyner worke chair" and "3 other chairs." In the chamber there were "two feather beds and bolster (one old)," "a whitish cotton rug an old torne sheet a part of a bed stud and bed cord," "1 pillow and pillow case," a "Red Coverlidd a bed blanket, much worne, three sheets," "three broken joynt stools and a Court Cubbard."

When the Inn Was a Puritan Ordinary

Scarcely the outfit of the St. Regis this! But the early ordinaries, in the country at least, were not intended for guests who would pass the night. Their chief function was to circulate the festive flip up to nine o'clock in the evening and to thaw out pious pilgrims before and after meeting on Sundays. Ordinaries in the large towns were a different matter. When Hugh Gunnison, proprietor of the King's Arms in Dock Square, Boston, sold out his house with its furniture and appurtenances in 1651 he realized £600, a right goodly sum for those days. The list of his household goods is of particular interest, not only for itself, but also because it shows that the custom of naming rooms obtained in the New England inn of the seventeenth century as it had in the old England inn of the sixteenth.

" In the chamber called the Exchange one halfe bedstead with blew pillows, one livery Cupboard coloured blue, one long table, benches, two formes and one carved chaire.

" In the Kitchen three formes dressers shelves.

" In the Larder one square Table banisters drssers & shelves round.

" In the Hall, three Small Roomes with

tables and benches in them one table about six foote long in the Hall and one bench.

"In the low parlor one bedstead one table and benches two formes, one small frame of a form and shelves, one Closet with shelves.

"In the room Vnder the closet one child's bedstead.

"In the Chamber called London, one bedsted two benches.

"In the Chamber over London one bedsted, one crosse table one forme one bench.

"In the Closet next the Exchange, shelves.

"In the barr by the hall, three shelves, the frame of a low stoole.

"In the upper p'lor one bedsted two chairs one table one forme bench and shelves.

"In the Nursey one crosse Table with shelvs.

"In the Court chamber one Long table, three formes one livery cupbord & benches.

"In the closet within the Court chamber one bedsted and shelvs.

"In the Starr chamber one long table, one bedsted, one livery Cupbord one chair three formes with benches.

"In the Garret over the Court chamber one bedsted one table two formes.

When the Inn Was a Puritan Ordinary

"In the garret over the closet in the Court chamber one bedsted one smale forme.

"In the foure garrett chambers over the Starr Chamber three bedsteds foure tables with benches.

"In the brewhouse one Cop, twoe fatts, one under back, one upper back, one kneading trough one dresser one brake.

"In the stable one Racke & manger.

"In the yarde one pumpe, pipes to convey the water to the brew house, fyve hogg styes, one house of office.

"The signe of the Kinges Armes and signe posts."

Except for a sign, — which all ordinaries were required by law to have, and taproom-fixtures, — which even the poorest of them did not lack, — this house of Gunnison's was very unusually equipped. It contained no less than thirteen "bedsteds!"

By 1675 ordinaries had so multiplied that Cotton Mather complained that every other house in Boston was an ale-house. And in 1696 Nathaniel Saltonstall of Haverhill, Massachusetts, protested thus to the Salem Court against the increase of ordinaries and ale-houses in the colonies: "Much Hon'd Gentlemen: I allways thought it great prudence and Christianity in our former leaders and rulers, by their laws to state the number of publique houses in towns and for regulation of such houses, as were of necessity thereby to prevent all sorts, almost, of wickednesses which daily grow in upon us like a flood. But alas! I see not but that now the case is over, and such (as to some places I may term them) pest-houses and places of enticement (tho not so intended by the Justices) the sins are multiplied. It is multiplied, too, openly that the cause of it may be, the price of retailers' fee etc. I pray, what need of six retailers in Salisbury, and of more than one in Haverhill, and some other towns, where the people, when taxes and rates for the country and ministers are collecting, with open mouths complain of povertie and being hardly dealt with, and yet I am fully informed can spend much time and spend their estates at such blind holes, as are clandestinely and unjustly petitioned for; and more threaten to get licenses, chiefly by repairing to a remote court, where they are not known or suspected, but pass for current, and thereby the towns are abused, and the youth get evil habits; and men sent out on country service at such places waste

When the Inn Was a Puritan Ordinary

much of their time, yet expect pay for it, in most pernicious loytering and what, and sometimes in foolish and not pot-valient firing and shooting off guns, not for the destruction of enemies, but to the wonderful disturbance and affrightment of the inhabitants, which is not the service a scout is allowed and maintained for. . . .

"I am now God's prisoner," the letter concludes, "and cant come abroad, and have waited long to speak of those and others but as yet cant meet with an opportunity. You have nothing here of personal animosity of mine against any man but zeal and faithfulness to my country and town, and to the young and rising generation that they be not too much at liberty to live and do as they list. Accept of the good intentions of, gentlemen, your humble servant, — N. Saltonstall."

Yet Cotton Mather and Nathaniel Saltonstall to the contrary notwithstanding there was almost no rioting in the Puritan ordinary. Had such been the case we should certainly find mention of it in Sewall's Diary, — and that incomparable picture of colonial Boston contains not more than half a dozen entries in all concerning tavern disorders. The longest is on the Queen's birthday in 1714: — "My neighbor Colson knocks at my door about nine P. M. or past to tell of disorders at the ordinary at the South End kept by Mr. Wallace. He desired me that I would accompany Mr. Bromfield and Constable Howard hither. It was 35 minutes past nine before Mr. Bromfield came, then we went, took Aeneas Salter with us. Found much company. They refused to go away. Said was there to drink the Queen's health and had many other healths to drink. Called for more drink and drank to me. I took notice of the affront, to them. Said they must and would stay upon that solemn occasion. Mr. Netmaker drank the Queen's health to me. I told him I drank none; on that he ceased. Mr. Brinley put on his hat to affront me. I made him take it off. I threatened to send some of them to prison. They said they could but pay their fine and doing that might stay. I told them if they had not a care they would be guilty of a riot. Mr. Bromfield spake of raising a number of men to quell them, and was in some heat ready to run into the street. But I did not like that. Not having pen and ink I went to take their names with my pencil and not knowing how to spell their names

When the Inn Was a Puritan Ordinary

they themselves of their own accord writ them. At last I addressed myself to Mr. Banister. I told him he had been longest an inhabitant and freeholder and I expected he would set a good example by departing thence. Upon this he invited them to his own house, and away they went. And we went after them away. I went directly home and found it 25 minutes past ten at night when I entered my own house."

The Judge of the Witches, as might have been expected, had little love for taverns. Sometimes, to be sure, he made pleasuring trips with his wife to the Greyhound Tavern in Roxbury, — a public house which had almost the odour of sanctity, situated as it was between the home of the saintly Eliot and that of the prayerful Danforth, — there to make a gala dinner upon boiled pork and roast fowls before riding home in the "brave moonshine." But his general attitude towards taverns and their proprietors was one of hostility as can be seen from an entry made in his diary September 20, 1771, when he wrote, "Thomas Hale was made a justice. I opposed it because there are five in Newbury already, *and he had lately kept an ordinary and sold rum."* The selling of liquor

Among Old New England Inns

was not at all to Judge Sewall's taste. Readers who have followed the story of this magistrate's many courtships in an earlier book of mine [1] will recall, however, that he had not the slightest objection to partaking of "Canary" once it had been sold.

[1] "The Romance of Old New England Churches."

CHAPTER II

MADAM KNIGHT: TRAVELLER AND TAVERN-KEEPER

EVERY one who has explored at all the annals of early New England has met with the name and the fame of Sarah Knight. The arduous journey from Boston to New York which this intrepid woman made in 1704 and an account of which she at that time committed to paper is far too remarkable not to have become a classic allusion among writers who treat colonial subjects. Yet one has to search far and long before one can find the diary as originally printed; and few who read therein Madam Knight's diatribes against many of the public houses at which she stopped during her journey realize that the lady herself became a tavern-keeper towards the end of her life.

It was of course a very unusual experience which this Boston-born woman invited when she set out on horseback, and with no proper escort, to make her journey to distant New York two long centuries ago. Some idea of the remoteness of that time is gained from remembering that Peregrine White, the first child born after the landing of the Pilgrims at Plymouth, had just died, that it was five years before the birth of Dr. Johnson, one year before the birth of Benjamin Franklin and twenty-seven years before the great Washington came as a little child among us.

Madam Knight's father and mother were among the first settlers of Charlestown and are both buried in the Copp's Hill cemetery, Boston. For many years they lived on North square, in a house which was later the residence of Samuel Mather. It was on the doorstep of this house that Captain Kemble saluted his wife, one Sabbath day, after returning from a three years' absence, thus calling down upon his head the penalty of two hours in the stocks "for lewd and unseemly conduct!" This was in 1673 when the daughter who was to make his name remembered was a child of seven.

The year of Sarah Kemble's marriage to Richard Knight cannot be determined, nor is there any data to show what manner of

Madam Knight

man he was. At the time of the famous journey he must have been either dead or abroad, however, for no husband properly protective would have allowed his wife to undertake so hazardous a trip merely for the sake of settling an estate.

To be sure the lady was not absolutely alone. The government post man gave her the benefit of his manly protection a part of the time and when he was not available she hired another guide. But the entertainment afforded at the ordinaries along the way was often of the rudest and the roads for the most part were exceedingly rough and wild.

The Vade Mecum for America, issued in 1732, gives the names of all the taverns on the road to New York going by way of New London and as this was almost exactly the route Madam Knight followed we may believe that she spent her first night, after leaving Boston, at the Dedham ordinary, afterwards kept by Nathaniel Ames, the celebrated almanack maker. The first license for this tavern is dated 1658.

The flavour of those far-away days may best be caught, if we follow Madam Knight's own crisp account of what she heard and saw during her trip. The journal's first date is

Among Old New England Inns

Monday, October 2, 1704: "About three o'clock afternoon, I began my Journey from Boston to New Haven; being about two Hundred Mile. My Kinsman, Capt. Robert Luist waited on me as farr as Dedham, where I was to meet ye Western post. I vissitted the Reverd. Mr. Belcher, Ye Minister of ye town, and tarried there till evening, in hopes ye post would come along. But he not coming, I resolved to go to Billingses where he used to lodg, being 12 miles further. But being ignorant of the way, Madm Belcher, seeing no persuasions of her good spouses or hers could prevail with me to Lodg there that night, Very kindly went wyth me to ye Tavern, where I hoped to get my guide, And desired the Hostess to inquire of her guests whether any of them would go with mee. But they being tyed by the Lipps to a pewter engine, scarcely allowed themselves time to say what clownish . . . [Here half a page of the MS. is gone] . . . Pieces of eight, I told her no, I would not be accessary to such extortion.

"Then John shan't go, sais shee. No, indeed shan't hee; And held forth at that rate a long time, that I began to fear I was got among the Quaking tribe, beleeving not

KIMBALL TAVERN, BRADFORD

Madam Knight

a Limbertong'd sister among them could out do Madm Hostes.

"Upon this, to my no small surprise, son John arrose, and gravely demanded what I would give him to go with me? Give you, sais I, are you John? Yes, says he, for want of a Better; And behold this John look't as old as my Host, and perhaps had bin a man in the last Century. Well, Mr. John, sais I, make your demands. Why, half a pass of eight and a dram, sais John. I agreed, and gave him a Dram (now) in hand to bind the bargain.

"My hostess catechis'd John for going so cheep, saying his poor wife would break her heart . . . [Here another half page of the MS. is gone] . . . His shade on his Hors resembled a Globe on a Gate post. Hiss habitt, Hors, and furniture, its looks and goings Incomparably answered the rest.

"Thus jogging on with an easy pace, my Guide telling mee it was dangero's to Ride hard in the Night (wh his horse had the sence to avoid) Hee entertained me with the Adventures he had passed by late Rideing, and eminent Dangers he had escaped, so that remembring the Hero's in Parismus and the Knight of the Oracle, I didn't know but I had mett with a Prince disguis'd.

"When we had Ridd about an how'r, wee come into a thick swamp, wch, by Reason of a great fogg, very much startled mee, it being now very Dark. But nothing dismay'd John: Hee had encountered a thousand and a thousand such Swamps, having a Universal Knowledge in the woods; and readily Answered all my inquiries wch were not a few.

"In about an how'r, or something more, after we left the Swamp, we come to Billingses, where I was to Lodg. My guide dismounted and very Complaisantly help't me down and shewd the door, signing me wth his hand to Go in; wch I Gladly did — But had not gone many steps into the Room, ere I was Interrogated by a young Lady I understood afterwards was the Eldest daughter of the family with these or words to this purpose, (viz) Law for mee — what in the world brings You here at this time a night? I never see a woman on the Rode so Dreadfull late in all the days of my versall life. Who are You? Where are you going? I'me scar'd out of my witts — with much more of the same Kind. I stood aghast, Prepareing

Madam Knight

to reply, when in comes my Guide — to him Madam turned, Roreing out: Lawfull heart, John, is it You? — how de do! Where in the world are you going with this woman? Who is she? John made no Ansr. but sat down in the corner, fumbled out his black Junk, and saluted that instead of Debb; she then turned agen to mee and fell anew into her silly questions, without asking me to sitt down.

"I told her she treated me very Rudely, and I did not think it my duty to answer her unmannerly Questions. But to get ridd of them, I told her I come there to have the post's company with me to-morrow on my Journey &c. Miss star'd awhile, drew a chair, bid me sitt, And then run up stairs and putts on two or three Rings (or else I had not seen them before) and returning, sett herself just before me, showing the way to Reding, that I might see her ornaments . . . I paid honest John wth money and dram according to contract and Dismist him, and pray'd Miss to shew me where I must Lodg. Shee conducted me to a parlour in a little back Lento wch was almost fill'd with the bedstead wch was so high that I was forced to climb on a chair to gitt up to ye wretched bed that lay on it; . . ."

Among Old New England Inns

Varied and exciting as had been Madam Knight's first day it was luxurious travelling compared with that of the day which followed. At her next stopping-place she was served " cabage of so deep a purple " that she concluded the cook must have " boild it in her dye-kettle! ". But " having here discharged the Ordnary for self and Guide (as I understood was the custom) About Three afternoon went on with my Third Guide, who Rode very hard; and having crossed Providence Ferry, we come to a River wch they Generally Ride thro'. But I dare not venture; so the Post got a Ladd and cannoo to carry me to tother side and hee ridd thro' and Led my hors."

The lady's sensations in the canoe are amusingly described. "It was very small and shallow, so that when we were in she seem'd redy to take in water which greatly terrified mee, and caused me to be very circumspect, sitting with my hands fast on each side, my eyes stedy, not daring so much as to lodg my tongue a hair's breadth more on one side of my mouth than tother, nor so much as think on Lott's wife, for a wry thought would have oversett our wherey: But was soon put out of this pain, by feeling the Cannoo on

BULL DOG TAVERN, PROVIDENCE

Madam Knight

shore, wch I as soon almost saluted with my feet; and Rewarding my sculler, again mounted and made the best of our way forwards." A little further on in that same day's journey Madam Knight actually did ford a river, however, knowing that she must either "Venture the fate of drowning, or be left like ye Children in the wood. So, as the Post bid me, I gave Reins to my Nagg; and sitting as steady as just before in the Cannoo, in a few minutes got safe to the other side." The end of this day's travel was marked "by the Post's sounding his horn, which assured mee hee was arrived at the Stage, where we were to Lodg: and that musick was then most musickall and agreeable to mee."

This tavern was Haven's in what is now North Kingston, Rhode Island, "a clean comfortable house," where Madam Knight was promptly served with "Chocolett made with milk in a little clean brass Kettle." The bed "was pretty hard Yet neet and handsome" and, had it not been for a topers' dispute in the adjoining kitchen, our lady traveller would have felt herself quite fortunate for the nonce in her fare. The next day, however, she was forced to ride twenty-two miles before coming to any tavern. And then the proprietor brusquely refused to give shelter! The name of this surly taverner was Davol spelled Devil in the old records. And Madam Knight, as we might have known, did not neglect the opportunity thus offered her to make sharp puns on this bad landlord's name. In New London she was the guest of Rev. Gurdon Saltonstall, minister of the place, and through his good offices, a young gentleman, Mr. Joshua Wheeler, was persuaded to guide her as far as New Haven. Here the doughty dame informed herself of the manners and customs of the place and at the same time worked right diligently at the affair she had come upon. Some of her descriptions of Connecticut life in that day are very interesting:

"On training dayes the Youth divert themselves by Shooting at the Target, as they call it, . . . where he that hits neerest the white has some yards of Red Ribbon presented him, wch being tied to his hattband, the two ends streeming down his back, he is Led away in Triumph, wth great applause, as the winners of the Olympiack Games . . ." Madam Knight's study of the Connecticut Indians is also diverting.

Madam Knight

After two months stay in New Haven our traveller resolved to push on to New York. " Being by this time well Recruited and rested after my Journy, and my business lying unfinished by some concerns at New York depending thereupon, I resolved to go there with my kinsman, Mr. Thomas Trowbridge of New Haven and a man of the town who I engaged to wait on me there." At Rye the little party lodged " in an ordinary wch a French family kept. Here being very hungry, I desired a fricasee wch the Frenchman undertakeing, mannaged so contrary to my notion of Cookery, that I hastned to Bed supperless." At this house Madam Knight did not even have a room to herself; after she had laid her down on the hard bed provided, she heard a rustling noise nearby and upon inquiry found that the maid was " making a bed for the men " on the floor not far from her own couch!

New York impressed Madam Knight as a less desirable place of residence than Boston, for she found that, — even two centuries ago, — its inhabitants " were not so strict in keeping the Sabbath." (At this time, too, it is worth noting, Boston had a population of ten thousand people as against New York's five thousand.) Madam Knight was herself a genial soul, though, and she describes with very evident appreciation the "Vendues" she attended and the "Riding in Sleys about three or four Miles out of Town where they have Houses of Entertainment at a place called the Bowery" in which she had a share.

Early in January she was again in New Haven and now, at length, she comes to "an accommodation and distribution" with those involved with her in the settlement of the estate. Accordingly in February she writes that "the man that waited on me to New York taking charge of me I set out for Boston. We went from New Haven upon the ice (the ferry not being passable thereby) . . . and went on without anything remarkabl till wee come to New London and I lodged again at Mr. Saltonstall's — and here I dismist my guide and my generos entertainer promised me Mr. Samuel Rogers of that place to go home with me. I stayed a day longer here than I intended by commands of the Honble Govenor Winthrop to stay and take supper with him whose wonderful civility I may not omitt. The next morning I Crossed ye Ferry to Groton, hav-

Madam Knight

ing had the Honor of the Company of Madam Livingston (who is the Govenors Daughter) . . . and divers others to the boat — And that night Lodgd at Stonington and had Rost Beef and pumpkin sause for supper. The next night at Haven's and had Rost Fowle!" Haven's appears to have been well named.

It was on March third that Madam Knight "got safe home to Boston," having been nearly a fortnight on the road. No wonder her "Kind relations and friends" flocked in to welcome her and hear the story of her "transactions and travails." She had been away five months in all and that in a day when men, much less women, scarcely ever travelled the 271 miles which the Vade Mecum gives as the post route to New York. Nothing but verse could adequately express her emotions so she wrote on the windowpane of her room:

> "Now I've returned to Sarah Knight's
> Thro' many toils and many frights
> Over great rocks and many stones
> God has presar'vd from fracter'd bones."

Hazardous and exhausting as had been this journey to New London it by no means

Among Old New England Inns

discouraged Sarah Knight, however. For when her only daughter Elizabeth married, some eight years later, the Colonel John Livingston "whose first wife was the Govenors Daughter" our traveller again made her way to the Connecticut town, where she successively speculated in Indian lands, managed a shop, cultivated a farm and, — last but not least, — kept a tavern. She bought her Norwich property in 1717 and the year following she was, with others, brought before Richard Bushnell, Justice of the Peace, for selling strong drink to the Indians. She tried to shift the blame of the liquor-selling upon her maid, Ann Clark, but refusing to acquit herself by swearing that Ann was solely to blame, she was sentenced to pay a fine of twenty shillings. All the while, however, Madam Knight was moving in good society in Norwich, and writing what was called poetry for the edification of her select circle of friends.

In 1722 she moved to the Livingston farm on the west side of the road from Norwich to New London and opened there a "place of entertainment for travellers" where she lived until her death September 25, 1727, in the sixty-second year of her age. She lies

Madam Knight

buried in the New London cemetery. The famous Diary was preserved in the family of Christopher Christophers of New London, whose wife, Sarah, inherited it, among other effects, from Madam Livingston, who was Sarah Knight's daughter. Later it passed, by inheritance, into the possession of Mrs. Ichabod Wetmore of Middletown, Connecticut, who allowed its publication in 1825 under the supervision of Theodore Dwight of New York. Reviewers generally regarded it, when first given to the world, as a clever forgery and it was classed in libraries as fiction. Now, however, it is highly prized as an authentic picture of early New England and its author is widely acclaimed one of the most interesting characters of her time.

CHAPTER III

THE FATHER OF THE TURNPIKE AND SOME RELATED TAVERNS

THE first post-road to New York, over which Madam Knight travelled in 1704, went by the way of Providence, Stonington, New London and the shore of Long Island Sound, a distance of two hundred and fifty-five miles. Just eighty years after that doughty dame's journey, Captain Levi Pease put on a regular stage between Boston and Hartford and the beginning of systematic communication between Boston and New York was established. Pease was a Connecticut man (born in Enfield in 1740) but after his marriage he removed to Massachusetts, and it is with a little Massachusetts town, Shrewsbury, near Worcester, that his fame is most intimately bound up. Shrewsbury, moreover, is particularly interesting to us because, at the time Pease started his stage route, there were no less than three noted

PEASE TAVERN, SHREWSBURY

The Father of the Turnpike

taverns in the place, — Farrar's, Baldwin's and Howe's.

Farrar's Tavern is now better known as the Pease Tavern for the reason that the "Father of the Turnpike" eventually came to be its landlord. But Major John Farrar, an army officer of considerable distinction, was in charge during the Revolution and during the visit made to the village in 1789 by General Washington while on his way to Boston. For all travellers to and from the New England capital the house was a popular resort, for it stood on the corner formed by the junction of the "great road" with the road to Westboro', about one mile from the Northboro' line, right in the current of travel. Very likely, therefore, it was at this tavern that John Adams overheard in 1774 the conversation which, tavern-hater though he was, so impressed him that he set it down with scarcely concealed pleasure: "Within the course of the year, before the meeting of Congress in 1774, on a journey to some of our circuit courts in Massachusetts, I stopped one night at a tavern in Shrewsbury about forty miles from Boston, and as I was cold and wet, I sat down at a good fire in the bar-

Among Old New England Inns

room to dry my greatcoat and saddlebags till a fire could be made in my chamber.

"There presently came in, one after another, half a dozen or half a score substantial yeomen of the neighborhood, who, sitting down to the fire, after lighting their pipes, began a lively conversation on politics. As I believed I was unknown to them all, I sat in total silence to hear them. One said: 'The people of Boston are distracted.' Another answered: 'No wonder the people of Boston are distracted. Oppression will make wise men mad.' A third said: 'What would you say if a fellow should come to your house and tell you he was going to make a list of your cattle, that Parliament might tax you for them at so much a head? And how should you feel if he was to go and break open your barn to take down your oxen, cows, horses and sheep?' 'What would I say?' replied the first, 'I would knock him in the head.' 'Well,' said a fourth, 'if Parliament can take away Mr. Hancock's wharf and Mr. Rowe's wharf, they can take away your barn and my house.'

"After much more reasoning in this style, a fifth, who had as yet been silent, broke out: 'Well, it's high time for us to rebel; we

The Father of the Turnpike

must rebel some time or other, and we had better rebel now than at any time to come. If we put if off for ten or twenty years, and let them go on as they have begun, they will get a strong party among us, and plague us a great deal more than they can now. As yet they have but a small party on their side.'"

With such talk as this stirring in Shrewsbury it is not to be wondered at that the town produced one of the most effective leaders of the Revolutionary War, General Artemas Ward. Ward was born in 1727 in the house afterwards known as the Baldwin Tavern, which his father had built two years before and which passed in 1755 into the possession of Henry Baldwin of Pelham, New Hampshire. Only a heap of stones now marks the site of Baldwin's tavern but it was in its day a fine house and a very noted resort. We cannot do better than linger for a little while over its traditions. One of these concerns a murder committed here on a certain night by a traveller who had taken a room with his ill-starred victim. In the morning the guilty party had fled but the hideous bloodstains on the bedstead testified that the dead man on the floor had met his end only after a terrible struggle.

Among Old New England Inns

One habitué of this tavern was old Grimes of Hubbardston, immortalized by Albert G. Green in a curious poem which praises more ingeniously than honestly a somewhat disreputable character. For Grimes was the kind of man who could, and did, ride his horse straight into the tap-room of the Baldwin Tavern in case he was too unsteady, — as not infrequently happened, — to dismount outside. The poem, however, with its curious division of theme, (the first two lines of each stanza refer, it will be noted, to the man's character and the last two to his clothing) is interesting enough to be quoted in full:

OLD GRIMES

Old Grimes is dead, that good old man,
   We ne'er shall see him more;
He used to wear a long blue coat
   All buttoned down before.

His heart was open as the day,
   His feelings all were true;
His hair was some inclined to gray
   He wore it in a queue.

Whene'er he heard the voice of pain,
   His heart with pity burned;
The large round head upon his cane
   From ivory was turned.

The Father of the Turnpike

Kind words he ever had for all,
  He knew no fell design;
His eyes were dark and rather small
  His nose was aquiline.

He lived at peace with all mankind,
  In friendship he was true;
His coat had pocket-holes behind,
  His pantaloons were blue.

Unharmed, the sin which earth pollutes
  He passed serenely o'er;
And never wore a pair of boots
  For thirty years or more.

But good old Grimes is now at rest
  Nor fears misfortune's frown;
He wore a double-breasted vest,
  The stripes ran up and down.

He modest merit sought to find
  And pay it its desert;
He had no malice in his mind
  No ruffles on his shirt.

His worldly goods he never threw
  In trust to Fortune's dances,
But lived (as all his brothers do)
  In easy circumstances.

His neighbours he did not abuse
  Was sociable and gay;
He wore large buckles on his shoes
  And changed them every day.

Among Old New England Inns

> His knowledge hid from public gaze,
>   He did not bring to view;
> Nor make a noise town-meeting days,
>   As many people do.
>
> Thus undisturbed by anxious cares,
>   His peaceful moments ran;
> And everybody said he was
>   A fine old gentleman.

If, however, you would have fact instead of poetry concerning old Grimes, see the History of Hubbardston. For he was no fictitious character; the ancient roof-tree on the Gardner road with which he is identified has burned down within the past six months.

After the Baldwins, father and son, had passed to their rewards, the tavern bearing their name came into the possession of Captain Aaron Smith, one of the Shrewsbury men who had fought at Bunker Hill and who afterwards followed Lafayette. When the Marquis came to Worcester in 1824 Aaron Smith, then in his eighty-ninth year, marched from his home to greet his old commander and present to him an elegant cane which he had carved from a grape-vine brought from the Jerseys. It is, however, with Captain Smith's share in the Shays Rebellion that the

The Father of the Turnpike

principal interest of his career lies for us. For it was in the court-yard of his tavern that the rebellious ones had their rendezvous and from that spot they hurled defiance at Judge Ward who then lived in the house directly opposite.

This insurrectionary movement was nurtured in Conkey's tavern, Pelham, by Captain Daniel Shays, an adventurous soul who lived within half a mile of that hostelry (built in 1758) and so found it very convenient to develop there a plan for resisting what seemed to him the tyranny of the judges. Shays saw, as did many another, that the people had been made very poor by the enormous expense attending the Revolutionary War. And as imprisonments multiplied for debts which there was small hope of ever being able to pay he conceived the notion of stopping all court action and so setting matters right. He had brooded too long, among his lonely Pelham hills, upon sufferings which only time and patience could remove; and these broodings, reinforced by a consciousness of power and inflamed by the drinks served before Landlord Conkey's blazing fire combined to make him a rebel of thoroughly dangerous type.

Among Old New England Inns

His following was confined very largely to Worcester county and among his men were many from Shrewsbury. Captain Aaron Smith rallied his old soldiers in response to Shays' command, and several others, who had fought in the Revolutionary War under General Ward, now took up arms against their old neighbour and commander, solely because he was the representative of the majesty of the law.

It took real courage to defy these desperate men when they presented themselves at the court-house steps and with drawn swords and fixed bayonets forbade Judge Ward to go about his business. Lincoln's History of Worcester credits the usually silent judge with a magnificent burst of eloquence as the bayonets of his former soldiers penetrated his clothing. He told them that "he did not value their bayonets; they might plunge them into his heart; but while that heart beat he would do his duty; when opposed to it his life was of little consequence; if they would take away their bayonets and give him some position where he could be heard by his fellow-citizens and not by the leaders alone who had deceived and deluded them, he would speak but not otherwise."

UPTON TAVERN, FITCHBURG

The Father of the Turnpike

Struck with admiration for their old commander's courage the bayonets were withdrawn and then, with great fervour and irresistible logic, Judge Ward proceeded to reason with the people, showing them that, though their grievances were not to be denied, they had taken an utterly wrong way to relieve them. His hearers were not a little impressed and they finally allowed Judge Ward to go in peace. Then, the Court having adjourned to a certain day in January, those under arms marched back to their headquarters in front of the Baldwin Tavern. Here, ere long, the militia found them out and dispersed them, sadder and wiser men, Shays having already left his followers to hide himself in obscurity.

Still another tavern, — in Fitchburg, Massachusetts, — is interestingly connected with the Shays Rebellion. This, the present home of Mrs. S. A. Fairbanks, was then known as the Upton Tavern and officers were in pursuit of rebels who fled there for protection. But the servants of the law did not find their men for they neglected to examine sufficiently the crooked little closet under the stairs in the front hall.

The Shays Rebellion crisis in Shrewsbury's

history was in 1787, — and Levi Pease's coach had for four years now been tooling through the village. It took great faith in the value of the enterprise to run empty wagons to Hartford and back as was done for some little time, but Pease had performed many hard things before and so knew how. During the Revolution he had often carried important messages at great peril of his life; it is related of him that on many a moonlight night he lay on his back and paddled his boat with his hands lest he be betrayed to some suspicious eyes. So he was just the man to start our first stage line. For money he turned to his friend Reuben Sykes, who had previously driven a stage with him from Somers to Hartford, — a distance of twenty miles, — and on October 20th, 1783, at six o'clock in the morning, Pease started from Boston, as did Sykes from Hartford, in " two convenient wagons " ! Each made the allotted trip in four days, the fare being ten dollars each way, and the transfer from Pease's coach to Sykes' being effected at Spencer, the highest point between Boston and Springfield. So successful did the enterprise soon grow to be that Pease became the owner of

The Father of the Turnpike

a Boston inn, on the spot where St. Paul's church now stands.

Still it was hard travelling in those earliest days if we may trust Josiah Quincy. " I set out from Boston," he says, " in the line of stages lately established by an enterprising Yankee, Pease by name, which in that day was considered a method of transportation of wonderful expedition. The journey to New York took up a week. The carriages were old and shackling, and much of the harness made of ropes. One pair of horses carried the stage eighteen miles. We generally reached our resting-place for the night, if no accident intervened, at ten o'clock and after a frugal supper went to bed with a notice that we should be called at three the next morning, which generally proved to be half-past two. Then, whether it snowed or rained, the traveller must rise and make ready by the help of a horn lantern and a farthing candle, and proceed on his way over bad roads, . . . Thus we travelled, eighteen miles a stage, sometimes obliged to get out and help the coachman lift the coach out of a quagmire or rut, and arrived at New York after a week's hard travelling, wondering at the ease as well as expedition of our journey."

Among Old New England Inns

Captain Pease was not a man to endure poor roads if he could help it, however, and so with his usual enterprise and energy he soon set on foot a movement which resulted in the first Massachusetts turnpike, laid out in 1808 from Boston to Worcester through South Shrewsbury. Much earlier than this he had bought better horses and more comfortable wagons, so that he was able to advertise in the Massachusetts Spy or the Worcester Gazette, under date of January 5, 1786:

"Stages from Portsmouth in New Hampshire to Savannah in Georgia.

"There is now a line of Stages established from New Hampshire to Georgia, which go and return regularly, and carry the several Mails, by order and permission of Congress.

"The stages from Boston to Hartford in Connecticut set out during the winter season, from the home of Levi Pease, at the Sign of the New York Stage, opposite the Mall, in Boston, every Monday and Thursday morning precisely at five o'clock, go as far as Worcester on the evenings of those days and on the days following proceed to Palmer, and on the third day reach Hartford; the first Stage reaches the city of New York on

The Father of the Turnpike

Saturday evening, and the other on the Wednesday evening following.

"The stages from New York for Boston set out on the same days, and reach Hartford at the same time as the Boston stages.

"The stages from Boston exchange passengers with the stages from Hartford at Spencer, and the Hartford Stages exchange with those from New York at Hartford. Passengers are again exchanged at Stratford Ferry and not again until their arrival at New York.

"By the present regulation of the stages, it is certainly the most convenient and expeditious way of travelling that can possibly be had in America, and in order to make it the cheapest, the proprietors of the stages have lowered their price from fourpence to three pence a mile, with liberty to passengers to carry fourteen pounds baggage.

"In the summer season the stages are to run with the mail three times in a week instead of twice in the winter, by which means those who take passage at Boston in the stage which sets off on Monday morning, may arrive at New York on the Thursday evening following, and all the mails during that season are to be but four days

Among Old New England Inns

going from Boston to New York, and so from New York to Boston.

"Those who intend taking passage in the stages must leave their names and baggage the evening preceding the morning that the stage sets off, at the several places where the stage puts up, and pay one-half of their passage to the place where the first exchange of passengers is made, if bound so far, and if not, one-half of their passage so far as they are bound.

"N. B. Way passengers will be accommodated, when the stages are not full, at the same rate, viz. three pence only per mile.

"Said PEASE keeps good lodging &C for gentlemen travellers, and stabling for horses."

Before he could afford the high rents of Boston, Shrewsbury was the centre of all this activity on Levi Pease's part. The Farrar Tavern came into his possession in 1794 and here he brought his family to live. In the northeast room upstairs the Free Masons held their meetings, — according to Miss Ward's very delightful "Old Times in Shrewsbury," — and the room is still called the "Masons' Room." Across the passage is what was formerly a dancing hall divided

The Father of the Turnpike

in the middle by a swing partition which could be raised and lowered at pleasure. Behind the house, in its salad days, was a large open shed for the protection of loaded wagons and, near-by, another shed containing benches and chairs where the teamsters were served. Under this shed, in the side of the house, slight holes were cut, one above the other to a window in the second story. These holes were large enough to hold on by and to admit the toe of a man's boot. Thus, by dexterous use of hands and feet, the men who must rise at cock-crow could let themselves out of the house without disturbing the members of the family.

The Exchange Hotel, still standing in Worcester and still used as a public house, was the Worcester office for Pease's stage line. Built in 1784 it was originally owned by Colonel Reuben Sykes, Pease's partner, and was called successively, the United States Arms, Sykes's Coffee House, and Sykes's Stage House. Washington stopped here for breakfast in 1789 when, says the chronicler, "he politely passed through town on horseback. He was dressed in a brown suit and pleasure glowed in every countenance as he came along." Here it was, too, that Lafay-

Among Old New England Inns

ette was staying on that occasion when Captain Aaron Smith tramped in from Shrewsbury and was affectionately embraced by his old-time commander.

In 1799 a company was formed to extend the turnpike from Worcester to Amherst. Thus was a new chain of taverns brought into the service. At Amherst the star house of the town was the predecessor on the same site of the present Amherst House. Ever since 1757 there has been a tavern on this spot, the first in the series being kept by David Parsons. His son, Gideon Parsons, Joel Dickinson, Solomon Boltwood and Elijah Boltwood were successively landlords, the last-named ranking for some thirty-odd years as one of the most genial publicans of Western Massachusetts. The registers in his day bore the names of many men of national and some of international fame, while in front of the fire at night sat doctors of divinity, learned lawyers, members of the General Court and of Congress. So gifted in his profession was "Uncle Elijah," however, that people of every station felt equally at home under his hospitable roof.

The tavern in his day was a two-story yellow building with a tap-room occupying

BOLTWOOD'S TAVERN (AFTERWARDS THE AMHERST HOUSE), AMHERST

The Father of the Turnpike

the entire front. On the second floor was a ball-room, arched overhead and extending to the roof. Here dinners of ceremony were served and old-time assemblies held. From a stout post in front of the house was suspended an imposing sign of a lion. About 1821, when Amherst College was established the wooden building was torn down and a handsome brick structure (which stood until 1879) entertained travellers in its stead. In 1838 Harvey Rockwood became the proprietor, — and the Boltwood Tavern was superseded by the Amherst House, — as the stage line had already been superseded by the railroad.

CHAPTER IV

GUBERNATORIAL AND OTHER TAVERN JUNKETS

AFTER writing the title of this chapter it occurred to me to look up the etymology of "junket" and see why the term consorts so naturally with adjectives like "gubernatorial," and "aldermanic." I found that the noun was originally spelled juncate, from the Italian *giuncata,* cheese; and that, from denoting a cheesecake in the time of Johnson it came to mean delicate food when used by Milton and to be spelled jun*ket* and describe "an entertainment by stealth" when employed by Swift. Now, though there is no evidence that the entertainments of which this chapter is to speak were conducted by stealth, it certainly is true that a great deal of the patronage by which the old-time taverns waxed rich came in connection with official business and was paid for by the public money. It is fairly clear, too, from the protests one meets in the pages of colonial

Gubernatorial and Other Tavern Junkets

history, that a disproportionate amount was often felt to be spent upon these entertainments. So we will let our title stand; it may serve to illuminate the real character of certain official expeditions even now under way.

About one hundred and seventy years ago there was a very famous junket from Boston to the western part of the Bay Province in order that the Council of Governor Jonathan Belcher might consult with the Indians of that section. An account of this trip which called itself "A Diary of Surpassing Interest" was published and because the thing is very rare and shows that our junket really had in it the elements of "a stolen entertainment" I herewith reproduce it. The tour must have been a great occasion at the several taverns where the official party halted for refreshments and to tarry over the night. Hardly a single one of the public houses here referred to is standing to-day though the names of several of the landlords will be familiar to readers of this book.

"On Wednesday morning, August 20th, 1735, about six o'clock," says the diary, "his Excellency, attended by a number of gentlemen, set out from Boston on a journey to Deerfield, about 120 miles. We got to

Among Old New England Inns

Larned's at Watertown ¼ after seven, 9 miles. Set out at 8 for Sudbury thro. Weston, got there at ½ hour after 9, 11 miles-20-, Set out again at 12, got to Colonel Woods at Marlborough ½ after 1, 10 miles. Set out at ½ after 2, got to Colonel Ward's at Shrewsbury, about 4, 10 miles, Set out at 5 to Col. Chandler's at Worcester about 5 miles, 25-

20
25
—
First day 45 miles

" 21st, Thursday 1 o'clock P. M. set out from Worcester, got to Leicester about 28 minutes after 2, 6 miles. Set out about 3 for Brookfield, got to a house in Brookfield about 4, 8 miles, Set out about ½ hour after, got to Col. Dwights at Brookfield a little before 6, 8 miles.

6
8
8
—
Second day 22 miles.

" 22nd. Friday about 8 set out from Brookfield for Cold Spring, got to Capta. Lyman's about ½ hour after 11, 15 miles, set out about ¼ after 2 for Hadley, got there about

Gubernatorial and Other Tavern Junkets

¼ after 5, 15 miles, got to Col. Stoddard's at Northampton over the Ferry about Sunset, 3 miles.

15	45
15	22
3	33
Third day 33	100 miles.

" 23rd. Saturday. Sabbath Day, tarry'd at Northampton.

" 25th. Monday morning about 10 o'clock a clock set out from Northamton for Hatfield, got to Captain Williams about 11, 5 miles, Set out at 2 for Deerfield, got there about ½ after 4. 15 miles, Monday 20 miles.

" 26th. Tuesday tarry'd at Deerfield. Deerfield 20 miles.

" 27th. Wednesday at Deerfield. There was a Tent erected of about 100 foot long, where the Govr dined with the rest of the Gentlemen, & where in the afternoon the Tribe of the Caguarogas (or French Mohawks) was sent for, & after the usual Salutation & Conference, they were dismist.

" 28th. Thursday at Deerfield. The same was Gone [through] to the Housetonacks, & to the Sattacooks & Mohegans together, in the forenoon. In the afternoon the Mohawks were sent for again, & had a conference. It lasted about an hour & an half.

"29th. Friday at Deerfield. The Housatonnocks were sent for, & had a conference, it lasted about an hour & an half, (in the forenoon.) Then the Mohawks were sent for, received their Presents after a short Conference, & dined with the Governor & Gentlemen in the Tent. & after Dinner the Govr took his Leave of them.

"30th. Saturday at Deerfield. The Housatonnocks were sent for & after some Conference received their Presents, & were Dismist. Then the Scattacooks were sent for & in like manner received their Presents, the Mohegans received theirs after Dinner without any further Conference. These three Tribes dined with the Governor.

"31st. Sabbath Day at Deerfield. In the forenoon the Revd. Mr. Sargent was ordained to preach the Gospel to the Tribe of the Housetonnock Indians. The Revd Mr. Ashley of Deerfield began with Prayer, the Revd Mr. Appleton of Cambridge preached 2 Tim: 2: 21. 'If a man therefore purge himself from these he shall be a Vessell unto Honour, sanctified & meet for the Master's Use & prepared unto every good work.' The

Gubernatorial and Other Tavern Junkets

Revd Mr. Williams of Hatfield gave the charge, & the Revd Mr. Williams of Springfield the right hand of Fellowship. In the afternoon the Rev Mr. Williams of Springfield preached from Is. ii., 4: 'And he shall judge among the nations and shall rebuke many peoples and they shall beat their swords into ploughshares & their Spears into Pruning Hooks.'

" September 1st Monday between 11 & 12 we set out from Deerfield for Fort Dummer, got their about 5, 25 miles.

Monday 25 miles.
Fort Dummer 145 miles.

" 2nd Tuesday we set out from Fort Dummer a little after 8, ferried across the River, got to Ensign Field's at Northfield about 11, 13 miles, set out from thence about ½ hour after 12, got to a River where we stopt, about 2, 10 miles, set out at ½ hour after, got to Mr. Rand's at Sunderland ¼ after 4, 12 miles, set out at 5, got to Kelloggs at Hadley Ferry, ¼ after 6, 10.

13
10
12
10
Tuesday 45 miles.

Among Old New England Inns

"The Gover. & others went over the Ferry to Northampton I lodged at Hadley, got to Col. Stoddards over the Ferry about 8 next morning, 3 miles.

"3rd Wednesday set out from Northampton about 9, got to Lieut. Ingerson's at Westfield ½ hour after 12, 17 miles. Set out for Springfield about 3, got to Springfield Ferry about 4, 6 miles; crossed the River, got to Mr. Sherriff Marshfield's ½ after 4, 1 mile, 7 miles.

$$\frac{\begin{array}{r}17\\7\end{array}}{}$$

Wednesday 24 miles.

"4th Thursday we set out from Springfield about ten o'clock, got to Scots' at the Elbow at 1, 15 miles, set out about ½ hour after 2, got to Col. Dwight's at Brookfield ½ hour after 5, 15 miles.

$$\frac{\begin{array}{r}15\\15\end{array}}{}$$

Thursday 30 miles.

"5th Friday, we set out from Brookfield about ½ hour after 7, got to Leicester about ¼ before 11, 16 miles. Set out about ¼ after,

Gubernatorial and Other Tavern Junkets

got to Col. Chandlers at Worcester about ¼ after 12, 6 miles.

16
6
—
22 miles.

" set out ½ hour after 2, got to Col. Ward's at Shrewsbury about ¼ before 4, 7 miles, set out about ½ hour after 4, got to Col. Woods at Marlborough about 6,

10
22
10
—
39
Friday about 4 miles.

"6th Saturday we set out from Marlborough ¼ after 7, got to Sudbury at 9, 10 miles; set out at 11, got to Larned's at Watertown ¼ before 1, 11 miles, set out ½ after 2, got to Boston at 4, 9 miles.

10
11
9
—
Saturday 30 miles."

There are several places named in the

journal upon which it may be well to remark. The house of Colonel Dwight was upon Foster's Hill in Brookfield. It was purchased, not many years ago, by the Quaboag Historical Society and measures were being taken to have it put into good repair when, one night, it burned to the ground.

Governor Belcher, in whose honour the Cold Spring here referred to was afterwards called Belchertown, had been in office several years at the time of this junket and was highly regarded by the people in spite of the fact that there was some opposition to him among the so-called favoured classes. In 1742 he was removed from his office in Massachusetts but was soon appointed governor of the province of New Jersey, where he was welcomed with open arms and did much to help Jonathan Edwards,[1] — in whose "Great Awakening" he had been deeply interested, — put Princeton University on its feet. The "Sabbath day" that the party "tarried at Northampton" was doubtless spent in hearing Edwards preach.

As for the errand which occasioned the junket: it had to do with a very real grievance of the Indians. Land speculators were

[1] See "Romance of Old New England Churches."

DWIGHT HOUSE, BROOKFIELD

FRARY HOUSE, DEERFIELD

Gubernatorial and Other Tavern Junkets

crowding them close and there was need that a judicial-minded body should listen to their story and do what they could to adjust matters.

Almost forty years earlier another famous case had been tried in this very locality by a junketing party from Boston. The house with which that trip is associated was later a tavern and, fortunately for us, is still standing. It is called the Frary House and is now owned by Miss C. Alice Baker, a descendant of Samson Frary, whose name the place bears.

The older part of the Frary House was built in 1689, the other half being added in 1748 when the whole house was used as a tavern. The spacious dancing hall of the place, which is thirty-three feet long and proportionately wide, was the scene of many a festive gathering in those tavern days and its spring floor still responds, at Miss Baker's private parties, to the impetus of the " light fantastic toe." Gaiety had no share, however, in the visit of officials that now concerns us.

Back in the earliest days of the house it was the home of some simple people in whose family there lived a young serving-woman,

Among Old New England Inns

Sarah Smith. Through this young woman the place is associated with one of those horrible child-murders occasionally to be found in New England history.

Though Sarah Smith pleaded not guilty to the charge of murdering her illegitimate baby the jury of twelve men, — Joseph Parsons, foreman, — decided against her and, Justice Winthrop having condemned her to hang on the following Thursday, such punishment was duly meted out to her. In accordance with the custom of the times Rev. John Williams preached a sermon before her on the day of the execution. But his words appear to have made no very profound impression upon her, for her ghost is said to have long haunted the house in which she committed her crime. Up to forty years ago it appeared with remarkable regularity, I am told.

Possibly, however, the apparition connected with the place really owes its origin to some unrecorded crime done during the days when the house was a tavern. Certainly the place has age enough to have survived several murders.

Its first Boniface was Salah Barnard who in 1763 bought it from David Arms for

Gubernatorial and Other Tavern Junkets

£175. His son Erastus was a tavern keeper also, pursuing this business until 1815. Miss Baker bought the estate May 24, 1890 and had the old house thoroughly restored. It enjoys the distinction of being the oldest house in Deerfield.

Governor Endicott's peregrinations were most laudably free from extravagance. The bills presented on his account by Joseph Armitage, who kept the tavern just half-way between Boston and Salem and therefore came in for considerable patronage from persons having business before the Courts of Essex County, were always modest. " From the Court of election 1651 till the end of October 1651 the governers Expenses " were:

" to beare and cacks	6 d
beare & cacks to himself and some other gentlemen	1 s 2 d
beare and cacks with Mr. Downing	1 s 6 d
beare & a cack	6 d
	3 s 8 d "

The lesser lights in the official train were not so abstemious for during the same period they ran up a bill for a considerably larger amount.

Among Old New England Inns

" to the Sargeants from the end of the Court of elections 1651 till the end of October 1651.

bear and cacks	1 s 2 d
for vitalls beare and logen	5 s
to Benjamin Scarlet the Governors man	8 d
bear & vittells	2 s
to the Sargents	1 s 9 d
beear & cacks	1 s
to a man that Carried a letter to warne a Court about the dutchmen	1 s 6 d
to the Sargeants	1 s 2 d
	14 s 3 d "

These bills were ordered to be paid in the following form:

" Mr. Auditer I pray you give a note to Mr. Treasurer for the payment of 17s 11d according to these two bills of Joseph Armitage. Date the 7th of the 11mo 1651.
Jo Endicott."

But these gubernatorial and other junkets were not always promptly paid for and this fact accounts for the preservation of many old-time tavern bills that, in the ordinary

Gubernatorial and Other Tavern Junkets

course of things, would have perished long ago. Armitage, for instance, had been for some years retired from the duties of tavern-keeper, when being in money difficulties, he attempted to collect a bill long overdue in the following petition:

"To the Honered Court now sitting at Salem: The Humble pitition of Joseph Armitage, Humbly sheweth that in the time that I kept Ordinary there was some expences at my Hows by some of the Honored magistrates & Deputys of this County as apears by the bills charged upon the Auditer Generall, which I never Receaved.

"Therefor your Humbell petticionir doth humbly request this Court that they would give me an order to the County Treasurer for my pay & so your poure petitioner shall ever pray for your prosperity
JOSEPH ARMITAGE."

Armitage's previous calling, — that of a tailor, — ought to have given him wide experience in collecting bad debts, but evidently he had not profited by the teachings of adversity for he was continually involved in pecuniary difficulties. His successor at this Lynn

Among Old New England Inns

"Anchor" was much more prosperous; though he made his house popular he collected money owed him and for forty years flourished as a tavern-keeper, — and otherwise. Thomas Marshall, for so this functionary was named, arrived in Lynn from London in the latter part of 1635 and, soon after, became a freeman of the colony. When Cromwell went into the business of saving England, Marshall felt a call to help him, and returning to the mother country sat on the right hand of the Lord Protector, — if his own statements can be relied upon. At any rate he had a "captain" before his name and the lustre of military glory all over it when he came back to Lynn after the war, eager to discuss with any traveller who would listen to him, his experiences while with Oliver. John Dunton promised to be a good victim when he passed that way in 1686, but Captain Marshall did not succeed in holding him long. If there was boasting to be done Dunton wanted to do it himself. He has left us this account of his call at the Anchor: "About two of the clock I reached Capt. Marshall's house which is half-way between Boston and Salem; here I staid to refresh nature with a pint of sack and a good fowl.

Gubernatorial and Other Tavern Junkets

Capt. Marshall is a hearty old gentleman, formerly one of Oliver's soldiers, upon which he very much values himself. He had all the history of the civil war at his fingers end and if we may believe him Oliver did hardly anything that was considerable without his assistance, and if I'd have staid as long as he'd have talked, he'd have spoiled my ramble at Salem."

Executions were great junket occasions at the old-time tavern for the gallows often stood very near the public house and our Puritan forbears had no qualms about sending to "everlasting punishment" one who had been proved guilty of crime. Apropos of the grewsome structure near what was long known as Porter's Tavern, Cambridge, one satiric rhymster wrote:

> "Cambridge is a famous town,
>   Both for wit and knowledge,
> Some they whip and some they hang,
>   And some they send to college."

An especially gala day in the University City was September 18, 1755, thus cheerfully described by a Boston gentleman who had just seen a negro woman burnt for com-

Among Old New England Inns

plicity in the murder of her master: "Execution day a clear but for the time of year a Cold day about 1 o'clock sat out for Cambridge saw ye execution Mark hanged and Phillis burnt then to Bradishes, & then to morses drank some punch with Mr. Moreley Tom Leverett Mr. Cooper Tom foxcroft Ned Emerson & others & walked down with Jonathan Bradish and then to mr. Moreleys house tarried till ten supped & refreshed nature sufficiently and then went home and went to bed & slept woke up very finely refreshed." The sermon that accompanied this occasion was preached by the Rev. Mr. Appleton on the appropriate text "The Way of the Transgressor is Hard."

Those old-time clergymen were so exasperatingly sure they were right! Nor did they make fine distinctions. To us of today it is almost inconceivable that Rev. Dr. Ezra Stiles could have written in the margin of his almanack for the year 1789, against the date February 13, " General Ethan Allen of Vermont died and went to Hell this day "—but there it stands. And this because a patriot of the highest integrity was a free-thinker! Allen and his men, by the bye, made their headquarters at the " Catamount "

Gubernatorial and Other Tavern Junkets

tavern, Bennington, Vermont. One of the rooms in this hostelry, which stood until 1871, was designated as the "council room." Here the brave band of Green Mountain Boys laid their plans for the capture of Ticonderoga and drank good New England rum the while. The old tavern account-book bearing Ethan Allen's unbalanced score is still preserved.

Auctions of human beings and public whippings were other junket occasions at the New England tavern. Criminals and paupers were both sold here the former to the highest bidder, the latter to the lowest; and lashes on the bared back were administered with neatness and dispatch. At Israel Clifford's tavern in Dunbarton, New Hampshire, one Gould, a sheep-thief, was sold at public auction for "damages and costs," taxed at £2-12-10 after having been vigorously "whipped thirteen stripes by Archibald Stark, Constable."

None of the many junkets with which we have had to do seems to me so revolting however as those which attended the sale of paupers. In the town of Wareham, on Buzzard's Bay, at the tavern of Benjamin Fearing such events frequently took place if we may trust Bliss's "Colonial Times on Buzzard's Bay." The sales were made, this writer tells us, in the tap-room of the inn, "where the landlord as he served the thirsty guests from his decanters, discussed with them the value of the services of the paupers, for whose keeping they had come to bid. The town records bear ugly testimony to the truth of this in the following words: "Jurned from the meeting house down to Benjamin Fearings house to vandue the poor." I hope I am right in saying that this revolting custom has quite passed away in New England though in Pike County, Pennsylvania, only eight years ago, signs were posted, "A Woman for Sale" and Mrs. Elmira Quick, seventy-seven years old, was put up, in Rutan's Hotel, "to be sold to the lowest bidder for keep for a year" while men clinked glasses in the bar-room.[1]

[1] "Stage Coach and Tavern Days," p, 221.

CHAPTER V

THE INNS OF OLD BOSTON

WHEN John Dunton, the voluble London bookseller whose praise of Ipswich fare we shall later encounter, took his pen in hand to describe a Boston landlord the result was as follows: " He is a person so remarkable that had I not been acquainted with him it would be a hard matter to make any New England man believe that I had been in Boston; for there was no house in all the town more noted, or where a man might meet with better accommodation. Besides he was a brisk and jolly man whose conversation was coveted by all his guests as the life and spirit of the company."

The date of this paragraph is 1686 and the man who inspired it was George Monk, host of the " Blew Anchor," which used to flourish on the ground now occupied by the Globe newspaper buildings and which, in early times, divided with the State's Arms

Among Old New England Inns

the magisterial patronage of the town. Robert Turner had been an earlier landlord here and Savage has preserved for us one record of entertainment during his day which is decidedly interesting; he tells us that " at the sign of the Blue Anchor Turner furnished lodgings and refreshments to members of the government, to juries, and to the clergy, when summoned into synod by our general court." That the law-makers did not stint themselves at the Anchor we are persuaded after seeing an old bill of an election banquet when two hundred and four diners consumed 72 bottles of Madeira, 28 of Lisbon, 17 of port, 10 of claret, 18 of porter and 50 " double-bowls " of punch, in addition to unspecified cider.

This inn was one of the most popular of the seventeenth century hostelries, but it was neither the oldest nor the most famous of the Boston taverns of that day. Cole's, licensed in 1634, antedates it by several years and was the first house of entertainment in the New England metropolis. It probably stood near the site well known to us today as the " Old Corner " of " Bookstore " fame. Here Samuel Cole, who is classified as a " comfit-maker," saw to the comfort of Miantonomoh

The Inns of Old Boston

when he and his dusky retinue visited Governor Vane in 1636 and here too, the Earl of Marlborough took up his residence when he came over to Boston on colonial business. Winthrop had urged his Lordship to accept the hospitality of the Governor's mansion but the haughty nobleman assured him that the house wherein he was staying was "exceedingly well-governed" and intimated that he would, therefore, remain where he was.

The distinguishing name of the second ordinary started in Boston cannot be given, but we know that its landlord was William Hudson, senior, that his license was issued in 1640, and that his previous occupation had been that of a baker. His name is on the list of those who were admitted freemen of the Colony in May, 1631, and we find him repeatedly noted as active in the town's affairs. His house was on the site afterwards given over to the "Bunch of Grapes," of which there will be much to say a few pages further on.

A very celebrated house of this period was that called the King's Arms, and kept by Hugh Gunnison at the head of what is now Adams (Dock) Square. The date when

Among Old New England Inns

Gunnison was first allowed to "sell beer" is 1642, and as he is then spoken of as one who keeps a "cooke's shop" it is plain that he must have begun very early to serve the public at this stand. In 1643 we find him humbly praying the court for leave "to draw the wyne which was spent in his house," explaining his reasonable request by saying that he felt it to be unfair as he knew it to be unprofitable to care for people who had purchased their liquor elsewhere. He asks this favour in order that "God be not dishonored nor his people grieved." With the coming in of Puritan rule in England, Gunnison diplomatically changed the name of his inn from the "King's Arms" to the "State's Arms;" when the Stuarts were restored the house resumed its old insignia.

A rival and a near neighbour of Gunnison's was William Hudson, Junior, whose house was at what is now the upper corner of Elm and Washington streets. He, too, was influenced by the coming in of Cromwell, though not in quite the same way as Gunnison. He, "with divers other of our best military men" crossed the ocean to take service in the Parliamentary forces, leaving the inn to the care of his wife. When he

The Inns of Old Boston

returned, after an absence of two years, it was to find her publicly accused of having been unfaithful to her marriage vows. Very likely some of the many sailors who frequented the house had stolen her heart away. For Dock Square was then what its name would indicate, the centre of the city's transportation. At high tide the water came nearly up to the houses here and from Hudson's to the dock below was but a stone's throw.

The most convenient inn for those who drew their wealth from the sea was, however, Ship Tavern, which stood on the southwest corner of what are now North and Clark streets. It was a brick building with a projecting second story and the date of its erection was surely as early as 1650. Thomas Hutchinson, father of the Governor, was some time its landlord, and in 1663 John Vyal presided over its destinies. Here King Charles's commissioners lodged when they came to America " to settle all disputes arising in the New England colony." In the course of their business, — and as a result of too liberal indulgence in Master Vyal's " best," — one of them, Sir Robert Carr, assaulted a constable in the public room of

Among Old New England Inns

the house and found a fresh dispute on his hands. He was immediately summoned by Governor Leverett to come to his house and answer the complaint lodged against him! Sir Robert Carr, however, was a resourceful gentleman; moreover, he remembered very well Leverett's affront to the commissioners in keeping his hat on his head when their authority to act was being read to the council. Very well, too, he knew that Leverett, who had served under Cromwell, would find as wormwood a flaunting of Stuart authority. So, with manifest joy, he replied to the summons as follows: " Sr, Yors I receyved last night in answer to wh as I am Sr Robert Carr I would have complied with yor desyres, but as I am wth ye Kyng's Commision, I shal not grant yor requests, both in respect of his Majestyes honor and my oune duty." Yet with all his insistence upon royal authority he could not make the colonists come around. His commission issued endless proclamations from the Ship Tavern and sounded trumpets without cease; but Boston folk went quietly on their way, unconscious, as it seemed, of the trouble they were making for themselves by refusing to be subdued.

The Inns of Old Boston

Characteristically, they persecuted in their turn. Nicholas Upshall, the noble Quaker who kept the Red Lion in North street, they threw into jail for his outspoken condemnation of the rigour with which the authorities were dealing with his sect. Upshall had come to New England on the Mary and John of Winthrop's fleet but he was very soon in durance, and eventually he was banished for having attempted to get food to two Quakeresses who were starving in Boston's jail. Prison treatment broke his health and he died as a result of it. Probably he is the only Boniface we shall meet who suffered death for conscience' sake.

With the birth of the Royal Exchange, which stood on the southwest corner of Exchange and State streets, came the dawn of that brilliant pre-Revolutionary Boston dear to writers of romance. By 1711 the business of entertainment was being carried on here but it was not until fifteen years later, when Luke Vardy had become landlord, that the place took on the colour which has made it famous. It was then the resort of all the young bloods of the town, who, brave in velvets and ruffles, in powdered hair and periwigs, swore by the king and drank deep draughts of life and liquor. From this inn, Benjamin Woodbridge and Henry Phillips, both scions of Boston's first families, adjourned to the Common in 1728 to fight a duel. Woodbridge had made a slighting remark about a friend of Phillips, and the latter had thrown the contents of his wine-glass in the insultant's face. Nothing but the death of one or both could wipe out this score. So it came about that, soon after sunrise the next morning, young Woodbridge was found lying dead among the wet grasses of the community cow-pasture as the price of his careless words. Phillips escaped on a man-of-war which was just weighing anchor. The immediate outcome of this crime was the enactment of a law whereby the convicted offender in a duel was " to be carried publicly in a cart to the gallows, with a rope about his neck, and set on the gallows an hour; then to be imprisoned twelve hours without bail," and finally executed. The person killed in a duel was denied " Christian burial " and interred " near the usual place of execution with a stake drove through his body."

British officers were very fond of patronizing the Royal Exchange, — perhaps because

The Inns of Old Boston

its high-sounding name appealed to their aristocratic fancy,— and an engaging story associated with the house is that of the instant capitulation here of Captain Ponsonby Molesworth, a nephew of Lord Ponsonby, to the charms of Susanna Sheaffe, eldest daughter of the Deputy. The youth was marching with his soldiery, resplendent in the red uniform of His Majesty's service. The maiden happened to be within the house and, attracted by the music, stepped to the balcony. At once Molesworth saw her and was captivated by her beauty. Pointing her out to a brother officer he exclaimed, "Jove! That girl seals my fate!" Apparently he felt quite sure that Susanna would find him irresistible and such proved to be the case; they were married almost at once.

Vardy's was a favourite resort of the Masonic fraternity, also, mine host being a brother of the order. At one of their festivals Joseph Green thus apostrophized him:

"Where's honest Luke, that cook from London?
For without Luke the Lodge is undone.
'Twas he who oft dispelled their sadness,
And filled the Brethren's hearts with gladness.
Luke in return is made a brother
As good and true as any other,

Among Old New England Inns

> And still though broke with age and wine,
> Preserves the token and the sign."

It was in front of this house that there occurred on March 5, 1770, the "famous Boston Massacre." As to just how the trouble began or what were the exact circumstances attending it accounts do not agree. The reports made at the town-meetings in Faneuil Hall and the old South Church conflict with those written at the time; and at the trial (at the October term following) of Captain Preston, the commander of the troops, and the soldiers implicated in the massacre, the testimony was such that they were acquitted. What we do know, however, is that a chance collision between a sentry and some youths quickly developed into an attack with stones, clubs, snow-balls and other missiles upon the guard of British soldiers, and that five individuals were killed and several were slightly injured as a result. The story goes that the sentinel was first attacked, as he stood guarding the Custom House where the king's treasure was deposited, and that, retreating up the steps as far as he could, he loaded his gun, shouting lustily the while for help. Then the cor-

The Inns of Old Boston

poral and six privates of the main guard who were stationed on what is now State street, opposite the door on the south side of the Town House, came to his relief. It was alleged that they did not fire upon the crowd until they were themselves first attacked. However that may be, the first blood of the Revolution was then shed. Thus it comes about that the Royal Exchange is shown in the background of Revere's well-known picture of the Boston Massacre and so may be classed, almost in spite of itself, among the important Revolutionary taverns.

A Boston inn with an incontestable right to this appellation was the Liberty Tree Tavern which stood on the east side of Washington street, between Essex and Beach streets. The "Book of Possessions" tells us that in 1635 this plot of ground was apportioned to Garrett Bourne for a house and garden. The year following Bourne became a freeman, built his house and took possession. He set out a variety of shade trees about his house, many of which were elms. In 1646, he transplanted an elm selected on account of its shape and vigour, a little distance northwest of his house. Garrett Bourne "built and planted better than he knew."

Among Old New England Inns

In about a century the house became noted as a tavern, and a little later on, as the meeting-place of the Sons of Liberty. In about the same time that transplanted elm became famous as the Liberty Tree, as the Sons of Liberty used to rally under its wide-spreading branches. It was under this tree that the first public act of resistance to British tyranny showed itself. At dawn, on the 14th of August, 1765, an effigy of Andrew Oliver, the stamp officer, was discovered hanging to one of the larger branches, which caused great excitement. The sheriff was ordered by the colonial Governor Hutchinson to remove the effigy from the tree. But such was the intensity of public feeling, he declared he dare not do so. It was creating a local revolution, and was removed by stratagem. The tree became famous about 1760, and was named the Liberty Tree about this time. On Feb. 14, 1766, it was pruned by the order of the Sons of Liberty.

The ground about the tree had become sacred soil, and was designated as Liberty Hall, and really became the original stamping ground of the Revolution, in defiance of the "stamp act." In 1767 a flagstaff was erected, which went up through the branches,

LIBERTY TREE TAVERN, BOSTON

The Inns of Old Boston

upon which was hoisted a flag as a signal for the assembling of the Sons of Liberty. In August, 1775, the Tories, encouraged by their British allies, and led on by one Job Williams, armed with axes, made a furious attack upon the Liberty Tree, and it was ruthlessly cut down. This vandal act caused great excitement. At the close of the Revolution a liberty pole was erected on the stump of the old tree which long served as a point of direction. This pole having served during the second war with Great Britain, and having gone into decay, another one was erected about the time of the arrival of General Lafayette as the guest of the nation in 1824. The modern brick building now on this site has embedded in its front wall a tablet with a Liberty Tree in bas-relief.

Of other famous Revolutionary inns there were, of course, several in Boston. The oldest of these was the Bunch of Grapes which goes back to 1712, if not earlier. The first landlord here of whom we know was Francis Holmes, and after him came William Coffin in 1731, Joshua Barker in 1749, Colonel Ingersoll in 1764, John Marston in 1767, William Foster in 1782 and James Vila in 1789. Upon the arrival of Governor William

Among Old New England Inns

Burnett in 1728, he was escorted from the Neck to the Bunch of Grapes by a large body of enthusiastic citizens, headed by the Lieutenant-Governor, the Council, and Colonel Dudley's regiments. Burnett had in his train also a tutor, a black laundress, a steward and a French cook upon whom, as we may readily believe, the Bostonians gazed with no little wonder.

Governor Pownall is another of the colonial grandees who frequented the house in its earlier days. There is a pleasant story of a kiss which he once delivered standing on a chair there. Pownall was a short, corpulent person but a great ladies' man, and it was his habit to salute every woman to whom he was introduced with a sounding smack upon the cheek. One day a tall dame was presented and he requested her to stoop to meet his proffered courtesy. "Nay, I'll stoop to no man, — not even to your Excellency," exclaimed the Amazon, with a haughty toss of her head. "Then I'll stoop to you, madam," readily retorted the gallant Governor, and springing to a chair beside her he bent over to do his obeisance.

A less ingratiating visitor to the inn was Sir William Phips who once threatened to

The Inns of Old Boston

thrash the landlord for some fancied slight. He could have done it, too, for he was a man of Herculean strength and his caning of Captain Short of the Nonesuch frigate and his assaults on the Collector of the Port Brenton left their mark upon the victims as well as upon history. When the voting in the General Court was proceeding in a way which did not please him he sometimes rushed into the chamber cane in hand and drove his opponents from their places! One writer [1] has given us a very vivid picture of him sitting at his window in the Bunch of Grapes, which no one else dared approach, and glaring out at the pedestrians on King (now State) street.

Much of interest was to be seen from that window, for the street was filled with "horses, donkeys, oxen and long-tailed trucks, and a sprinkling of one-horse chaises and coaches of the kind seen in Hogarth's realistic pictures of London life. And to these," adds Samuel Adams Drake, who has written delightfully of old Boston Taverns as of most other colonial subjects, "should be added the chimney-sweeps, wood-sawyers, market-women, soldiers and sailors, who are

[1] Frederick Walter Norcross in the New England Magazine.

now quite as much out of date as the vehicles themselves are. As there were no sidewalks, the narrow footway was protected, here and there, sometimes by posts, sometimes by an old cannon set upright at the corners." Thus the traveller coming to the Bunch of Grapes could alight from his horse, coach or chaise at the inn's very threshold, directly under the gilded cluster of suggestive fruit which dangled temptingly over the doorway of the inn.

One of these bunches of grapes now hangs in front of the lodge-room door of St. John's Lodge in the Masonic Temple, Boston, by reason of the fact that it was in the tavern they originally adorned that St. John's Lodge, the first Masonic lodge in America, was organized July 30, 1733 by Henry Price, a Boston tailor, who had received authority from Lord Montague. The house lived up to its sign, it is interesting to note, for it was known far and wide as "the best punch-house in Boston." When the time came to distinguish between conditional loyalty and loyalty at any cost, the Bunch of Grapes became the resort of the High Whigs, who made it a sort of political headquarters where patriotism was the password. And

The Inns of Old Boston

when public feeling was still further intensified by military occupation and bayonet rule, a scarlet coat was an inflammatory signal in that tap-room.

Upon the evacuation of Boston by the royal troops, this house was naturally the very centre of rejoicing and Stark's victory at Bennington was celebrated here with peculiar fervour. " In consequence of this news," writes one who was an actor in the affair, " we kept it up in high taste. At sundown about one hundred of the first gentlemen of the town, with all the strangers then in Boston, met at the Bunch of Grapes, where good liquors and a side-table were provided. In the street were two brass field-pieces with a detachment of Colonel Craft's regiment. In the balcony of the Town-house all the fifes and drums of my regiment were stationed. The ball opened with a discharge of thirteen cannon and at every toast given three rounds were fired and a flight of rockets sent up. About nine o'clock two barrels of grog were brought out into the street for the people that had collected there. It was all conducted with the greatest propriety and by ten o'clock every man was at his home." When Stark himself came to town he was royally entertained by the patriotic Marston, and when Lafayette returned from France in 1780 with the news that his country would lend us her aid he, too, was received here with all honours.

A charming picture of the kind of entertainment furnished at this inn has come down to us. For the dinner, served at two o'clock, — to which the guests would have been summoned by the ringing of a bell in the street — there would be perhaps twenty persons. Once seated, they chatted together pleasantly while discussing salmon in season, veal, beef, mutton, fowl, ham, vegetables and pudding. Each had his pint of Madeira set before him and each served himself to that portion of the joint he liked best, all the carving being done at the table. Five shillings a day was the usual charge for this excellent fare.

Less picturesque than some of the Revolutionary gatherings, but quite as important to the progress of America, was the meeting in this tavern of the Ohio Company, which, under General Rufus Putnam and other Continental officers carried on at Marietta the first concerted movement of New England towards the Great West.

The loyalists gathered in great numbers at

The Inns of Old Boston

the British Coffee House. Here was performed in 1750, by an amateur company of red-coated officers, Otway's "Orphan," an event which caused the enactment of a law prohibiting, under pain of severe penalties, the performance of stage plays in Boston. And here, in 1751, was formed the first association in Boston to take unto itself the name of club. It was called the Merchants Club, though crown officers, members of the bar, army and navy men and gentlemen of high social rank as well as merchants were admitted to membership. For a long time this club represented the ripest culture and the most brilliant wit in the colonies. But when the clouds of the Revolution began to gather, the Whigs took themselves off to the Bunch of Grapes over the way. Thus we find John Adams writing, under date of 1771: "Spent the evening at Cordis's, in the front room towards the Long Wharf, where the Merchants' Club has met these twenty years. It seems there is schism in that church, a rent in that garment." There was indeed as James Otis had discovered not long before.

Here, one evening in 1769, Otis received the drubbing that was to cost him his reason.

Among Old New England Inns

The brilliant young orator had delivered his famous speech against the Writs of Assistance only a few days before, and in this speech he had so criticized Customs Commissioner Robinson that his friends feared harm might come to him as a result. But Otis had no forebodings of evil. Had not the Boston mob carried him on their shoulders? There was only exultation in his thoughts, therefore, as he strolled down King street to the British Coffee House on the evening that was to mark his undoing. Very likely, though, he was wondering in his subconscious mind, as he made his way along the uneven street, who could have written the note which requested a meeting at the Coffee House at that hour.

He was to learn only too soon. Outside the inn he paused beneath the broad sign to speak with a friend. Then he went within. Immediately he was jostled into a corner and set upon by a party of roughs at whose head he recognized his enemy, Robinson! Otis's friend did what he could in the way of rescue, but he was promptly overpowered and hurried into the street. Meanwhile the great orator had been thrown to the floor where he was left, stunned and bleeding,

The Inns of Old Boston

with a great cut in his forehead. Futile now were his rare gifts. His brain became clouded as a result of the blows he had received, and ultimately he became insane. Thus the Tories accomplished by brute force what they were never able to do by argument, — the silencing of the most potent voice ever raised against royal encroachment. Otis's gifts of satire alone would have won for him their hearty hatred. Once when Governor Bernard had interrupted him to ask whose authority he was just then citing, he had replied coolly, " He is a very eminent jurist, and none the less so for being unknown to your Excellency."

Yet Otis refused to pose as a martyr, and never alluded to his sufferings, save for some such purpose as John Adams records, apropos of the complaints of William Molyneux. That gentleman had been petitioning the legislature for favours which it did not choose to grant, and for several evenings he had wearied the company with the recital of his grievances, ending his story always by saying " That a man who has behaved as I have, should be treated as I am is intolerable."

Otis listened for some time without retort, but at length, perceiving that the whole club was out of patience, he jumped up and said gayly, " Come Will, I too, have a list of grievances; will you hear it? " Expecting sport all cried out, " Ay! ay! let us hear your list."

" Well, then in the first place I resigned the office of Advocate General which I held from the crown, which produced me — how much do you think? "

" A great deal, no doubt," said Molyneux.

" Shall we say two hundred sterling a year? "

" Ay, more I believe," said Molyneux.

" Well, let it be two hundred. That for ten years is two thousand. In the next place, I have been obliged to relinquish the greater part of my business at the bar. Will you set that at two hundred pounds more? "

" Oh I believe it is much more than that! " was the answer.

" Well, let it be two hundred. This, for ten years, makes two thousand. You allow then I have lost four thousand pounds sterling? "

" Ay, and more too," said Molyneux.

Otis went on: " In the next place I have lost a hundred friends among whom were men of the first rank, fortune and power in

The Inns of Old Boston

the province. At what price will you estimate them?"

"D—n them!" said Molyneux, "at nothing. You are better off without them than with them."

A loud laugh from the company greeted this sally.

"Be it so," said Otis. "In the next place I have made a thousand enemies, among whom are the government of the province and nation. What do you think of this item?"

"That is as it may happen," said Molyneux, reflectively.

"In the next place you know I love pleasure, but I have renounced pleasure for ten years. What is that worth?"

"No great matter: you have made politics your amusement."

A hearty laugh.

"In the next place I have ruined as fine health as nature ever gave to man."

"That is melancholy indeed; there is nothing to be said on that point," Molyneux replied.

"Once more," continued Otis, holding down his head before Molyneux, "look upon this head!" (There was a deep half-closed

scar in which a man might lay his finger —)
" and, what is worse, my friends think I have a monstrous crack in my skull."

This made all the company look grave and had the desired effect of silencing Molyneux, who was really a good companion. Yet, notwithstanding his wrongs, Otis was so generous that, when Robinson had apologized, he magnanimously refused the damages awarded him by the court.

Another inn frequented by Otis and one which will probably outlive all its contemporaries in the endurance of its fame is the Green Dragon, which Daniel Webster once pronounced the "headquarters of the Revolution." Here Warren, John Adams and Paul Revere all assembled and plotted and here used to resort hundreds of patriots for the express purpose of conferring with their chiefs. The house was kept in 1712 by Richard Pullin; in 1715 by Mr. Pattoun; in 1734 by Joseph Kilder; in 1769 by John Cary and in 1771, when it became the place of meeting of the Revolutionary Club, by Benjamin Burdick. In the local events which preceded the encounter at Lexington the men who met here all had important parts to play. Says Revere: "In the fall

THE GREEN DRAGON, BOSTON

The Inns of Old Boston

of 1774 and winter of 1775 I was one of upwards thirty, chiefly mechanics, who formed ourselves into a committee for the purpose of watching the movements of the British soldiers and gaining every intelligence of the movements of the tories. We held our meetings at the Green Dragon Tavern. This committee was astonished to find all their secrets known to General Gage, although every time they met every member swore not to reveal any of their transactions except to Hancock, Adams, Warren, Otis, Church and one or two more."

Doctor Church proved to be the traitor among them.[1]

The men of the Green Dragon group it was who gave the alarm on the eve of the battle of Lexington, who spirited away cannon under General Gage's very nose and who, again and again, in the course of the war, performed swiftly and well dangerous pieces of work. Dr. Warren was the idol of the crowd, and between him and Revere a very warm friendship sprang up. When he sent the silversmith word, therefore, that he must instantly ride to Lexington he knew that the alarm would be spread with all

[1] See "Romance of Old New England Roof-Trees."

possible dispatch " through every Middlesex village and farm." It was in this inn that a great mass of Boston mechanics voted with acclamation to urge the adoption of the Constitution by the Federal Convention. The walls of the Green Dragon so shook as they made this resolve, that Samuel Adams exclaimed whimsically, " Well if they want it they must have it."

The tavern stood on Union street and was a two-storied brick building with pitch roof, showing above its entrance a metal dragon. The site of this most famous of Boston inns is now marked by a tablet having the fabled monster sculptured thereon in bas-relief. During the British occupation of Boston, the several lodges of the regiment held their meetings here. Thus there are associations of many kinds connected with the house.

No one of these is more interesting than the celebration here of that Pope Day which cost Governor Hancock one thousand dollars. Boston had long observed the anniversary of the momentous Gunpowder Plot by processions from the North and South End respectively. Each section had its marchers and its Pope, and when the two met there was sure to be a riot, for the rivalry between these

The Inns of Old Boston

two districts was exceeding bitter. From these combats, in the course of which the rival effigies of the papal sovereign were always dragged from their thrones and fists, stones and clubs circulated freely, there arose a degree of ill-feeling which Hancock feared might prove very prejudicial to the patriot cause. So, having in vain endeavoured to suppress the disagreements, he formed the brilliant idea of setting the bickerers all down together at a great feast spread in the Green Dragon. His plan worked like a charm, and though the spread cost him a great deal of money, — which he never spent without pain, — he had the satisfaction of knowing that it put an end to the riots which had long disturbed the community.

Another famous hostelry of eighteenth century Boston was the Cromwell's Head which stood near King's Chapel on School street. It was kept by Anthony Brackett in 1760, by his widow in 1764, and later by his brother Joshua. Marquis de Chastellux, of Rochambeau's auxiliary army, lodged here when he was in Boston in 1782, and had the felicity to make the acquaintance of Paul Jones. It speaks badly for the gallantry of the little admiral that he is said to have read to the company in the coffee-room of this house some verses composed in his honour by Lady Craven.

When Boston town fell into the power of the "British hirelings" it seemed for a time as if it might go hard with this hostelry. For its sign, which bore the grim features of the Lord Protector, hung so low over the footway that pedestrians had been compelled either to bow before it or whack their heads against its heavy board, alternatives equally detestable to Kingsmen. When their time of might dawned, therefore, mine host Brackett was obliged to take down his sign and retire it for a time from public life. But on the very day of the evacuation it was replaced! Brackett's "bill" was from a plate made by Paul Revere. At its head stood a facsimile of the sign stating that besides board, lodging, and fare one might have wine, punch, porter and liquor, with due care for one's horse for certain pounds, shillings, and pence.

Lieutenant-Colonel George Washington, then a young man who had just begun to make a name for himself, put up at this tavern in 1756. He had been sent to New England by Governor Dinwiddie to confer

The Inns of Old Boston

with Governor Shirley about matters military. By one who saw him then he is described as exceeding tall with large hands and feet and a patrician air which commanded homage.

Twenty years later, when Washington was again in the vicinity of Boston, he was chiefly associated with the George or St. George Tavern which stood on the Neck, near the Roxbury line. This inn was surrounded by an estate of eighteen acres which included a stretch of field and marsh from Roxbury on the south to the great creek on the west. It had orchards and gardens about it and commanded a good view of both Boston and Cambridge Bay. In 1775 it was a military centre for just below it the Americans had thrown up their entrenchments. Despite the fact that the inn was well within range of the British musketry General Washington used to visit it daily during the siege and, standing on its low porch, was wont to view the enemy's position through his field-glasses. His uniform, with its buff-coloured facings, was an easy mark for the British sharpshooters, and several of their bullets, which lodged in the veranda posts, bore evidence of their zeal and vigilance.

Among Old New England Inns

The sign at this inn depicted a globe with a man breaking through the crust, like a chicken from its shell. Apropos of this we have a characteristic story of Continental soldiery. A regiment had just made a forced march from Providence and hungry, weather-beaten and broken with fatigue they reached this inn. When the wag of the crowd espied the man on the sign with his motto, " Oh, how shall I get through this world," he exclaimed, with a rueful look at his own battered person, " 'List, darn ye! 'List, and you'll get through this world fast enough."

With the Hancock Tavern in Corn Court, where Talleyrand is said by some to have stayed during his visit to Boston in 1795 there is connected a story of romantic if tragic interest. The diplomat took a fancy to a delicately-worked pen-knife in the landlord's possession and offered to buy it whereupon it was given to him with the compliments of mine host. Soon after leaving America Talleyrand went to Homburg and there became enamoured of a beautiful baroness known to the world as Cordelia. This woman in her turn admired the penknife and with a kiss and a jest her lover

HANCOCK TAVERN, BOSTON

gave it to her. Later he deserted her and she was found dead on the floor of her apartment with an open note addressed to M. de Talleyrand on the table by her side. "I have burned all your letters," this note read. "They do no honour to my memory nor to your heart. You are the author of my death; may God forgive you as I do."

The lovely baroness had stabbed herself to the heart with that pen-knife which had once been the property of a Boston boniface.

CHAPTER VI

SOME REVOLUTIONARY TAVERNS

THE tavern was the breeding-place *par excellence* of the Revolution. What more natural than for a lot of men, sitting around a blazing fire and talking by the month of their wrongs, to say finally to each other "Let us rebel!" Flip all around and then more flip would be drunk to this resolution; after which our sturdy forefathers would go home in the light of the twinkling stars full to the brim of patriotism, — and of New England rum. But they were by no means beside themselves with either. It was an age of hard drinking and hard thinking and very careful plans were laid ere the first seditionary step was taken.

Occasionally, of course, the landlord was on "the other side." Such was the case with Captain Jones, keeper of the Golden Ball Tavern in Weston, Massachusetts, in whose house the British spy, John How, received

GOLDEN BALL TAVERN, WESTON

Some Revolutionary Taverns

hospitality while out on a mission for General Gage previous to the battles of Lexington and Concord.

It was a fine spring morning early in April, 1775, that a loutish-looking fellow presenting the appearance of a Yankee farmer, strolled into the stable yard of the Joel Smith Tavern in the centre of Weston and asked for work. When questioned as to what he could do, he said he was an expert gunsmith, and from that led the talk into warlike channels. But he was a little *too* glib, and he was soon told that no Britishers were wanted for hire there. He protested vehemently that he was not a Britisher, but the men of this public house would have none of him, asserting that they knew perfectly well by his talk that he was a Britisher and a spy.

By this time quite a crowd had gathered in the tavern-yard and, to escape from their anger, How hurried up the road. His instructions had been to examine the bridges and fording-places, as well as to find out the state of public feeling and he was in the midst of the former occupation when Captain Jones of the Golden Ball caught sight of him. To the captain's question as to what he was doing down there, How replied that he was looking for flagroot; but when he found that Jones was a Royalist in his sympathies he revealed his true character, and was promptly taken into the tavern and provided with a good dinner. Hardly had he finished the meal, however, when there came word that the mob were after him, and he was hastily escorted by Jones's negro servant to the house of Mr. Wheaton, another Royalist who lived in a remote part of the town. There he safely spent the night while thirty baffled men searched every nook and corner of the Golden Ball in the hope of finding him, contenting themselves, when sure he was not there, with drinking a new barrel of rum Jones offered them. In a day or two How pushed on to Worcester and, the next week, turned up at Concord with his observation primed for any sign of military stores he might come upon. Meanwhile he had sent back word to General Gage that if he attempted to march artillery over the Weston road not a man would come back alive. This little incident at Weston it was, then, which caused the Tory general's change of plan, and brought on the battle of Concord.

The builder of the famous Golden Ball

Some Revolutionary Taverns

Inn (erected in 1751) was Colonel Elisha Jones, an ardent Tory, who, at the time of his death, three months before the battle of Concord, commanded the Royal Middlesex Regiment. His Weston estate, which is now the home of General Paine, was confiscated during the Revolution, as was most other Tory property, and the tavern was kept in the family only by Landlord Jones consenting to take the oath of allegiance. He kept it, too, so far as is known. Certainly Paul Revere did not find the atmosphere of the house at all oppressive when he spent a night there while on his way to receive the prisoners taken at Saratoga, whom he conducted to Winter Hill.

The Buckman Tavern, on the right of the Bedford road in Lexington, saw the assembling, preparatory to the battle of Lexington, of the minutemen who belonged to Captain Parker's company. From here, too, the British were fired upon, and in the house, which still stands, may be seen to-day shot-holes to attest that the regulars fired back.

The object of the British in marching to Concord was to destroy the stores John How had told them were there. Almost as soon as Major Pitcairn reached the town he went to a tavern where he had often lodged, sometimes in disguise, and finding the door closed, forced his way in and put innkeeper Jones under guard while the place was searched. He must have felt richly rewarded, for his men found three 24-pounders, completely furnished with everything necessary for mounting, which the Major very speedily put out of commission. Then he demanded that mine host serve him breakfast! One of the buildings which now forms part of the modern Colonial Inn was a storehouse at this time, and was also visited in 1775 by John How.

From the earliest days, Concord had been quite rich in taverns. On the spot where the present public library stands Sergeant William Buss long kept an old-time ordinary. Buss was a most estimable — not to say extraordinary — person, for, not desiring to sell "strong waters," he asked the selectmen to exempt him from that duty when they gave him an inn license in 1660 or earlier. Just where he drew the line is not clear, because it is hardly possible that the selectmen, in granting his request, sustained him to the extent of permitting him to sell neither fermented nor distilled liquor. Buss

Some Revolutionary Taverns

was, however, supplemented in his ministrations by Major Simon Willard, whose duties included the exercise of the "trainband" as well as the sale of wine and "strong water."

This Simon Willard was a good deal of a man. He came to America from Kent county, England, and was at Cambridge, Massachusetts, as early as 1634. With the Rev. Peter Bulkeley, he joined in the purchase of the tract of territory we know as Concord, and he soon became an important person in the direction of matters there, being possessed of considerable means as well as of strong common sense. About 1660 he went to Lancaster, and in 1672 to Groton, in both of which towns he has left his impress upon history. In King Philip's war, he led a company, with distinction to them and to himself, and in times of peace he was closely identified with the militia of the Massachusetts Bay Colony. His first wife was Mercy Shays, and his second and third were sisters of President Dunster of Harvard College. His seventeen children have done much to preserve the name and the fame of their progenitor. The old Willard house at Concord survived until about thirty years ago, when it was destroyed by fire. Its site is now marked by a tablet not far from the first south bridge. In 1666 John Hayward kept the Black Horse Tavern on the main street and for years afterwards he welcomed the travelling public there. Before the Revolution, Ephraim Jones presided over an ordinary near the west end of the Main street burying ground, and adjacent to the old wooden jail; feeding the prisoners was part of this tavern-keeper's business.

Most interesting for our purposes, however, because still standing, is the Wright Tavern, established in 1747, and a public house during the War of the Revolution, — even as it is to-day. Here some of the English officers made their headquarters during their few hours' sojourn in the town on April 19th, and here, tradition says, Maj. John Pitcairn, who commanded the British marines, observed as he stirred his brandy and sugar, "In this way we will stir the blood of the Yankees before night." This place was also the rendezvous of the Concord Minutemen while awaiting, on that same morning, tidings of the advance of the English, and hither came Captain Smith

Some Revolutionary Taverns

and his company from Lincoln to report. The Wright Tavern, therefore, has every claim to the reverence it annually receives from thousands of pilgrims, who there rest from their labours, and partake of needed refreshment in the course of "doing" Concord. Its age alone would make it worthy of veneration. Opened about 1747 by a militia captain named Ephraim Jones, it passed in 1751 into the possession of Thomas Munroe, formerly of Lexington, who made the place, — as Jones had done before him, — a very popular resort for town officials and others. Amos Wright began to be landlord here in 1775 and, though he was the head of the house for only a short time, his name clings. At present the property belongs to the "First Parish Society," into whose care it was willed by the late Reuben Rice and Judge E. Rockwell Hoar. Its old fireplaces are now reopened, and the inside of the house is restored to somewhat of its former antique appearance. Externally it has changed surprisingly little from the aspect it presented away back in 1775, when Doolittle and Earle painted it as the background for their picture showing the royal troops drawn up in Concord square.

Among Old New England Inns

The prices formerly charged at this house are interesting. When ordinaries were first established in Concord a meal cost a sixpence, but in 1779 it was enacted in a neighbouring town that there, — and very likely here, also,

"A mug of West India flip should cost 20 pence.

"A mug of New England flip should cost 12 pence.

"A good dinner should cost 12 pence.

"Breakfast and supper, each, should cost 15 pence.

"Lodging should cost 4 pence."

At the Munroe Tavern in Lexington the brutality which disgraces the English soldiery of April 19, 1775, first became evident. Percy reached this tavern with reinforcements about two o'clock in the afternoon. One party of his men entered the house and, after compelling the inmates to serve them to whatever they wanted, ruthlessly shot down John Raymond, an infirm man residing in the family, only because he had become alarmed at their roughness and brutal conduct, and attempted to leave the house for a place of greater safety.

At Cooper's Tavern, in Arlington, Jabez

WRIGHT TAVERN, CONCORD

COOPER'S TAVERN, ARLINGTON

Some Revolutionary Taverns

Wyman and Jason Winship, two aged citizens who had come, unarmed, simply to inquire the news " were most barbarously and inhumanly murdered by the British, being stabbed through in many places, their heads mauled, skulls broken and their brains dashed out on the floors and walls of the house." [1]

Arnold's Tavern, Weymouth, Massachusetts, is another house of Revolutionary interest, for here was organized on March 9, 1775, the committee of correspondence for that and neighbouring towns. Of this committee Dr. Tufts was chairman and Captain White, Major Lovell, Major Vining and Mr. Joseph Colson other members.

At Sawtell's Tavern, Shirley, in the old Bay State, the rights of New England people to representation when they had paid taxes were vigorously asserted. Obadiah Sawtell kept the house, and when the General Court was formed, he was sent as the town's first representative. He was a delegate, too, to the convention which adopted the Constitution of the United States. How extensively persons from outside appeared

[1] Deposition of Benjamin and Rachel Cooper, taken May 10 1775, while the facts were fully known.

Among Old New England Inns

at Shirley for accommodation, tradition does not inform us, but the tavern was the place where, on gala days, the townspeople conducted their games and sports, and here, too, the veterans of the French and Indian wars long made their boasts of valour.

Greenwich, Connecticut, has a Revolutionary tavern of quite unusual interest, for it was from here that General Israel Putnam, "old Put," rushed out (in 1779) with his face half shaved, to take that daring ride down the stone steps, the story of which is one of our most cherished American traditions. In those days the house was the Israel Knapp Tavern, one of the most popular hostelries on the main road between Boston and New York. Along this road Sir Edmund Andros journeyed to take his seat as the Governor of New England in 1686; in 1775 a messenger bearing the news of Lexington spurred his horse past the inn, and Washington and Lafayette were only a few of the others who made the highway historically famous by passing over it. To-day automobiles by the score speed along here every hour and their passengers stop for refreshment at the Putnam Cottage tea-room,

ARNOLD'S TAVERN, WEYMOUTH.

SAWTELL'S TAVERN, SHIRLEY

Some Revolutionary Taverns

even as their ancestors were wont to do at Israel Knapp's taproom.

The house probably dates back two hundred years. Certainly the land on which it stands was bought in 1692 by one Timothy Knapp, and the interested student may find in the Greenwich land records the following deed, dated 1729:

" Know all men by these presents that I Timothy Knap of Greenwich in the County of fairfield & Colony of Connecticut for ye love good will & fatherly afection which I have and do bear to my loving & dutiful son Israel Knap of the same place County and Colony aforesd do fully freely & absolutely give & grant unto my aforesd son Israel Knap his heirs excrs or admrs for ever soitin pearsal or pearsals of land within ye bounds of greenwich the half of my now Dwelling hous and the one half of my home lot & ye one half of a barn when it is bilt & finished & the one half of my orchard & the land on south side of the street that is bounded north by the streets & east by the land of Ebeneezer Mead & south by the land of Sam'l Mills & west by ye meads lands for him ye sd Israel Knap his heirs asigns for to have &

to hold ye above bargained premises with all Rights privalidgs and apurtanances to ye same belonging or in any wis apurtaining & do promis to warrant secure & defend the above bargained premises from all former bargains seals rents taxes or in cumbrances what so ever made or contracted before the Daye & Date hereof always provided that sd Israel Knap is not to sell nor let out sd premises to any man or persons who so ever during the life of his father & for the confirmation of this above written Deed of gift I have hereunto sett my hand & seal this twenty first Day of March anno qui Domini 1729

"Signed sealed & delivered In the presents of Caleb Knap Jue. John Marshal Entered Aprill ye 19th Day 1729 by Joshua Knap Recorder

The tenth day of April anno domini 1729 then appeared the person of Timothy Knap did acknowlidg the above written deed of gift to be his free and voluntary act & deed

"Gershom Lockwood Justice of ye peace."

The deed of this transfer seems worth giving in full because it establishes the claim of this house to a place among the very few early New England taverns which still entertain the public. To it, as to the Williams Tavern at Marlboro, the Wayside Inn at

Some Revolutionary Taverns

Sudbury, and the West Brookfield Tavern, the automobile has given a new lease of life.

The really interesting history of this house begins, however, with the Revolution. Greenwich was debatable ground all through that struggle and British soldiers were almost as much there as our own men; similarly there was a considerable number of people resident in the town who had Tory sympathies. Among these was Israel Knapp himself, and it is said that his tavern was for a long time the secret meeting-place of those who strove to defeat the Colonies' cause. Thereby hangs a highly romantic though rather dismal tale.

Israel Knapp's favourite son, Timothy, shared the Tory proclivities of his father, but he was deeply in love with the beautiful daughter of the patriot, Jonathan Mead, who lived nearby. It is believed that the girl returned his affection but she felt that loyalty to her father's cause compelled her to refuse Timothy's offer of marriage, and the youth, not unnaturally, was deeply hurt by this. As he left the house the evening of her refusal to give him the answer he so ardently desired he exclaimed, reproachfully, though with some anger as well,

"One day you will speak to me, but I shall never answer you."

One evening, shortly afterwards, when he was approaching the Mead home, probably to make another attempt to win the girl of his choice, her father, mistaking him for one of the British marauders of whom the town was full, shot him through the heart. In an agony of love and remorse, the girl threw herself upon his lifeless body and besought him to speak to her. But he could not respond either to her voice or to her warm caresses. His body lies buried on the grounds of his father's tavern.

"Old Put" had himself been doing the gallant the night before he was surprised by the British at this inn. The story goes that he had escorted a pretty maiden, Mistress Bush of Cos Cob, to a dance in that part of the town known as Pecksland, and that it was in the wee small hours of the morning when he retired. Next morning he slept considerably later than was his habit, and he had only shaved one side of his face when the news came that a large force of British and Tories was approaching along the Post Road from New York. With the lather still on his face, Putnam saddled his horse, ha-

Some Revolutionary Taverns

stened to the Congregational meeting house, — which was only a few rods west of the Knapp Tavern, — and drew up his little body of Continentals. Resistance by such a small number was futile, however, and after the first volley he ordered his men to look to their own safety as best they could. Then he started on a gallop towards Stamford for reinforcements.

The nearest way was down some steps cut for pedestrians in the rocks of what is now known as Put's Hill. The British thought that they had surely captured the American general when they saw him spurring his horse to this precipitous place. But " old Put " was equal to anything, and without a second's hesitation he galloped down the steep incline, turning in his saddle to shake his fist at the astounded dragoons, who dared not follow him, and to call, " Darn ye, I'll hang ye to the next tree when I get ye." That very day he returned with reinforcements and captured a considerable number of prisoners.

Since the Revolution, the Knapp Tavern has been the property of various owners, though it was held until 1812 by Margaret Knapp, daughter of the old tavern-keeper.

Among Old New England Inns

Then the Tracey family held it for more than fifty years and, in 1901, the late Colonel Herschel Adams, — whose wife, Helen Reddington Adams is a descendant of John Reddington, a Greenwich soldier of the Revolution, — bought the place and was instrumental in turning it over to the Putnam Hill Chapter, D. A. R. as their headquarters. The house is tastefully furnished with choice pieces of the Colonial and Revolutionary period, nearly all of which have well-authenticated histories. Of particular interest is a desk in the reception room, which was long the property of Colonel Barrett, who led the American troops at Concord. Upon this desk Putnam, while a guest of Colonel Barrett, once wrote a letter to Washington.

KNAPP TAVERN, GREENWICH

INTERIOR OF KNAPP TAVERN (NOW PUTNAM COTTAGE)

CHAPTER VII

SOME RHODE ISLAND TAVERNS IN WHICH HISTORY WAS MADE

THE smallest of the New England states is very rich in historic taverns. Allusion has already been made to the Roger Mowry Tavern which no longer survives but which stood on Abbott street, Providence, nearly two hundred and fifty years — from the dark days of King Philip's war to the dawn of the twentieth century! This is a very long time in our land of rapid changes, so long a time indeed that it is small wonder that scarcely a trace of the original building could be seen in the house as it last looked. But the huge stone chimney and the rear view of the tavern from the top of the hill upon which it stood proved amply satisfying to one in search of evidence of antiquity.

Another Providence tavern of venerable association is connected with the first overt act of rebellion credited to our colonist forebears. This is the Sabin Tavern, formerly located on South Main street, Providence, in one room of which the party met to organize the expedition which destroyed the *Gaspee*. This act took place nearly three years before the Concord and Lexington fight but the sturdy patriots of Rhode Island were so filled with resentment against the overbearing conduct of the *Gaspee's* officers that they resolved to strike an effective blow. The obnoxious schooner was commanded by Lieut. William Dudingston, and its advertised mission was "to prevent breakers of the revenue laws, and to stop the illicit trade, so long and so successfully carried on in the colony."

The manner in which these orders were carried out was what chiefly offended. For the *Gaspee's* commander insultingly overhauled all vessels sailing up and down the bay, not excepting market boats; and he even went to the length of molesting and plundering people on shore. In the Providence *Gazette* of March 28, 1772, we find the following reference to one of these depredations: "A number of men belonging to the armed schooner that has been for some time past cruising in the river interrupting

SABIN TAVERN, PROVIDENCE

Some Rhode Island Taverns

the traders, firing on Oyster boats &c we are told landed on the Narragansett Shore a few days since & carried off several Hogs belonging to the inhabitants, and also a Quantity of Fire wood." Individuals apprehended by the *Gaspee* within the bay were sent " to Boston for trial, contrary to an act of Parliament, which required such trials to be held in the Colonies where seizures were made."

This was not for a moment to be tolerated and Darius Sessions, the deputy-governor, began to be besieged with complaints, all of which asked for information concerning the real authority of this British commander in taking charge of the navigable waters of the state. Thereupon Chief Justice Hopkins was asked for an opinion. He gave it: " no commander of any vessel has a right to use any authority in the body of the Colony, without previously appearing to the governor and showing his warrant for so doing, and also being sworn to a due exercise of his office."

Naturally this decision precipitated a spirited correspondence between Governor Wanton and Lieut. Dudingston. Subsequently all the letters which passed between them were submitted to Admiral Montague, who was in command of the British fleet at Boston. But, following a custom not yet outgrown, the Admiral stoutly upheld his "man" replying to the governor "that he Dudingston, has done his duty and behaved like an officer, and it is your duty as a governor to give him your assistance and not endeavor to distress the King's officers for strictly complying with my orders. I shall give them directions," he continued, "that in case they receive any molestation in the execution of their duty, they shall send every man so taken in molesting them to me. I am also informed, the people of Newport talk of fitting out an armed vessel to rescue any vessel the King's schooner may take carrying on an illicit trade. Let them be cautious what they do for as sure as they attempt it and any of them are taken I will hang them as pirates."

This was the threat which inspired the gathering at Sabin's tavern. A favourable opportunity to strike an effective blow was supplied by the grounding of the *Gaspee* about seven miles below Providence, while chasing the sloop *Hannah* commanded by Benjamin Lindsay. The *Hannah* continued

Some Rhode Island Taverns

up the river and arrived about sunset at her wharf in Providence. Then, in the words of Col. Ephraim Bowen, one member of the *Gaspee* party, " Lindsey immediately informed Mr. John Brown, one of our first and most respectable merchants of the situation of the *Gaspee*. He concluded that she would remain immovable until about midnight, and that now an opportunity offered of putting an end to the trouble and vexation she daily caused.

" Mr. Brown immediately resolved on her destruction, and he forthwith directed one of his trusty shipmasters to collect eight of the largest long boats in the harbor, with five oars each; to have the oars and row locks well muffled, to prevent noise and to place them at Fenner's wharf, directly opposite to the dwelling of Mr. James Sabin, who kept a house of board and entertainment for gentlemen. About the time of the shutting up of the shops, soon after sunset, a man passed along the main street, beating a drum, and informing the inhabitants of the fact that the *Gaspee* was aground on Namquit Point, and would not float off until three o'clock the next morning; and inviting those persons who felt a disposition to go and destroy that troublesome vessel, to repair in the evening to Mr. James Sabin's house.

"About nine o'clock I took my father's gun, and my powder horn and bullets and went to Mr. Sabin's, and found the southeast room full of people, where I loaded my gun and all remained there until about ten o'clock, some casting bullets in the kitchen and others making arrangements for departure, when orders were given to cross the street to Fenner's wharf, and embark; which soon took place and a sea-captain acted as steersman of each boat; of whom I recollect Capt. Abraham Whipple, Capt. John B. Hopkins (with whom I embarked) and Capt. Benjamin Dunn. A line from left to right was soon formed, with Capt. Whipple on the right, and Capt. Hopkins on the right of the left wing.

"The party thus proceeded until within about sixty yards of the *Gaspee,* when a sentinel hailed, 'Who comes there?' No answer. He hailed again and no answer. In about a minute Dudingston mounted the starboard gunwale, in his shirt, and hailed, 'Who comes there?' No answer. He

Some Rhode Island Taverns

hailed again, when Capt. Whipple answered as follows:

"'I am the sheriff of the county of Kent [expletives]. I have got a warrant to apprehend you [ditto] so surrender — — —!'

"I took my seat on the main thwart, near the larboard row-lock, with my gun by my right side, facing forwards.

"As soon as Dudingston began to hail, Joseph Bucklin, who was standing on the main thwart, by my right side, said to me, 'Eph, reach me your gun and I can kill that fellow.' I reached it to him accordingly; when, during Capt. Whipple's replying, Bucklin fired, and Dudingston fell; and Bucklin exclaimed, 'I have killed the rascal.'

"In less than a minute after Capt Whipple's answer the boats were alongside of the *Gaspee,* and boarded without opposition. The men on deck retreated below as Dudingston entered the cabin.

"As soon as it was discovered thatt he was wounded, John Mawney, who had for two or three years been studying physic and surgery, was ordered to go into the cabin and dress Dudingston's wounds and I was directed to assist him. . . .

Among Old New England Inns

"Dudingston called for Mr. Dickinson to produce bandages and other necessaries for the dressing of the wound, and when finished, orders were given to the schooner's company to collect their clothing and everything belonging to them, and put them into the boats as all of them were to be sent on shore. All were soon collected and put on board of the boats, including one of our boats. They departed and landed Dudingston at the old Still house wharf at Pawtuxet, and put the chief into the house of Joseph Rhodes. Soon after, all the party were ordered to depart, leaving one boat for the leaders of the expedition; who soon set the vessel on fire, which consumed her to the water's edge."

Col. Bowen's account of this affair, written when he was eighty-six years old, is illuminatingly supplemented by John Mawney's recollections of the night's work, published about 1825 in the Providence *American and Gazette*. He heard the drummer passing through the streets, he tells us, and, attracted by the extraordinary announcement he was making, hurried to the Sabin Tavern. After some persuasion Mawney consented to join the expedition as surgeon;

Some Rhode Island Taverns

and it is over his professional duties on the eventful evening that he lingers with most pride in his narrative.

"When I was summoned to the cabin," he says, "I found Lieut. Dudingston in a sitting posture, gently reclining to the left, bleeding profusely, with a thin white woollen blanket loose about him, which I threw aside, and discovered the effect of a musket ball in the left groin; and thinking the femoral artery was cut, threw open my waistband, and taking my shirt by the collar tore it, when Mr. Dudingston said, 'Pray, sir, don't tear your clothes; there is linen in that trunk."

Undoubtedly Mawney's work was skilful though he was only a student, for after the wound had been dressed Lieut. Dudingston offered him a gold stock-buckle as a testimonial of his gratitude and when he refused to accept this urged upon him a silver one which he wore with pride until his death.

Three days later the Providence *American and Gazette* published the bare facts of the *Gaspee's* destruction, but hours before the press had presented the thing in outline the story was well known throughout the Colony and in neighbouring colonies as well.

Among Old New England Inns

In that era the newspaper came straggling after instead of anticipating the events of the day.

Of course every possible endeavour was made to apprehend the offenders, the initial reward of one hundred pounds sterling being increased to five hundred pounds " to any person or persons who shall discover the persons guilty " and a hundred pounds additional for the discovery and apprehension of the person " who acted or called themselves or were called by their accomplices the head sheriff or the captain." Notices of these rewards were freely distributed throughout the towns in the Colony but without other effect than that accorded the King's proclamation which was posted on the hay-scales near the northeast corner of the Market house, and which Mr. Joseph Aplin, a distinguished lawyer, struck down with his cane immediately after reading. Even the Royal Commission especially appointed to search out the participators in this bold deed could find out nothing!

Yet the people of the town knew well about the details of the affair and such letters as this quoted by Mr. Edward Field

Some Rhode Island Taverns

in his "History of Rhode Island" passed freely through the mails:

"PROVIDENCE, Ye 23rd June 1772.
"DEAR BROTHER:
"If I had no other motive to embrace this opportunity of writing to you yet gratitude would oblige me. . . . Doubtless you have heard of the skirmish down the river, and of the burning of the armed Schooner and badly wounding the captain; so I shall write no more concerning the affair (though I was on the wharf when the boats were manned and armed and knew the principal actors), lest it should be too much spread abroad; and perhaps you have seen the thundering proclamation in the newspaper and the reward of £100 sterling offered to any person or persons who shall discover the perpetrators of the said villainy, as it is called.

"The clock strikes eleven. We take no note of time but from its loss. . . .
"From your affectionate brother
"and sincere friend
SOLOMON DROWN JUNR."

With Rhode Island's next brave strike in behalf of liberty the David Arnold Tavern at Old Warwick is connected. The deed in question was the capture of the British General Prescott by Major William Barton of Warren on the night of July 5, 1777.

For some six months previous to this, Providence had been in a state of most intense excitement owing to the arrival at Newport, early in December, of the British fleet and troops commanded by Sir Henry Clinton. To defend the inhabitants of the colonies from the depredations of the soldiers (who were wont to come on shore and indulge in the wildest kind of revelry), and to guard against any surprise or attack on the town, state troops were posted at various points along the shores of Narragansett Bay. In the month of June, 1777, a regiment of Rhode Island troops, under the command of Col. Stanton, was stationed in the town of Tiverton. Maj. Barton was an officer of this regiment.

Barton had previously served at Newport, and was familiar with the island and its surroundings as well as with the offenses which had been there committed by the men from the British ships. Moreover, he ardently admired Gen. Charles Lee, who was now

Some Rhode Island Taverns

a captive in the hands of the enemy. (Lee, it should be parenthetically explained, was not known for nearly a century later as "the most worthless character which the Revolution brought to notice.") Resentment, then, against the British, a loyal zeal to rescue Lee, and desire to distinguish himself, were motives which worked together in Barton's mind, and caused him to carry out a plan second to none in the Revolution for boldness and adroit performance.

Prescott, as Maj. Barton knew, frequently spent the night at the house of a man named Overing about five miles above Newport on the west road leading to Bristol Ferry. Because Prescott's errand at this house was one of which he had no reason to be proud, the guard was only a slight one. Barton's plan, therefore, was to cross Narragansett Bay from the mainland, seize Prescott and carry him to the American camp.

Not long after Barton had hit upon this idea, he received from a man named Coffin, who had escaped from the island, many details concerning the Overing house. Thus he had at last sufficient information to enable him successfully to carry out his project. For a time he kept the plan to himself, but at last he went to Col. Stanton and unfolded it to him. To his delight this officer promised him all possible aid. Barton declined to explain to his friends the details and object of his night-errand so that the utmost confidence was called for on their part. This much, however, he did tell them; that it was necessary for the purpose of the mysterious affair, that five whale-boats be provided. In a few days these were forthcoming. The only thing now needed was men.

The regiment was ordered paraded, and the colonel having thus provided his subordinate with an opportunity to ask for volunteers, forty, the necessary number, were quickly chosen. With them and the following order from his colonel, Barton proceeded to do his work:

"HEADQUARTERS CAMP AT TIVERTON,
"5th July, 1777.
"LIEUT. COL. BARTON,
"You will proceed to the Island of Newport and attack the enemy when and where you think proper and make Report to me of your proceeding.
"JOS: STANTON, JR. *Colo.*"

Some Rhode Island Taverns

Not until two days after the beginning of active operations did Barton explain to his volunteers the nature of the enterprise upon which they had embarked! But though they were greatly astonished at the boldness of the plan, not one of them wished to withdraw, and it was, therefore, with the full quota of men that he proceeded with his perilous undertaking on the evening of July 9th. No plunder, no liquor, silence and implicit obedience were the conditions imposed as the forty-one men embarked on the five boats waiting at Warwick Neck with oars already muffled. Barton's boat took the lead. To distinguish it from the others a pole was set up on which was tied a white handkerchief. He was followed swiftly and silently as he made his way close to the western shore of Prudence Island, taking care to avoid the enemy's ships, which lay near Hope Island. Yet they went quite near enough to hear the sentinel call in the black night "All's well!"

When the landing was made at that point on the shore nearest the Overing house, one man was left with each boat and instructed to push off in case any break in the plans should occur. Then the five divisions pushed on up to the house. There were three entrances and it was arranged that all were to be attacked while one group of men guarded the road and another acted on emergencies.

No sooner was the front gate opened, however, than a sentinel advanced and demanded, "Who come there?" No reply was made and the party kept on; a second time the sentinel inquired, "Who comes there?"

"Friends," retorted Barton, who was now nearly up with the guard.

"Advance and give the countersign," was the response.

"We have none," said Barton, "but have you seen any deserters tonight?"

This naïve retort so surprised the guard that John Hunt, one of the party, was able to overpower the man and take away his gun before he had time to realize that these were enemies and not friends. Told to preserve silence under penalty of instant death, he became as one dumb.

To enter the house and capture Prescott was the work of only a few moments, for Mr. Overing, much frightened, immediately indicated the room where he was soon found,

Some Rhode Island Taverns

sitting in his nightclothes on the side of the bed.

"Are you General Prescott?" demanded Barton.

"Yes," replied the man.

"You are my prisoner."

"I acknowledge it, sir," replied Prescott.

The general was then told that he must accompany them at once, and, though he begged for time to dress, he was allowed opportunity to put on only a few garments. Time was very precious just then. Had Major Barrington, the general's aid, who in an attempt to give the alarm jumped from the window of the chamber where he had been sleeping, not been captured by the men outside, the whole affair might have miscarried.

There was none too much time as it was, for scarcely had the little party made their way through the meadows to the boats when three cannon and three rockets, the signal of alarm, came from the island; some of the household had spread the news and the whole camp was aroused. Barton and his party proceeded on their way unmolested, however, and Prescott said admiringly as they rowed past the British vessels lying at anchor, " Sir, I did not think it possible you could escape the vigilance of the water-guards."

From the landing-place to David Arnold's tavern at Warwick neck was not much of a walk, but Prescott, whose bare feet had been scratched by the blackberry vines in the meadow they had recently crossed, begged so hard for a pair of shoes that a pair was obtained for him from one of the officers at the Warwick neck station. Samuel Cory, of the expedition, was directed by Barton to take the shoes to the general and put them on. There was some difficulty about this as Prescott kept protesting that his feet were so swollen the shoes would not fit. " My orders were to put the shoes on General Prescott, not to see that they fitted," said Samuel grimly, as he vigorously executed the order.

Upon their arrival at the tavern, the two prisoners were assigned rooms and carefully guarded. Next morning at breakfast Prescott ate little, and Mrs. Arnold, the landlord's wife, thinking he did not like her fare, made some remark on the subject. But the British general assured her that he had no appetite. He likewise had no cravat,

DAVID ARNOLD TAVERN, WARWICK

PELEG ARNOLD TAVERN, NEAR WOONSOCKET

Some Rhode Island Taverns

and Mrs. Arnold, noticing this, kindly gave him one of her best white handkerchiefs to remedy this defect of toilet. Soon after the morning meal, the two distinguished prisoners were driven under guard to Providence, in a coach General Spencer had sent out for this purpose. From Providence, Prescott was forwarded to General Washington's headquarters in New Jersey, and in the spring he was exchanged for General Lee, as Barton had hoped would be the case.

Peleg Arnold's tavern at what is now Union village, near Woonsocket, is another Revolutionary tavern rich in historic associations. As a house of entertainment the place dates back to 1739, when Lieut. Thomas Arnold, the father of Peleg, was licensed to keep a public house. Situated as it was on the "Great Road" leading to Worcester, it was widely patronized by weary travellers, and when the father died in 1765 Peleg began to carry on the business. To his door, ten years later, rode a dusty messenger with the exciting news of Concord and Lexington, news which so aroused the tavern-keeper that throughout the Revolution his house was the centre of all the patriotic enterprises of that section.

Among Old New England Inns

Here the town-meeting was held and here men were recruited for service in the army. Here, too, a little later, were deposited arms for distribution among the North Smithfield soldiery. When Peleg Arnold died, he had for many years been Chief Justice of the Supreme Court of Rhode Island.

Another Justice Eleazer Arnold was also a Rhode Island tavern-keeper and a man of unusual qualities. His license to keep a public house is dated August 14, 1710, and the privilege then extended is thus formally recorded:

"Whereas the Lawes do Provide that no Person Inhabiting on our Collony shall keepe any Publick house of Entertainment for strangers, Travilers or others, nor Retale Strong drinke, unless they have a licence from the Councill of ye Respective Towne whereunto they do belong; And Whereas you Justice Eliezer Arnold Inhabitant of this Towne of Providence, in ye Colloney of Rhode Island & Providence Plantations in New England haveing desired of ye Towne Councill of sd Providence that they Would Grant unto you a licence in order to that Purpose, whereby you might be in a Capacitye to keepe a house of that Order & for

Some Rhode Island Taverns

that imploy: The Towne Councill of said Providence being mett, & haveing Considered your Request, and to ye end that strangers, Travilers & other Persons may be accomodated with suteable Entertainment at all times as Ocation Requires do by these presents Grant un to you ye abovesd Justice Eliezer Arnold licence & libertye to keepe a Publick house of Entertainment in sd Providence Towneshipp at your dwelling, for the Entertaineing of Strangers, Travilers & other Persons, both horse and foote, Carters, Drovers, &c: at all times for & duiring the full & just Terme of one yeares Time forward from ye day of the date of these presents: And that at all times duiring the said Terme of time you do (within your Prescinks) well & truely Observe, do & keepe good Orders according as ye lawes do Require Persons Who are licenced to keepe such houses to do & Performe. Dated August ye 14th: 1710."

This old house has been designated for generations as " The Stone Chimney House " by reason of its huge fireplace and chimney of stone. It has been said that this form of construction was used on the side to the northwestward, north and northeastward to protect the house from the fire-arrows of Indians who dwelt in the primeval forest that there stretched out. This explanation, too, is given for the mortar-laid shingles on the roof. Unfortunately for the story, however, there are facts to show us that the relation between Eleazer Arnold and his redmen neighbours were most unusually friendly. Within the tavern when he died was "an old bed the Indians used to lie on!"

For its time Justice Arnold's tavern was unusually spacious. It had four rooms on the lower floor and on the second floor were two chambers one of which contained a fireplace. The living-room was large and commodious with its huge fireplace, the great "summer" beam upon which the guns were wont to be placed, and over the fireplace a strong eye-bolt to which could be attached a block and tackle to aid in hauling great logs to the fire. Mantelpieces, as one careful student of colonial days has pointed out, were no part of the interior furnishings of really old houses. "Whatever was arranged about the walls was hung on long hooks made of natural branches, fitted according to the ingenuity of the owner." The date of

ELEAZER ARNOLD TAVERN, NEAR QUINSNICKET, LINCOLN

GREENVILLE TAVERN, SMITHFIELD

Some Rhode Island Taverns

this house is 1687, and here Justice Arnold long held his court.

The Greenville Tavern, Smithfield, Rhode Island, dates back to 1730, and with its second-story piazza, overhanging roof and huge chimney certainly suggests old-time revelries and romantic rendezvous. Divers merry parties were wont to congregate in this old inn and sip flip or cheering toddy around its blazing fire. Mr. Edward Field quotes an ancient rhyme which throws into sharp relief one such congenially occupied group:

"Landlord, to thy bar room skip,
  Make it a foaming mug of flip —
  Make it of our country's staple,
  Rum, New England sugar maple,
  Beer that's brewed from hops and Pumpkins,
  Grateful to the thirsty Bumpkins.
  Hark! I hear the poker sizzle
  And O'er the mug the liquor drizzle,
  And against the earthen mug
  I hear the wooden spoon's cheerful dub.
  I see thee, landlord, taste the flip;
  And fling thy cud from under lip,
  Then pour more rum, the bottle stopping,
  Stir it again and say it's topping;
  Come, quickly bring the humming liquor,
  Richer than ale of British vicar,

Among Old New England Inns

Better than Usquebaugh Hibernian
Or than Flacus' famed Falernian,
More potent healthy, racy, frisky,
Than Holland's gin or Georgia's whisky.
Come, make a ring around the fire
And hand the mug unto the squire;
Here, Deacon, take the elbow chair,
And Corporal Cuke, do you sit there;
You take the dye tub, you the churn,
And I'll the double corner turn.
See the fomenting liquor rise
And burn their cheeks and close their eyes;
See the sidling mug incline,
Hear them curse their dull divine
Who on Sunday dared to rail
Against B —'s flip or Downer's ale
Quick, landlord, fly and bring another,
And Deacon H. shall pay for 'tother
Ensign and I the third will share,
Its due on swop for the pyeball mare."

From this highly convivial verse, we discover that though there was seldom much furniture in a typical tap-room, a flip-iron was an indispensable fixture. This, when heated, gave to certain mixtures a burnt, bitter flavour which was much liked. The ingredients stirred together varied in different parts of the colonies but one much

Some Rhode Island Taverns

approved by Rhode Island palates consisted of home-brewed beer sweetened with sugar molasses or dried pumpkin and flavoured with a liberal dash of rum.

An era which could enjoy such barbarous drinks not unnaturally encouraged barbarous customs. Certainly no softer adjective may fitly characterize the shift marriages which took place in Rhode Island, not far from one of the taverns we have here been discussing. In the records of the town of Warwick appears the following entry:

"These are to signify unto all ministers of justice that Henry Strait Jun of East Greenwich in ye colony of R. I. and Prov. Plantation took Mary Webb of ye town of Warwick in ye colony afousd. widow in only a shift and no other Garment in ye presns of Avis Gordon May Collins and Presilar Crandall and was Lawfully Married in sd Warwick ye first of August 1725 by me Recorded ye 5th of Nov 1725 Pr John Wickes T. C."

In South Kingstown this same curious custom prevailed and it is there recorded that "Thomas Cullenwell was joyned in Marriage to Abigaile his wife the 22d of February 1719-20. He took her in marriage after she had gone four times across the Highway in only her shift and hair lace and no other clothing. Joyned togather, in marriage per me George Hassard Just."

The third record, which is somewhat fuller, shows us what this extraordinary wedding custom meant to its participants:

" In the town of Newport in the Colony of Rhode Island and on the 13th of September 1714 John Gavett of the town and county above said did meet with Sarah Stephenson, widow, in the street within the town abovesaid stark naked save only her shift and they being lawfully published the said John Gavett did accept in marriage the above said Sarah Stephenson stark naked save only her shift without housing or lands or any personal state whatever, and in said street I did join together in marriage the above said John Gavett and Sarah Stephenson on the day and year above said as witness my hand and seal hereto affixed.

" NATH'L SHEFFIELD *Assistant.*"

Let it not be thought, however, that this custom was peculiar to Rhode Island. Such was far from being the case; shift marriages

Some Rhode Island Taverns

for the purpose of escaping the debts contracted by the bride's deceased husband took place in many of the colonies, — certainly in Pennsylvania and in all the New England states. And a pitiful commentary they are upon the crude civilization of our tavern-loving forbears.

CHAPTER VIII

THE TAVERNS THAT ENTERTAINED WASHINGTON

OF all the distinguished guests with whose names tavern traditions are proudly linked, Washington is, of course, the most eminent. The tavern that can boast of having given him shelter for a night has ten times the chance of preservation accorded the ordinary old building. One writer indeed believes that the Washington tavern business is greatly overdone and, in speaking of an inn interesting chiefly for its age, points out triumphantly that it is " innocent of Washington associations." Just here, however, we will take the other tack and trace carefully the hostelries honoured by the President's party during his official visits to New England.

" Thurs. Oct. 15, 1789," says his Diary, " I commenced my journey about 9 o'clock for Boston and a tour through the Eastern

States. The Chief Justice, Mr. Jay — and the secretaries of the Treasury and War Departments accompanied me some distance out of the city. About 10 o'clock it began to Rain and continued to do so till 11, when we arrived at the house of one Hoyatt, who keeps a Tavern at Kingsbridge, where we, that is, Major Jackson, Mr. Lear and myself with six servants, which composed my Retinue dined. After dinner, through frequent light showers we proceed'd to the Tavern of Mrs. Haviland at Rye. . . . Oct. 16 About 7 o'clock we left the Widow Haviland's and after passing Horse Neck, six miles from Rye, we breakfasted at Stamford [Connecticut] which is 6 miles further. At Norwalk, which is six miles further we made a halt to feed our horses. . . . From thence to Fairfield where we dined and lodged, is 12 miles. October 17. — A little after sunrise we left Fairfield, and passing through Et. Fairfield, breakfasted at Stratford, which is ten miles from Fairfield. . . . At this place I was received with an effort of Military parade; and was attended to the Ferry, which is near a mile from the center of the Town, by sevl. Gentlemen on horseback. . . . From the ferry

Among Old New England Inns

is about 3 miles to Milford." The tavern in Milford, — now no longer standing, — was kept by Andrew Clark, — and not very well kept either. Lambert's history tells us that, during his New England tour of 1789, Washington twice put up here. The house had been opened very early in the town's history by one Tomlinson who, in 1656, was sued by the authorities because "he had broken the jurisdiction order by selling strong water, wine and beer at greater prices than was allowed, and kept a disorderly house in that he suffered young men and maids to come there and dance and play at shuffle board." Washington's criticism of the house was that he did not find the food good, — and that it had no silver spoons! Not much relishing his supper of boiled meat and potatoes, he called for a bowl of milk, which was brought him, with a pewter spoon that lacked a handle. He asked for a silver spoon, but was told the house afforded none, whereupon he gave the servant-maid a two-shilling piece and told her to go and borrow one. She accordingly borrowed one for him at the minister's.

"From Milford," the Diary continues, "we took the lower road through West

Haven and arrived at New Haven before two o'clock; we had time to walk through several parts of the City before Dinner. . . . The Address (of the Assembly) was presented at 7 o'clock and at nine I received another address from the Congregational Clergy of the place. Between the rect. of the two addresses I received the Compliment of a visit from the Govr. Mr. Huntington — the Lieut. Gov. Mr. Wolcott — and the Mayor Mr. Roger Sherman."

Sunday finds the President enjoying the hospitality of the town's best tavern. "Went in the forenoon to the Episcopal church," the Diary records, "and in the afternoon to one of the Congregational Meeting-Houses. Attended to the first by the speaker of the Assembly, Mr. Edwards, and a Mr. Ingersoll, and to the latter by the Governor, the Lieut. Governor, the Mayor and Speaker. These gentlemen all dined with me (by invitation) as did Genl. Huntington, at the House of Mr. Brown, where I lodged, and who keeps a good Tavern. Drank tea at the Mayor's. . . . At 7 O'clock in the evening many Officers of this State, belonging to the late Continental army, called to pay their respects to me."

Among Old New England Inns

The keeper of this "good tavern" had not been very long in the business, it appears, for in the columns of the Connecticut *Journal* for April, 1786, we find the following: "Jacob Brown, one of the proprietors of the stages, informs the public that he has opened a house of entertainment in the City of New Haven." "This house must have faced the Green," says Mr. Henry T. Blake, secretary of the New Haven Colony Historical Society, "for in May, 1787, Mr. Brown advertised that 'he has removed from the house lately occupied on the Green to Colonel Hubbard's elegant stone house near the old market where those who wish to take passage in the stage and others may be decently entertained.'" This second house it was to which Washington came, and it is still standing at the junction of Church, George and Meadow streets. To-day, too, as in Washington's time it dispenses liquid refreshments. Only now its wares are served without lodging, over the counter, by the glass,—and they are of Teutonic appeal. The house was built by Dr. Hubbard, who died in 1794, and was, in its day, one of the most elegant private residences of the town.

That Saturday evening of Washington's

visit it was again thronged with handsomely-dressed gentlemen. A constant succession of civic, ecclesiastical and military dignities streamed through its spacious parlours. At seven the Committee of the Legislature appeared; at eight the Governor and the mayor made their bows and at nine the Reverend President of the College and the Congregational ministers arrived. Later numerous worthy citizens of the town paid their respects to the nation's head.

After the Sunday dinner at Brown's to which the Diary refers, the President heard the great Jonathan Edwards preach. His entertainers had expected that the distinguished theologian would furnish a sermon suitable to the extraordinary occasion, but Edwards, with characteristic other-worldliness announced that his text was, "Train up a Child in the way he should go and when he is old he will not depart from it." He added immediately that, in speaking on these sacred words, he would address himself principally to the children in the galleries! In this connection it is pleasant to find a charming story of the President's encounter, that afternoon, with one of those very children. He went, as the Diary records, to drink tea with the Mayor, Mr. Sherman. Roger Sherman's house is still standing, on Chapel street, next to the Union League Club building. Its door on that faraway occasion was opened, as the President was leaving, by Mr. Sherman's little daughter Mehitabel. Washington, putting his hand on her head remarked kindly, " You deserve a better office, my little lady!" "Yes, sir," she replied with a courtesy, " to let you *in*."

One earlier visit to New Haven the President had made. This was in the summer of 1775, when on his way to take command of the Continental forces at Cambridge. On this occasion he stopped at the house of Isaac Beers, then situated on the lot where the New Haven House now stands. The proprietor was the son of Mr. Nathan Beers, who was killed in his own house by the British troops during their invasion of New Haven in 1779. The house had been kept by Mr. Beers as a place of public entertainment since about 1760; and until he retired from inn-keeping in 1778 was the most prominent hostelry in New Haven. Public dinners were frequently held here, and John Adams records that when he stopped there in 1774 on his way to the Continental Con-

Taverns That Entertained Washington

gress he " talked of politics with Mr. Beers." While Washington was a guest at this house he was aroused very early in the morning to review the company of one hundred and sixty Yale students which had been formed, soon after the battle of Lexington, to serve the cause of the United Colonies.

" Left New Haven at 6 O'clock," we find to be the entry of October 19, " and arrived at Wallingford (13 miles) by half after 8 o'clock, where we breakfasted and took a walk through the Town. . . . About 10 o'clock we left this place, and at the distance of 8 miles passed through Durham. At one we arrived at Middletown, on Connecticut River, being met two or three miles from it by the respectable citizens of the place, and escorted in by them. While dinner was getting ready I took a walk around the Town from the heights of which the prospect is beautiful. . . . Having dined, we set out with the same escort (who conducted us into town about three o'clock for Hartford, and passing through a Parish of Middletown and Weathersfield we arrived at Harfd. about sundown. At Weathersfield we were met by a party of the Hartford light horse and a number of Gentlemen from the same place with Col⁰ Wadsworth at their head, and escorted to Bull's Tavern where we lodged."

This tavern, the most noted in Hartford, was called the Bunch of Grapes from its carved sign bearing that device. It stood at or near the point of intersection of Asylum street with the west side of Main street.

M. de Chastellux, who visited the house during the Revolutionary War, commented on it as " a very good inn; kept by Mr. Bull, who is accused of being rather *on the other side of the question;* a polite method of designating a tory."

The punctiliousness with which Washington fulfilled all his engagements in the course of this triumphal tour is very impressive. Occasionally, of course, the weather interfered with plans made but when such was the case we find the matter carefully explained in the Diary. Accordingly there is recorded on Wednesday, October 21, " By promise I was to have Breakfasted at Mr. Ellsworth's at Windsor, on my way to Springfield, but the morning proving very wet, and the rain not ceasing till past ten o'clock, I did not set out until half after that hour; I called, however, on

Taverns That Entertained Washington

Mr. Ellsworth and stay'd there near an hour — reached Springfield by 4 o'clock, and while dinner was getting, examined the Continental Stores at this place. A Col°. Worthington, Col°. Williams, Adjutant General of the State of Massachusetts, Gen. Shepherd, Mr. Lyman and many other Gentlemen sat an hour or two with me in the evening at Parson's Tavern, where I lodged, and which is a good House."

Until ten years ago this building stood at the west end of Court street though sadly shorn of its barns, sheds and dance-hall, all of which were prominent features in Washington's day. At that time it was a huge, rambling, unpainted structure with a lofty wing, which, when afterwards detached, was called the "light-house." Zenas Parsons was succeeded as landlord by Eleazer Williams and when James Monroe came to Springfield, early in his presidency, he found John Bennett in charge. Soon afterwards, the property was sold to Erastus Chapin, and, in 1819, a company of public-spirited townspeople bought its site for a square and moved the main part of the old tavern to its last resting-place at the foot of Court Street.

Among Old New England Inns

For the President's party in 1789, Palmer was the next stop, breakfast being taken " at the House of one Scott." This tavern is sometimes called "Scots at the Elbow," probably from its situation near the " ford " afterwards the "bridge" over the Quabog river. It was for many years a very famous inn.

Brookfield came next in the itinerary and the tavern which had the honour of entertaining Washington at dinner (October 23, 1789) is still standing, near the centre of West Brookfield village, directly on the main street. Built in 1760 by David Hitchcock, it was occupied by him as a hostelry till 1811. He, therefore, was the host at Washington's visit. Ten years later he entertained for the night another President, John Adams, on his way to Quincy, his home-town. Lafayette was entertained here in 1825 and there is a tradition that Jerome Bonaparte and his lovely American wife passed a night here soon after their marriage. Nowadays the tavern is a favourite resort of automobile parties, who find its combination of old-time atmosphere with modern improvements, of fragrant traditions with excellent food very attractive.

YE OLDE TAVERN, WEST BROOKFIELD

Taverns That Entertained Washington

This is, indeed, one of the few "taverns that entertained Washington" which I can cordially recommend to the twentieth-century wayfarer. Most of them are not inns any longer, and of such as are, the least said the better, — too often.

From Brookfield, — where the President received an "Express which was sent to me by Govr. Hancock giving notice of the measures he was about to pursue for my reception on the Road and in Boston, with a request to lodge at his House," the party pressed on "to Spencer, 10 miles further, and lodged at the House of one Jenks, who keeps a pretty good tavern."

The bread at this tavern was particularly good, if one may trust the landlord's wife; she used to tell the story that the General at breakfast remarked, "Madam, your bread is very beautiful."

"Commenced our course with the Sun," says the Diary on October 23, "and passing through Leicester met some Gentlemen of the Town of Worcester, on the line between it and the former to escort us.... We were received by a handsome Company of Militia Artillery in Uniform, who saluted with 13 Guns on our entry and departure. At this place also we met a Committee from the Town of Boston . . . On the Line between Worcester and Middlesex I was met by a troop of light Horse belonging to the latter, who escorted me to Marlborough, where we dined, and thence to Weston where we lodged."

Washington's stopping-place in Marlborough still welcomes guests; and to-day, as in his time, it is known as the Williams Tavern. Erected in 1665 by Abraham Williams, it has ever since been a popular resort for travellers. In early days court was held here, and the old-time cells may still be seen in the basement. The Duke de la Rochefoucault was once entertained here, and when Landlord Pease — of whom we have already heard — started his first line of mail-coaches in 1786 this house was one of the principal stopping-places on the mail route between Boston and New York.

The Weston tavern patronized by Washington in 1789 was that of John Flagg.

"On October 24," the Diary continues, "dressed by Seven o'clock, and set out at eight — at ten we arrived in Cambridge, according to appointment; but most of the Militia having a distance to come, were not

Taverns That Entertained Washington

in line till after eleven; they made however an excellent appearance, with Genl. [John] Brooks at their Head. At this place the Lieut. Govr. Mr. Saml. Adams, with the Executive Council, met me and preceded my entrance into town — which was in every degree flattering and honourable. To pass over the Minutiæ of the arrangement for this purpose, it may suffice to say that at the entrance I was welcomed by the Selectmen in a body. Then following the Liet Govr. and Council in the order we came from Cambridge (preceded by the Town Corps, very handsomely dressed), we passed through the Citizens classed in their different professions, and under their own banners, till we came to the State House; from which across the Street an Arch was thrown; in the front of which was this Inscription — 'To the Man who unites all hearts' — and on the other — 'To Columbia's favorite Son' — and on one side thereof next the State House, in a pannel decorated with a trophy, composed of the Arms of the United States — of the Commonwealth of Massachusetts — and our French Allies, crowned with a wreath of Laurel, was this Inscription — 'Boston relieved March 17th, 1776.'

Among Old New England Inns

This Arch was handsomely ornamented, and over the Center of it a Canopy was erected 20 feet high, with the American Eagle perched on the top. After passing through the Arch, and entering the State House at the S° End and ascending to the upper floor and returning to a Balcony at the N° end; three cheers was given by a vast concourse of people who by this time had assembled at the Arch — then followed an ode composed in honour of the President; and well sung by a band of select singers — after this three Cheers — followed by the different Professions and Mechanics in the order they were drawn up with their colours through a lane of the People, which had thronged abt. the Arch under which they passed. The Streets, the Doors, windows and tops of the Houses were crowded with well dressed Ladies and Gentlemen. The procession being over, I was conducted to my lodgings at a Widow Ingersoll's, (which is a very decent and good house) by the Lieut. Govr. and Council — accompanied by the Vice President, where they took leave of me. Having engaged yesterday to take an informal dinner with the Govr. [John Hancock] to-day, but under a

WILLIAMS TAVERN, MARLBOROUGH.

Taverns That Entertained Washington

full persuasion that he would have waited upon me so soon as I should have arrived — I excused myself upon his not doing it, and informing me thro' his Secretary that he was too much indisposed to do it, being resolved to receive the visit. Dined at my Lodgings, where the Vice-President favored me with his Company."

"Oct. 25. — Attended Divine Service at the Episcopal Church whereof Dr. Parker is the Incumbent in the forenoon and the Congregational Church of Mr. Thatcher in the afternoon. Dined at my lodgings with the Vice-President. Mr. Bowdoin accompanied me to both Churches. Between the two I received a visit from the Govr. who assured me that indisposition alone prevented his doing it yesterday, and that he was still indisposed; but as it had been suggested that he expected to *receive* the visit from the President which he knew was improper, he was resolved at all haz'ds to pay his Compliments to-day.

"Oct. 26. — The day being Rainy and Stormy, myself much disordered by a cold and inflammation in the left eye, I was prevented from visiting Lexington (where the first blood in the dispute with G. Brit'n was drawn). Rec'd the Complim'ts of many visits today. Mr. Dalton and Genl. Cobb dined with me, and in the Evening drank Tea with Govr. Hancock and called upon Mr. Bowdoin on my return to my lodgings.

"Oct. 27. — At ten o'clock in the morning received the visits of the Clergy of the Town; at eleven I went to an Oratorio (at King's Chapel) and between that and 3 o'clock rec'd the Addresses of the Govr. and Council — of the Town of Boston — of the President etc. of Harvard College and of the Cincinnati of the State; after wch at 3 o'clock I dined at a large and elegant Dinner at Faneuil Hall, given by the Govr. and Council, and spent the evening at my lodgings."

The evident satisfaction with which Washington throughout his Boston stay refers to "my lodgings" is particularly interesting when one recalls that underneath this phrase lurks a sly thrust at pompous John Hancock. On the raw chill day of the President's arrival the Governor's suite and a throng of the townspeople were on hand to welcome him, but the Governor himself failed to put in an appearance. He did not wish to recognize a superior personage within his

Taverns That Entertained Washington

official jurisdiction! Consequently he allowed the crowds to contract what was for years known as "the Washington cold" while awaiting him. But Washington had as high a sense of personal dignity as did Hancock; he had also a much nicer appreciation of when it is improper to show personal pique. Finally, therefore, he rode between the throngs on State street, past the State House to his cold dinner at Mrs. Ingersoll's on Tremont street near what is now Scollay square. And there all that day he kept his room, refusing flatly an invitation to dine with Hancock. The following morning the Governor realized his fiasco and, though suffering from gout, caused himself to be carried to Ingersoll's to present his apologies in person. Madame Hancock always insisted that her husband was really too ill to leave his house on the day of Washington's entry, but the impression that Hancock intended to slight the man who had been elevated, instead of him, to the place of President has none the less endured. The one person who came out of the affair with flying colours appears to have been the cook at Ingersoll's who, at the last minute, secured some very excellent fish for the distinguished guest's dinner and so saved the credit of Boston hospitality.

The boarding-house thus honoured stood at the juncture of Tremont and Court streets for many years. If its walls could have spoken, we should have for quotation a delicious description of that historic encounter between Hancock and Washington the day after the President's arrival! The visit was preceded by the following note:

" Sunday 26th October,
" half-past twelve o'clock.
" The Governor's best respects to the President. If at home and at leisure, the Governor will do himself the honor to pay his respects in half an hour. This would have been done much sooner had his health in any degree permitted. He now hazards everything, as it respects his health, for the desirable purpose."

To which the President replied: —

" Sunday, 26th October, one o'clock.
" The President of the United States presents his best respects to the Governor, and has the honor to inform him that he shall

Taverns That Entertained Washington

be at home till two o'clock. The President need not express the pleasure it will give him to see the Governor; but, at the same time, he most earnestly begs that the Governor will not hazard his health on the occasion."

When Hancock arrived, swathed in red flannel, and was carried by two men into the President's drawing-room Washington was most gracious, however. He gave full weight to the excuse of unmerciful gout and, in the afternoon, returned the visit with all courteous haste. But he returned to his lodgings to sleep, though Hancock had extended, and he had accepted, an invitation to be his guest while in Boston.

Salem was the next town which the President honoured with his presence for a time. His description of the journey thither is interesting: "October 29. Left Boston about 8 o'clock. Passed over the Bridge at Charles-town, and went to see that at Malden, but proceeded to the College at Cambridge, attended by the Vice-President, Mr. Bowdoin, and a great number of Gentlemen. . . . From Boston, besides the number of citizens which accompanied me to Cam-

Among Old New England Inns

The Ipswich tavern thus honoured above its fellows was built in 1693 or thereabouts, and was first used as a tavern in 1724 by Increase How, whose widowed daughter, Susanna Swasey, there carried on the inn for many years, marrying meanwhile Capt. George Stacey of Marblehead (June 30, 1763) and afterwards, Capt. Richard Homan of the same town. Upon Mrs. Homan's death, her stepson, George Stacey of Biddeford, conveyed to her son, Major Joseph Swasey, his interest in the tavern. The major had served with honour in the Revolutionary War, and Swasey's Tavern was for many years a notable feature of the town. Its taverner was town clerk as well and because of his sudden death during the progress of a town meeting (April, 1816) was long remembered in Ipswich. In 1805, his tavern became the property of John Heard, whose son Augustine sold the place to Zenas Cushing, from whose heirs it was purchased by Dr. William E. Tucker, the present owner. Originally the house was three-storied and hip-roofed, but it has been so remodelled that no trace of its antiquity remains.

In Newburyport, Washington was greeted

Taverns That Entertained Washington

with overwhelming enthusiasm. The Essex *Journal* and New Hampshire *Packet* of November fourth reports the visit thus, "Friday last the BELOVED PRESIDENT OF THE UNITED STATES made his entry into this town; and never did a person appear here, who more largely shared the affection and esteem of its citizens. He was escorted here by two companies of cavalry, from Ipswich and Andover, Marshall Jackson, the High Sheriff of the County of Essex, the Hon. Tristram Dalton, Esq., Major General Titcomb, and a number of other officers, as well as several gentlemen from this and neighboring towns. On his drawing near, he was saluted with thirteen discharges from the artillery after which, a number of young gentlemen placed themselves before him, and sang as follows:

"'He comes! he comes! the Hero comes!
  Sound, sound your trumpets, beat, beat your drums;
  From port to port let cannons roar,
  He's welcome to New England shore.
  Welcome, welcome, welcome, welcome
  Welcome to New England's shore.'

"The lines in the first verse which call for the beating of drums and roaring of cannon were instantly obeyed after the pronunciation of each word: and to the vocal was joined all the instrumental music in both choruses, which were repeated: — Then the President, preceded by the several companies of Militia and artillery of this town, the musicians, selectmen, High Sheriff, and Marshall Jackson, . . . passed to the house prepared for his reception. Here a feu de joy was fired by several companies of militia."

The Newburyport house which extended hospitality to Washington is still standing, and is now the public library of the town. Up to the time of Washington's visit, its owner had been Nathaniel Tracy, an interesting character who made vast sums during the Revolutionary War from his fleet of privateers. Besides this elegant home on State street, he at one time owned Craigie House in Cambridge, well known as Washington's headquarters and the home of the poet Longfellow. Tracy's cellars were always stocked with the choicest wines and all the appointments of his table were sumptuous in the extreme. Thomas Jefferson often stayed with him, and many other distinguished people were glad to visit at his

Taverns That Entertained Washington

home. But, just before Washington's visit, he became hopelessly involved in financial difficulties and selling his estates, retired to his farm-mansion near-by. Thus it was that the house which his father, Patrick Tracy, had built for him, passed temporarily into the hands of the Honourable Jonathan Jackson, Patrick's son-in-law; and since it was to Jackson's care as United States marshal that arrangements for Washington's Massachusetts visit had been entrusted, some of the unoccupied rooms in this house were furnished and made ready for the accommodation of the town's eminent visitor.

From Newburyport the President proceeded to Portsmouth " and was received," says the Diary, " by the President of the State of New Hampshire, the Vice-President, some of the Council — Messrs Langdon and Wingate of the Senate, Colº Parker, Marshall of the State and many other respectable characters; besides several Troops of well cloathed Horse in handsome Uniforms and many officers of the Militia also in handsome (red and white) uniforms of the Manufacture of the State. With this cavalcade we proceeded, and arrived before 3 o'clock at Portsmouth where we were received with every token of respect and appearance of cordiality, under a discharge of artillery. The streets, doors and windows were crowded here as at all the other places; and alighting at the Town House odes were sung and played in honor of the President. The same happened yesterday at my entrance into Newbury port. . . . From the Town House I went to Colonel Brewster's Ta'n, the place provided for my residence." This house is no longer standing, having burnt down in 1813 after a very interesting and varied career described at length in the chapter devoted to Portsmouth Taverns.

In none of the New England towns he visited, did Washington enjoy himself more than at Portsmouth. On the evening of his arrival the State House was beautifully illuminated and rockets were let off from the balcony. The next morning found him attending divine service at the Queen's Chapel, and in the afternoon he listened to a laudatory address delivered by Dr. Buckminster at the North Church. On Monday the President went on an excursion down the harbour in a barge rowed by seamen dressed in white frocks and accompanied by another barge containing an amateur band which

Taverns That Entertained Washington

"did their possible" at frequent intervals. The Diary says that "having lines, we proceeded to the fishing banks a little without the harbor and fished for cod, — but it not being of proper time of tide, we only caught two, — with which about ten o'clock we returned to town."

Of those two trophies Washington drew from the water but one. The other was hooked by Zebulon Willey, who was fishing in the vicinity and who, when he observed the President's bad luck, came alongside and handed over his line with a big one already on it waiting to be hauled in. It proved to be a very good pull for Zebulon, for the President gave him a silver dollar and all his after life he had a first-rate fish story to tell.

When the lines had been finally drawn up, the distinguished guest was rowed by the white-jacketed sailors straight to the hospitable vine-hung door, at Little Harbour, of Colonel Michael Wentworth and his wife who had been Martha Hilton. From this point they returned to town by carriages, passing, on the way, the residence of Captain John Blunt who had first met Washington on the famous "Crossing the Delaware" occasion. Blunt had for many years owned and sailed a coasting-vessel which plied between Portsmouth and Philadelphia, and he knew the Delaware nearly as well as the Piscataqua. Accordingly, when Washington, that winter day, observed the floating ice of the river, and asked if there were no one in the boat acquainted with the stream, Blunt's name was immediately spoken, and he was personally requested by the President to take the helm. Undoubtedly, therefore, there were pleasant reminiscences interchanged when the President and his pilot met again in 1789 on the Little Harbour road. Dinner and tea that day were taken at the beautiful Langdon home.

The President sat two long hours for his portrait the next morning, after which he called on President Sullivan at the famous Stavers Inn. Thence he proceeded to the home of his secretary, Tobias Lear, to pay his respects to that gentleman's aged mother. The crowd about the door while this extraordinary event was going on is said to have been the greatest Portsmouth has ever known. And well it might be; you and I would have been eager also to catch some glimpse of the party in the southwest par-

Taverns That Entertained Washington

lour of the old Lear house during that delightful hour when the President held the little relatives of his favourite private secretary upon his knee and talked to the venerable Mrs. Lear of her son's admirable service. Lear, to be sure, had not always been a man up to Washington's standard of punctuality. He apologized to his employer twice in a very few weeks for tardiness by explaining that his watch was wrong; but Washington had replied, " Mr. Lear, you must get a new watch, or I must get a new secretary," and the secretary saw the point.

The evening following the call at the Lears' found the President at " the Assembly, where there were about seventy-five well dressed and many very handsome ladies, among whom (as was also the case at the Salem and Boston assemblies) were a greater proportion with much blacker hair than are usually seen in the southern States." Early the next morning the honoured guests quietly left town " having earnestly entreated that all parade and ceremony might be avoided on my return. Before ten I reached Exeter, fourteen miles distance. This is considered as the second town in New Hampshire and stands at the head of the tide waters of the

Among Old New England Inns

Piscataqua river. . . . It is a place of some consequence, but does not contain more than one thousand inhabitants. A jealousy subsists between this town (where the Legislature alternately sits) and Portsmouth, which had I known it in time, would have made it necessary to have accepted an invitation to a public dinner; but my arrangements having been otherwise made I could not."

Haverhill, therefore, was the next town whose hospitality the cavalcade accepted. The account of this visit which has come down to us from the graphic pen of George Wingate Chase, makes very interesting reading. The President journeyed in an open carriage, he tells us, drawn by four horses accompanied only by his secretary, Mr. Lear, Major Jackson and a single servant. Mr. Lear, upon a beautiful white horse, rode in advance of the carriage, which was occupied by Washington and Mr. Jackson, and driven by the President's private coachman. The tavern used was variously called "Mason's Arms," from its sign of freemasonry, and Harrod's, after its proprietor; it stood on what became later the site of the Town Hall. The President had been earnestly invited to be the guest of Mr. John

Taverns That Entertained Washington

White, whose daughter had often been a visitor at his own home in Philadelphia, but in Haverhill, as so often before during this journey, he expressed his preference for a public house, observing with a smile that he was "an old soldier and used to hard fare and a hard bed."

On alighting at the tavern, he was introduced to a number of the town's prominent citizens and then, after a short rest, he took a walk to see the sights of the place, remarking repeatedly, as he made his way along the street now named after him, upon the pleasantness and beauty of the scenery, the thrift and enterprise of the citizens. "Haverhill is the pleasantest village I have passed through," he delighted his entertainers by observing.

With Washington's stay here is associated more of those charming stories about his fondness for children. Among his visitors with their fathers, were Mary White and Betsey Shaw, two bright little maidens of eight who were playmates and fast friends. While engaged in easy conversation with the gentlemen, the President called the little girls to him, and taking one upon each knee, soon completely dispelled their shyness by his kind words and gentle manner. During the interview he drew from his pocket a glove and smilingly inquired, "Which of the little misses will mend my glove?" Both were naturally eager for the honour, so they were told to do it between them and given each a hearty kiss upon the lips when they returned the glove, neatly repaired, half an hour later. The news of this reward spread rapidly, and not long after the visitors' departure, there came a timid knock at the door, and two more little maidens entered, requesting permission to kiss the President's hand. Washington saw the point, and gladly expressed willingness to *exchange* kisses with the little beggars. His duties towards the children of Haverhill were not yet all performed, however, for scarcely had he retired to his room,—early, in accordance with his usual custom,— when he heard a great uproar downstairs and learned that it proceeded from a small boy who said he "*must* see George Washington." Doubtless, the little fellow had listened to so many stories from his mother's lips about the "great Washington" that he expected to find the President some superhuman thing. At all events he only stared

Taverns That Entertained Washington

dumbly when let into Washington's presence. Very kindly he was asked what he wanted.

"I want to see George Washington," stammered the little fellow.

The President smiled. "I am George Washington," he said, patting the lad's head gently, "but, my little friend, I am only a man."

The landlord's little daughter, too, won a kiss that night for deftly applying the family warming-pan to the "best bed" in Washington's room.

Yet better than any of these stories about children one likes, I think, the incident attending Washington's departure on the ferry-boat early the next morning. Among those who had tried hard to obtain an interview with the President was Bart Pecker, an old soldier who had been in the famous "Washington Life Guards," but who, with declining years, had become so addicted to drink that he was not regarded as a credit to the community. Although he pleaded hard for a chance to speak to Washington, whom he declared he was "well acquainted with" he was purposely kept in the background on account of his habits and shabby appearance. But just as Washington was stepping upon the ferry-boat Bart's patience gave way and with a fierce ejaculation that he *would* " speak to the General," he pushed through the crowd and thrusting out his hand, cried excitedly, " General, how do you do? "

Apparently Washington recognized the voice for, turning quickly, he grasped the outstretched hand and, quietly slipping a gold-piece into it, said, " Bart, is this you? Good-bye, good-bye."

From Haverhill the distinguished party journeyed to " Abbot's tavern in Andover, where we breakfasted, and met with much attention from Mr. Phillips, President of the Senate of Massachusetts, who accompanied us through . . . to Lexington where I dined, and viewed the spot on which the first blood was spilt in the dispute with Great Britain, on the 19th of April, 1775. Here I parted with Mr. Phillips and proceeded on to Watertown. . . . We lodged in this place at the house of a Widow Coolidge near the Bridge, and a very indifferent one it is." The Andover tavern was excellent, however, and there is a very pretty story of Washington's stay there. His riding-glove had again become torn and he

ABBOTT TAVERN, ANDOVER

Taverns That Entertained Washington

asked his landlord's little daughter to mend it for him. This she did so neatly that, when she returned the glove, Washington took her upon his knee and gave her a kiss. Which so elated Miss Priscilla Abbott that she would not allow her face to be washed again for a week! This old tavern, long the residence of Samuel Locke, is still standing, and is in an excellent state of preservation though no longer used for the entertainment of the public.

Needham, Sherburn, Holliston, Milford and Menden were the places next along the route, and by the end of this day (November 6) the party has reached Taft's at Uxbridge, having travelled thirty-six miles. Taft's inn made a very good impression upon the President; we find him writing, the day after his stay there, this characteristic letter to the proprietor:

"HARTFORD 8 November, 1789

"SIR — Being informed that you have given my name to one of your sons, and called another after Mrs. Washington's family, and being, moreover, very much pleased with the modest and innocent looks of your two daughters, Patty and Polly, I do for these reasons send each of these girls a piece of chintz; and to Patty, who bears the name of Mrs. Washington, and who waited more upon us than Polly did, I send five guineas, with which she may buy herself any little ornaments she may want, or she may dispose of them in any other manner more agreeable to herself. As I do not give these things with a view to have it talked of, or even to its being known, the less there is said about it the better you will please me; but that I may be sure the chintz and money have got safe to hand let Patty, who I dare say is equal to it, write me a line informing me thereof, directed to 'The President Of the United States at New York.' I wish you and your family well, and am your humble servant,   GEORGE WASHINGTON"

Jacob's Inn in Thompson, Connecticut, "not a good house;" Colonel Grosvenor's in Pomfret and Perkins Tavern in Ashford are next noted in the Diary which then says: "It being contrary to law and disagreeable to the People of this State to travel on the Sabbath day — and my horses, after passing through such intolerable roads, wanting rest I stayed at Perkins Tavern (which by the bye is not a good one) all day — and a meeting-house being within a few rods of the door, I attended morning and evening service and heard very lame discourses from a Mr. Pond."

Washington's temperate allusion to the Connecticut Blue laws does him great credit. For the tithing-man who reminded him of them was not an over-courteous person, and insisted with more stubbornness than reverence that the Head of the Nation pause in his journey home to observe the Sabbath rest. As for the Ashford Tavern, it was a good house later if not just then. And it still stands, though now deserted. Since 1804 it has been known as Clark's Hotel, and for more than ninety years one of this family owned it. Then, in 1897, it was sold to Henry F. Hall, a wealthy lawyer of Wallingford, who intended to make it into a commodious home for summer boarders, but was prevented by illness from carrying out his plan. Now the building is becoming a prey to the elements though it is on the much-travelled Hartford and New York turnpike and once, as we have seen, entertained Washington.

"The house of one Fuller at Worthington, in the township of Berlin" provided the next breakfast after Hartford had been left behind, and "Smith's on the plains of Wallingford" was another stopping-place. New Haven was reached before sundown. "At this place," says the Diary, "I met Mr. Elbridge Gerry in the stage from New York, who gave me the first cert'n ac'ct of the health of Mrs. Washington. November 11. Set out about sunrise and took the upper road to Milford, it being shorter than the lower one through West Haven. Breakfasted at the former. Baited at Fairfield; and dined and lodged at Maj. Marvin's 9 miles further. November 12 — A little before sunrise we left Maj. Marvin's, and breakfasting at Stamford, 13 miles distant, reached the Widow Haviland's, 12 miles further; where, on acct. of some lame horses, we remained all night."

The following day finds the President back "at my house in New York, where I found Mrs. Washington and the rest of the family all well — and it being Mrs. Washington's night to receive visits, a pretty large company of ladies and gentlemen were present." The "tour through the Eastern States" had consumed almost exactly a

Taverns That Entertained Washington

month, and had made glad, — or sad, according to their deserts, the hearts of some twoscore landlords.

Rhode Island, it will be noted, had had no share in this tour. The truth was that the citizens of that state were a good deal averse to the new government and did not ratify the Constitution until May 29, 1790. This done, however, their state was at once included in the new order of things, and the President determined to make a short tour there just as he had done to the other parts of New England.

Accordingly we find the Pennsylvania *Packet* of August 28, 1790 printing: " The President arrived at Newport at eight o'clock on Tuesday morning (August 17) at which time he was welcomed to the state by a salute from the fort. From the landing place he was attended to his lodgings by the principal inhabitants of the town, who were severally presented to him. He then walked round the town, and surveyed the various beautiful prospects from the eminences above it. At four o'clock he was waited on by the most respectable citizens of the place, who conducted him to the Town Hall, where a very elegant dinner was provided, and sev-

Among Old New England Inns

eral toasts drank. After dinner he took another walk accompanied by a large number of gentlemen. On Wednesday morning at nine o'clock the President and his company embarked for Providence."

The ancient chariot in which Washington rode from place to place during his visit to Providence is still preserved and the Golden Ball Inn in which he had his headquarters also survives. This house was dedicated in 1783, an elaborate advertisement in the *Gazette* of Dec. 13 informing the citizens of Providence that "the Golden Ball Inn, opposite the State House, is ready for guests, and the proprietor, Henry Rice, is ready to please all who will honor him with their presence in the new inn." Mr. Rice's custom came promptly. The commanding position of the house, on the hill, and its size and imposing appearance drew to its doors whatever rich and distinguished travellers might be passing through. Over the entrance door hung a large beautiful golden ball, and within were broad curving staircases, and large and sunny rooms of varied shape. One item of equipment to which the proprietor pointed with pardonable pride

Taverns That Entertained Washington

was the wooden buttons by which all the doors could be fastened securely.

A famous early entertainment given in this house was the Lafayette Ball of 1784. The young Marquis had brought over with him from France several young gentlemen of aristocratic birth, and they and he were promptly made free of all the fine homes in Providence. Finally, as an event of particular elegance, this party at the Golden Ball was arranged. When the evening arrived all the beauties of the town were on hand, elegant in rich flowered brocades over short, quilted petticoats of silk or satin, with square-cut bodices and powdered hair to set off, as did their high-heeled slippers with silver buckles, their exquisite women's charms. A miniature of one of the guests thus apparelled has come down to assure us that the Golden Ball was a famous resort in its day. The men at that party were scarcely less gorgeous, for they wore silken hose and knee breeches adorned with silver buckles, while rich brocaded coats, lace ruffles and powdered hair made them still further irresistible. The ball room that night was brilliantly lighted with hundreds of wax tapers which shed their soft glow over the gay scene, and to the music of fifes, bugles and fiddles Providence belles and the young noblemen from o'er seas danced the flying hours away.

It was therefore, to a house already famous that Washington came that August of 1790. The room which he occupied on the second story was later used by President Monroe and President John Quincy Adams during visits to Providence, and in 1824 Lafayette again stopped here. The name of the house has been changed twice since its salad days, first to the Roger Williams House and later to the City Mansion House, generally known as the Mansion House. Until within a few years it remained a house of entertainment and it still stands, in an excellent state of preservation owned by a man who is very proud of its connection with Washington.

CHAPTER IX

THE WAYSIDE INN

THOSE of us who love the flavour of colonial days and delight in surviving monuments of that time cannot be too thankful for the preservation and continued use as an inn of the Red Horse Tavern in Sudbury. Sudbury was a great tavern town originally, and Longfellow, when he spoke of Landlord Howe's establishment simply as " a " wayside inn was giving it a perfectly correct description. For it was then only one of many. But, through the genius of the Poet of America this tavern has since become " *the* " Wayside Inn, the most widely known and deeply loved of all the old taverns in New England.

Happily it is really old and undeniably quaint. Sudbury was one of the first towns settled by our Puritan forbears, Rev. Edmund Browne, who named the place after the Suffolkshire home of his childhood, being among the passengers who sailed on "the good shipp *Confidence*" April 24, 1638 and settled here in "the wilderness." The place, however, had rich natural advantages, and these lusty young men from old England were soon prosperous as a result of their choice of a home.

John How was among the first in the settlement to be admitted a freeman. In England he had been a glover, but, there being slight demand for gloves in new towns of the seventeenth century, he turned his attention in 1661 to the trade of tavern-keeper. Very early, therefore, we find a How keeping a tavern. Longfellow, in accounting to an English friend for the coat of arms and justice authority with which his Landlord Howe is endowed said (Dec. 28, 1863) "Some two hundred years ago an English family by the name of Howe built in Sudbury a country house, which has remained in the family down to the present time, the last of the race dying two years ago. Losing their fortunes, they became innkeepers, and for a century the Red Horse has flourished, going down from father to son. . . . This will account for the landlord's coat of arms and for his being a jus-

WAYSIDE INN, SUDBURY

The Wayside Inn

ice of the peace, things that must sound strange to English ears."

As a matter of fact, however, there was nothing strange about an inn-keeper in colonial New England being both a gentleman and a squire. John How was a selectman as early as 1642 and in 1655 he was appointed to see to the restraining of youth on the Lord's day. Nor was this at all incompatible with his week-day uses. But Longfellow knew that an English reader would not understand this. James Fenimore Cooper, writing a quarter of a century earlier, knew it also for he says, " The inn-keeper of Old England and the inn-keeper of New England form the very extremes of their class. The one is obsequious to the rich, the other unmoved and often apparently cold. The first seems to calculate at a glance the amount of profit you are likely to leave behind you; while his opposite appears only to calculate in what manner he can most contribute to your comfort without materially impairing his own. . . . He is often a magistrate, the chief of a battalion of militia, or even a member of a state legislature. He is almost always a man of character; for it is difficult for any other to obtain a license to exercise the calling."

The first Landlord How was emphatically "a man of character." The proximity of his tavern in Marlborough to the Indian plantation brought him into intimate contact with the redskins, but he soon won their confidence and good will by his uniform kindness. Once he settled a dispute regarding a pumpkin-vine, which sprang up on the premises of one Indian while bearing its fruit upon that of another, in an impressively statesmanlike manner. Calling for a knife he divided the pumpkin squarely in halves, giving equal portions to each claimant!

It was not John How, though, whose inn Longfellow celebrated. His place was in Marlborough as has been said and his sign that of the Black Horse, while "the Wayside Inn" was the enterprise of his grandson and displayed a prancing steed of brilliant red over its doorway. According to some authorities, David How opened his house in 1714; certain it is that it was in full swing two years later, for Sewall, that incomparable diarist records that he started with a friend for Springfield on the 27th of

The Wayside Inn

April of that year, "treated at N. Sparhawk's, and got to How's in Sudbury about one-half hour by the sun."

The original house was a small one, generally supposed, says Mr. Homer Rogers, who bought the estate after the death of the last How, to be the L in the rear of the present edifice. David How kept the tavern until his death in 1746, when it passed into the hands of his son, Ezekial, by whom it was enlarged as increased demand for rooms made necessary. The business done by the house at this time was considerable, for it was on the great highway by which the mail travelled westward from Boston and passengers were glad to pause for a night here while pursuing the wearisome journey to the further part of the state and beyond. The fiery steed on the front of the sign was to distinguish the house from the Black Horse Tavern in Marlborough while on the back were later added the initials of the first three owners:

"D. H. 1686
E. H. 1746
A. Howe . . . . 1796"

While Ezekial Howe was the landlord

Among Old New England Inns

there was established the following price-list of charges at this Sudbury tavern:

```
"Mug best India flip . . . . 15
 New England do    . . . . 12
 Toddy in proportion . . .
 A good dinner . . . . . 20
 Best supper and breakfast . . 15 each
 Common do. . . . . . . 12
 Lodging . . . . . . . 4"
```

The nature of the entertainment for which these modest prices were asked may be gathered from this description written by President Dwight of Yale early in the nineteenth century: "The best old-fashioned New England inns were superior to any of the modern ones which I have seen. The variety was ample and the food was always of the best quality. The beds were excellent; the house and all its appendages were in the highest degree clean and neat; the cookery was remarkably good; and the stable was not less hospitable than the house. The family, in the meantime, were possessed of principle, and received you with the kindness and attention of friends. Your baggage was as safe as in your own house. If you were sick you were nursed and befriended

TAP-ROOM, WAYSIDE INN, SUDBURY

The Wayside Inn

as in your own family. No tavern-haunters, gamblers or loungers were admitted any more than in a well-ordered private habitation; and as little noise was allowed. . . . In a word you found in these inns the pleasures of an excellent private house. To finish the story, your bills were always equitable, calculated on what you ought to pay, and not upon the scheme of getting the most which extortion might think proper to demand."

Yet the tap-room was an important part of every tavern's equipment and that of the Inn in Sudbury was, and is, one of the most interesting apartments in the whole house. In one corner, over the bar, is the wooden portcullis raised or lowered according to the demand for liquid refreshment and we may still see here the ancient floor worn by the feet of hundreds of good fellows now gone to their long home; overhead are heavy oak timbers dating back to the days when flip reigned instead of cocktails. Upstairs you are shown the travellers' rooms which people of no particular importance occupied in common and the state chamber still decorated with its wall paper of bluebells wherein slept Lafayette on his journey to

Among Old New England Inns

Boston in 1824. Above is the garret where slaves were accommodated and which was used as a store-house for grain at the time when an Indian invasion was feared. Originally, too, the dance-hall was in one of these upper rooms.

A day passed under this roof one hundred and fifty years ago would have spread before us all the colour and movement, all the picturesque charm and interest of a typical New England tavern. A great deal earlier than we would then have thought pleasant, we should have been awakened by the rumbling of heavy market-wagons taking into Boston the produce of the rich Connecticut valley. There was no time on the down trip for the drivers to loiter by the way but in the afternoon, on the return, we should have found the canvas-topped wagons filling the road in front of the house while their owners refreshed themselves with excellent toddy in the tap-room and the horses partook of satisfying oats in the comfortable barns near by.

Yet the real event of the day was, of course, the coming, about breakfast-time, of the mail coach from Boston. We would be on the porch awaiting it, for the music of

The Wayside Inn

the horn would have heralded its approach and no one with blood in his veins would willingly miss the spectacle of its arrival, as the dexterous driver wheeled into the yard and brought his foaming bays to a standstill at the front door. Every one in the house arose to that occasion! Yet in a trice it is all over. The black stable boys have taken out the horses, the genial host has welcomed the travellers, — stiff and taciturn as might be expected of men who have ridden since three o'clock on an empty stomach, — and interest is transferred to the dining-room tables spread with bountiful breakfast cheer. A half hour later came the speeding of the parting guest to give one another thrill, for a journey had considerable hazard about it back in the eighteenth century.

Of the soldiers who marched up to the Red Horse, stacked their muskets and retired to the tap-room for rest and comfort many tales might be told. In 1724, during Lovewell's war, the steel-capped and buff-coated men who patrolled the roads of the vicinity made the place their rendezvous, and during the French and Indian war troops hurrying to the frontier stretched out and snatched a rest under the old oaks in front of the house. When the Worcester minutemen, led by Timothy Bigelow, were hurrying down to Lexington, they, too, tarried for a brief space at this ancient landmark.

Ezekial How himself had a not unimportant share of Lexington's glory. He was at this time lieutenant-colonel of the Fourth Regiment of Middlesex County Militia, of which James Barrett of Concord was colonel. In the May of the following year the legislature made him colonel, which commission he held until 1779 when he resigned. The number of Sudbury men in actual service at Concord and Lexington was three hundred and two. "The inhabitants of Sudbury never can make such an important appearance probably again," a Revolutionary soldier has written of the event.

The first news of trouble came to the town between three and four in the morning of that first Patriots' Day, carried to the Sudbury member of the Provincial Congress by an express from Concord. Immediately the church bell was rung, musketry discharged and the six companies of the town mustered into service. By nine o'clock all

The Wayside Inn

the men had reached Concord, and Landlord How had distinguished himself for particular gallantry in the affair at the old North Bridge. It does not, however, appear that he took further part in the active operations of the Revolution, though he continued to command his militia company and rendered important service as a member of the various committees charged with the makeup of quotas and the preparation of muster rolls. It was, therefore, altogether fitting that Washington should honour Sudbury and its inn with a brief visit during his triumphal progress through New England in 1789, stopping here for lunch and warmly shaking hands with the veteran landlord who had been one of the heroes of Concord.

Colonel How died in 1796 and again we turn to an inventory for intimate insight into life of a century ago. His appraised the famous coat-of-arms at $4, his firearms at $8, his library at $10, the clock at $30, a silver tankard at $25, the "other plate" at $30, and the homestead of 240 acres of land at $6,500 thus bringing the entire appraisal up to $9,531.48. By the will it is made clear that the inn then consisted of new and old parts, for the Colonel speaks of "a new kitchen at the west end of the dwelling-house, with the lower room adjoining thereto, also the long chamber over the aforesaid room, with the north-west bed chamber in the old part of said dwelling-house." The residue of the estate, after many minor legacies and several personal articles bequeathed to "my well-beloved granddaughter, Hepsibah Brown," was left to the Colonel's third son, Adam How.

Adam How was the antiquarian of the family and he spent a great deal of time tracing the family line back to the nobility of England. Apart from this, however, he did little to add to the lustre of the name. He kept the inn until 1830 when he was succeeded by his son, Lyman, whom Longfellow thus describes:

> "Proud was he of his name and race,
> Of old Sir William and Sir Hugh
> And in the parlour, full in view,
> His coat-of-arms, well-framed and glazed,
> Upon the wall in colours blazed;
> He beareth gules upon his shield,
> A chevron argent in the field,
> With three wolf's heads, and for the crest
> A Wyvern part-per-pale addressed

The Wayside Inn

Upon a helmet barred; below
The scroll reads, ' By the name of Howe.' "

It is with this Landlord Howe that the "Tales" are bound up. So, before passing to them let us see, if we can, what manner of man the original of Longfellow's Boniface really was. Rather imposing in appearance we find him, dignified and grave appropriately, it would appear, a leader of the Congregational choir in his town, a member of the school committee and justice of the peace. Because he was all his life a bachelor he left no Howe to survive him in carrying on the inn; but this was perhaps just as well because, during his time, the railroad came to supersede the stagecoach and ere his death, the stream of guests at the Red Horse had shrunk almost to a vanishing point. In the year following this good man's departure, we find the following interesting entry in Longfellow's diary, " Drive with Fields to the old Red Horse Tavern in Sudbury — alas! no longer an inn! A lovely valley, the winding road shaded by grand old oaks before the house. A rambling, tumble-down old building, two hundred years old; and till now in the family of the Howes, who have kept an inn for one hundred and seventy-five years. In the old time, it was a house of call for all travellers from Boston westward." Ten days later the poet writes Fields: "The Sudbury Tales go on famously. I have now five complete, with a great part of the 'Prelude.'"

The first series of the poems was published on Nov. 25, 1863 under the title "Tales of a Wayside Inn," which Charles Sumner suggested in place of the "Sudbury Tales" of the initial advertisement. All the characters described in the series are real but they were never at any inn together. The musician was Ole Bull; the poet, T. W. Parsons, the translator of Dante; the Sicilian, Luigi Monti; the theologian, Professor Treadwell of Harvard; the student Henry Ware Wales. Parson, Monti and Treadwell were in the habit of spending the summer months at the Sudbury Inn and Longfellow also had known the place in its palmy days, as is shown by the following entry made by him in the year 1840: "The stage left Boston about three o'clock in the morning, reaching the Sudbury Tavern for breakfast, a considerable portion of the route

The Wayside Inn

being travelled in total darkness, and without your having the least idea who your companion might be." Thus he was able to reproduce vividly the fragrant atmosphere of the place in that time

> "When men lived in a grander way
> With ampler hospitality."

Longfellow's description of the inn fits just as well now as it did fifty years ago:

> " Across the meadows bare and brown,
> The windows of the wayside inn
> Gleam red with firelight through the leaves
> Of wood-bine hanging from the eaves
> Their crimson curtains rent and thin.
>
> " As ancient in this hostelry
> As any in the land may be, . . .
> A kind of old Hobgoblin Hall, . . .
> With weather stains upon the wall
> And stairways worn, and crazy doors,
> And creaking and uneven floors,
> And chimneys huge and tiled and tall.
> A region of repose it seems,
> A place of slumber and of dreams,
> Remote among the wooded hills!
> For there no noisy railway speeds,
> Its torch-race scattering smoke and gleeds;

Among Old New England Inns

But noon and night, the panting teams
Stop under the great oaks that throw
Tangles of light and shade below,
On roofs and doors and window sills.
Across the road the barns display
Their lines of stalls, their mows of hay,
Through the wide doors the breezes blow,
The wattled cocks strut to and fro,
And, half effaced by rain and shine,
The Red Horse prances on the sign."

Gone, however, are many priceless furnishings of the house, among them that little desk in the tap room whereon the score of the drinkers was wont to be set down. Gone, too, from the window sash is that rhyme inscribed June 24, 1774 by " William Molineaux Jr., Esq.,"

"What do you think,
  Here is good drink,
Perhaps you may not know it,
If not in haste do stop and taste,
You merry folks will show it."

Yet there is no one of us, I take it, who would not prefer Longfellow's poem about this inn to the mere goods and chattels it once possessed. And better than any young blade's offhand verse is the great poet's allusion in his Prelude to

> "The jovial rhymes . . .
> Writ near a century ago,
> By the great Major Molineaux,
> Whom Hawthorne has immortal made."

For, has not he "immortal made" this most fascinating of all old taverns?

CHAPTER X

ENTERTAINMENT FOR MAN AND BEAST

Those of us who have been brought up with the idea that our Puritan ancestors liked to be uncomfortable have only to read Samuel Sewall's Diary to be fully persuaded of the contrary. Sewall, to be sure, was of redder blood than many men of his time; and yet his delight in " roast fowl at Compton's " (an Ipswich inn very noted in its day) and in the almonds tendered him by the ladies of his roving fancy did not prevent him from standing up in the Old South Church to confess his sin in having accepted " spectral evidence " at the trial of the witches, nor from keeping one day annually for fast and prayer in remembrance of that event. No, Puritans both believed deeply and enjoyed deeply. Study of tavern bills makes it quite clear that they keenly appreciated such comfort as could be had in those days.

WINN HOUSE, WOBURN

PAXTON INN, PAXTON

Entertainment for Man and Beast

So, by no illogical sequence, it was considered an honour to a Puritan to keep a good tavern. John Adams, travelling through Connecticut in 1771, found that Landlord Pease "was the great man of the town; their representative &C as well as tavern-keeper, and just returned from the General Assembly at Hartford." Lieut. Winn was proud to keep a Woburn tavern with his family arms displayed as a signboard, General Paxton was glad to have his portrait painted on the sign of the inn named after him, and Dr. Nathaniel Ames of Dedham, Massachusetts, was a person of such position that it is hard to tell whether one should characterize him as a druggist, an almanack-maker or an inn-keeper. The almanac was a capital advertisement for his house, at any rate, — as witness the following in the issue for 1751:

" ADVERTISEMENT

"These are to signify to all persons that travel the great Post-Road South West from Boston that I keep a House of Publick Entertainment Eleven Miles from Boston, at the Sign of the Sun. If they want refresh-

ments and see cause to be my guests, they shall be well entertained at a reasonable Rate.
                                N. AMES."

Upon this advertisement hangs a tale well worth telling. The old hostelry in Dedham had been kept as early as 1658 by Lieutenant Joshua Fisher, surveyor, apothecary, innholder and officer of "ye trayne band." His son and successor was Captain Fisher, who was also called Joshua. About 1735 one of the latter's daughters married Dr. Nathaniel Ames, our friend of the advertisement, who, since 1726, had been successfully publishing the almanacs which bear his name. Ames' wife and infant son died soon after his marriage, and he thereupon entered into a lawsuit with the families of his sisters-in-law for what would have been their share in the land and inn.

The turning-point of the suit hung upon the term "next of kin." Ancient common law and English law militated against the ascension of property, that is the inheritance by a father or mother from a child; in absence of husband, wife or lineal descendant, property passed on to the "next of kin," which might be a distant cousin. The Prov-

Entertainment for Man and Beast

ince Laws, however, substituted, by general interpretation, the so-called civilian method of counting kinship, by which the father could inherit. So Dr. Ames thought that he had a case; and though he was twice defeated in the courts he stood out pluckily for what he believed to be his rights with the result that, in 1748, after himself preparing unaided both case and argument, he triumphed before the "Superior Court of Judicature, etc., of the Province of Massachusetts Bay!" Thus it was that what had been Fisher's Tavern came to bear the name of Ames.

To win his case was not enough for this excitable person, however. He had suffered a good deal in mind and purse by the law's delay and his keen wits, darting about for an effective way of making Chief Justice Dudley and his associate Lynde smart for their failure to unite with Judges Saltonstall, Sewall and Cushing he hit upon the idea of caricaturing the Court. Accordingly he had painted and hung in front of his inn a sign which cost him forty pounds, — and some subsequent trouble. For the sign represented the whole court sitting in state and big wigs before an open book entitled

PROVINCE LAWS. The dissenting judges are shown with their backs to the book. Of course the learned gentlemen heard of the sign, and, of course, they sent a sheriff to bring it before them. But Dr. Ames, who happened to be in Boston at the time, also heard of the sheriff's errand and rode out to Dedham in all haste. When the officer of the law arrived he found on the pole where the lampoon had hung only this legend: "A wicked and adulterous generation seeketh after a sign, but there shall no sign be given it."

With this episode as a starter, and the almanac in which to follow up the advantage, the tavern became more famous than ever. The almanac-maker lived here for fifteen years and here were born, by his second wife, Dr. Nathaniel Ames and Hon. Fisher Ames, both men of distinction in their time. Richard Woodward did the honours of this house in September, 1774, for the famous Suffolk Convention where was chosen the committee that drafted the first resolutions in favour of fighting things out with Great Britain. And during the Revolution, as during the French and Indian War, this tavern was the centre of

Entertainment for Man and Beast

whatever went on for the cause of freedom. All the well-known patriots, including Washington, Lafayette, Hancock and Adams are said to have often eaten and drunk within its walls. It has now been dust for almost a century, though, and its sign-board, too, perished long ago. But in that entertaining book, " The Almanacks of Nathaniel Ames 1726-1775," the author, Sam Briggs, gives an illustration of the painting from a drawing found among Dr. Ames' papers after his death.

Before leaving the subject it is interesting to read Ames' own allusion, in the Almanack of 1752 to the disappearance of the Sign:

" The Affairs of my House are of a Publick Nature, and therefore I hope may be mentioned here without offence to my *Reader:* The Sign I advertised last Year by Reason of some little Disappointments is not put up, but the Thing intended to be signified by it is to be had according to said Advertisement. And I beg Leave further to add, that if any with a View of Gain to themselves or Advantage to their Friends, have reported Things of my House in contradiction to the aforesaid Advertisement,

I would only have those whom they would influence consider, that where the Narrator is not honest, is not an Eye or Ear Witness, can't trace his story to the original, has it only by Hear-say, a thousand such witnesses are not sufficient to hang a dog: & I hope no Gentleman that travels the Road will have his Mind bias'd against my House by such idle Reports."

This bold challenge seems to have had its due effect, for, in a letter dated Monday morning, June 11, 1753, which Mr. Field quotes, custom that was to have gone elsewhere is given to Ames's Tavern.

"Before I heard from you this morning," says the letter-writer in question, "the Gentlemen had concluded to dine at Gay's but I took the pains to see 'em again & we have agreed to have the Dinner at your house. I hope you will have evrything in that agreeable & genteel order that will Recommend your house to the Gentlemen & my preference of it before Gays acceptable to them & the Ladys.

"I am your hble Servant
"EZEKIAL PRICE

We propose Bacon
        Lamb

Entertainment for Man and Beast

Chicken
Green Peas &ctr Asparagrass
Sauces &ctr for the Dinner

"There will be about twelve chaises including those we meet so that you will provide for 24 persons. We are to meet some Company from Newport who will set out tomorrow & the next day being Wednesday we shall set out & be at your house abt 10 o'clock unless the Weather is so bad we can't proceed."

There is no evidence of any public-house in Lancaster, Massachusetts, — afterwards a famous tavern town, — until 1690 when Nathaniel Wilder received official permission to "Retale wine, Beere, Ale, Cyder, Rum, &c." His home was a garrisoned house on the southeast slope of George Hill, and he remained the sole innholder until his death in 1704, after which the business was carried on for a time by his widow. During the next twenty-five years, however, the list of those "privileged to sell" was a long one, among the most prominent people on it being Justice John Houghton, who lived opposite the State Industrial School grounds. In the Middlesex Court Files is preserved the following letter from Houghton which is of interest for its picture of tavern-days in Lancaster away back in 1715:

"To Capt. Samuel Phipps of Charlstowne.

"WORTHY SR. After my Humble Service & Due Respects Presented to ye Hon'r'able Justices of ye County of Middlesex, together with yourselfe, these are to acquaint you that I am under such Indisposition of Body that I could not attend this Last Session of ye General Assembly, nor can I as yet Possibly (with comfort) come to pay my excise nor to Renew my Licence, but I have sent ye money for ye last years excise by Joseph Bradbrook, the Bearer hereof, which I hope will be to acceptance & in case yo'r Hon'rs shall see cause that my Licence may be continued I hope you will abate neer one halfe of ye excise for Doubtless I have paid very Deare considering what I have Drawne Compared with other Townes. I had but one Hogshead of Rum ye last year & that wanted about 12 Gallons of being full when I bought it: & it wants severall Gallons of being out now besides about 10 or 12 Gallons Lent out & were it not that I am concerned with writing of Deeds &

Entertainment for Man and Beast

Bonds & other Publique Concerns of ye Town affaires, which Occasion Persons often to come to my House, in order to Signing & Issuing such things, I should not be willing to be concerned with a Licence; for what drinks I sell I do it as cheap as at Boston & besides ye first cost I pay twenty shillings pr Hogshead for carrying it up, besides the Hazard; & as for Cyder there is none to be had, nor like to be this year at any price, fruit is so scarce, & for wine I never sold 5 Gallons in all ye yeares I have had a license. So that my Draught being so Little (there being no Road or thoroughfare for travilers through our towne) I hope your Hon[rs] will consider ye Premisses & do therein as in your Wisdom & Justice it shall seem meet, which will oblidge

"Your Humble Servant
"JOHN HOUGHTON
"Dat. Lan[r] July y[e] 27th: 1715."

This letter must not be taken to mean that Lancaster folk did not drink, however. The trouble is that they manufactured and consumed large quantities of fermented beverages, — at home. The orchards of the town were very famous, and cider became a product of such commercial importance that, when a highway was being constructed, it was expressly stipulated that the road should be of such width as to make it " feasible . . . to carry comfortably, four oxen with four barrels of cider at once." In an old memorandum book of Judge Joseph Wilder is " an acompt of Cyder made in the y^r 1728 " for his neighbours. There were 616 barrels in all of which 61 went to " the Reverend Mr. John Prentice!"

The people of Hadley, conscious of the evil effects of liquor houses, were in no haste to have an ordinary, and when the subject was agitated in January, 1663, they proceeded with great caution, choosing a committee of ten to consider the matter, and to report to another of seven; the latter were to report to the town and the town was then to choose the man most fit to keep an ordinary. Yet after all this no man was chosen, and until 1668, when we find that Richard Goodman had his license " continued " there is no further mention of the matter. After 1668 there is no notice, for almost a quarter of a century, of an inn or ordinary in either Hadley or Hatfield, but during this period Joseph Kellogg, the ferry-man, had liberty

Entertainment for Man and Beast

to entertain such travellers as passed that way. Moreover, in September, 1684, Deacon Philip Smith was licensed to sell wine to persons "in real need,"— meaning the sick, — and in March, 1678, Samuel Partrigg had liberty to sell liquors "to the neighbors," and in 1681 "for the helpfulness of neighbors;" four years later this privilege was extended to the retailing of wine.

A famous Hadley liquor-case of this period was that of Doctor John Westcarr complained of *by the Indians* for having sold to them contrary to a law made by the General Court in May 1657 forbidding such traffic — to an Indian, — under the penalty of 40 shillings for every pint. Doctor Westcarr, when examined by Captain John Pynchon, confessed that he had had two barrels of liquor in the spring and, upon being asked what he did with it, said that he had used most of it in preparing medicines. The testimony of half a dozen Indians proved so convincing to the court, however, that Dr. Westcarr was heavily fined.

Of the custom of sharing rooms in primitive taverns early travellers give conflicting accounts. Madam Knight's testimony we have already read, and an English officer put himself on record to the effect that " the general custom of having two or three beds in a room to be sure is very disagreeable; it arises from the great increase of travelling within the last few years, and the smallness of their houses, which were not built for houses of entertainment." Captain Basil Hall, on the other hand, declared that even at remote taverns his family had exclusive apartments; while in crowded inns it was never so much as suggested to him that other travellers should share his quarters.

The cost of these quarters was for the most part very reasonable. When John Tripp and his wife put up at the Bowen Inn, Barrington, Rhode Island, they were presented with the following bill:

	s.	d.
To 1 Dinner		9
To Bread and Cheese		7
To breakfast and dinner	1	3
To 1 Bowl Toddy		9
To lodging you and wife		6
To 1½ Bowl Toddy	1	1½
To ½ Mug Cyder		1½
To lodge self and wife		6
To 1 Gill Brandy		5½

Entertainment for Man and Beast

To breakfast	9½
Mug Cyder	1½
To ½ Bowl Toddy	4½
Dinner	8
To 15 Lb. Tobacco at 6d	7 6
To ½ Bowl Toddy	4½
To ½ Mug Cyder	1½
To Supper	6

Typical fare and typical treatment at one of this better class of taverns is thus described by Adam Hodgson: "Every ten or fifteen miles you come either to a little village composed of a few frame houses, with an extensive substantial house, whose respectable appearance, rather than any sign, demonstrates it to be a tavern, (as the inns are called,) or to a single house appropriated to that purpose and standing alone in the woods. At these taverns you are accosted, often with an easy civility, . . . by a landlord who appears perfectly indifferent whether or not you take anything *for the good of the house.* If, however, you intimate an intention to take some refreshment, a most plentiful repast is, in due time, set before you, consisting of beef-steaks, fowls, turkies, ham, partridges, eggs, and, if near the coast, fish and oysters, with a great variety of hot bread, both of wheat flour and Indian-corn, the latter of which is prepared in many ways and is very good. The landlord usually comes in to converse with you and to make one of the party; and as one cannot have a private room, I do not find his company disagreeable. He is, in general, well informed and well behaved, and the independence of manner which has often been remarked upon, I rather like than otherwise, when it is not assumed or obtrusive, but appears to rise naturally from easy circumstances, and a consciousness that, both with respect to situation and intelligence, he is at least on a level with the generality of his visitors. At first I was a little surprised, on enquiring where the stage stopped to breakfast, to be told, at Mayor Todds; — to dine? At Col. Brown's — but I am now becoming familiar with these phenomena of civil and political equality. . . ."

At the Ellery Tavern, Gloucester, as in many another old New England hostelry, the intercourse between the landlord and the lawmakers was so familiar that mine host had every reason to think himself quite as good as anybody. The selectmen of the town regularly held their meetings at this

Entertainment for Man and Beast

inn and in 1744 the annual salary of the five men chosen for the office was five dollars apiece the rest being taken out in tavern charges, which amounted to thirty pounds old tenor. The following year the citizens evidently thought they would economize, and they accordingly voted the selectmen a salary of five pounds old tenor apiece and " to find themselves." This particular house offers a beautiful example of the overhanging second story and the lean-to, or sloping-roofed ell. It was built in 1707 by Parson White, but James Stevens afterwards made a tavern of it and there held sway until 1740 when it came into the hands of Landlord Ellery.

In the town of Cambridge, Massachusetts, also, the selectmen met at a tavern, the one chosen frequently being the Blue Anchor which had been established as an ordinary as early as 1652. Their bill there for 1769 amounts to nearly five pounds.

By what seems to-day an interesting paradox " Ordination Day " was perhaps the most profitable tavern-gathering in the year. Then the visiting ministers were entertained by an especially good brew called " ordination beer " and sometimes there was even

Among Old New England Inns

an "ordination ball" in the evening, for which the sanction of the cloth had been obtained. The bill at one Hartford ordination Mrs. Earle gives as follows:

	l.	s.	d.
To keeping Ministers		2	4
2 Mugs Tody		5	10
5 Segars		3	
1 Pint Wine			9
3 Lodgings		9	
3 Bitters			9
3 Breakfasts		3	6
15 Boles Punch	1	0	
24 dinners	1	16	
11 bottles wine		3	16
5 Mugs flip		5	10
5 Boles Punch		6	
3 Boles Tody		3	6

With unconscious humour this bill is endorsed "all paid for except the Minister's Rum."

Very often a tavern would be famed far and wide for its particular variety of drink. Brigham's Tavern at Westborough used to prepare mulled wine in this perfectly irresistible fashion: a quart of boiling hot Madeira, half a pint of boiling water, and six

ELLERY TAVERN, GLOUCESTER

BRIGHAM'S TAVERN (NOW THE WESTBOROUGH HOTEL),
WESTBOROUGH

Entertainment for Man and Beast

eggs beaten to a froth, all sweetened and spiced. Nutmeg was a favourite flavouring and fashionable ladies and elegant gallants always carried the delicate dainty in their pockets. Some New England taverns were famous for their spruce, birch and sassafras beer, boiled with quantities of roots and herbs, with birch, spruce or sassafras bark, with pumpkin and apple parings, with sweetening of molasses or maple syrup. One song writer of colonial times declared joyously,

" Oh, we can make liqour to sweeten our lips
Of pumpkins, of parsnips, of walnut-tree chips."

Everybody appears to have drunk and frequently the most unexpected persons, dropped, liked Silas Wegg, into poetry on the joys of drinking. For instance in 1757 S. M. of Boston whom there is reason to think was Samuel Mather, the son of Cotton Mather, sent to Sir Harry Frankland, the hero of Agnes Surriage's romance, a box of lemons with these lines: —

" You know from Eastern India came
The skill of making punch as did the name.
And as the name consists of letters five,
By five ingredients is it kept alive.

Among Old New England Inns

To purest water sugar must be joined,
With these the grateful acid is combined.
Some any sours they get contented use,
But men of taste do that from Tagus choose.
When now these three are mixed with care
Then added be of spirit a small share.
And that you may the drink quite perfect see
Atop the musky nut must grated be."

Of making many flips there was no end. Each landlord had his own opinion as to the proper way of mixing this indispensable article and every tavern bill one finds is punctuated with entries charging it up to the thirsty traveller. John Adams said that if you spent the evening in a tavern you found it full of people drinking drams of flip. Certainly the old tap-rooms were cheerful and inviting gathering-places with the landlord cheerily presiding over his cage-like counter, surrounded by cans and bottles and glasses, jars of whole spice and loaves of sugar with rows of suggestive looking barrels in the background

"Where dozed a fire of beechen logs that bred
Strange fancies in its embers golden-red,
And nursed the loggerhead, whose hissing dip
Timed by wise instinct, creamed the bowl of flip."

Entertainment for Man and Beast

The loggerhead, more commonly called the flip iron, was a regular part of the chimney furniture in "ye olden time:" it was constantly kept warm in the ashes all ready to impart at short notice the puckering bitterness and curious scorched taste beloved of our ancestors. Sometimes, at Hallow E'en, parties of twentieth century young people get out the paraphernalia of Colonial tippling and try how it all seems; but I have yet to meet a modern who enjoyed the results. We of to-day are too far from the digestions of our ancestors to delight in their drinks.

CHAPTER XI

TAVERN SIGNS — AND WONDERS

THE custom of naming the tavern and placing before its door a signboard with a more or less appropriate device was brought to New England from Holland and the mother country. There was, indeed, a time when our laws required such a sign; and in France Louis XIV expressly prescribed that "Tavern keepers must put up Synboards and a bush: Nobody shall be allowed to open a tavern in the said city and its suburbs without having a sign and a bush." The "bush" here referred to was just what the name would imply, set on a pole or nailed to the tavern door. Hence the proverb "Good Wine needs no bush."

The variety and incongruity of tavern signs eventually became a matter of note and prompted the following curious rhyme in the *British Apollo* in 1710:

SIGN OF THE HANCOCK TAVERN, BOSTON

Tavern Signs — and Wonders

> "I'm amazed at the signs,
> As I pass through the town,
> To see the odd mixture,
> A Magpie and Crown,
> The Whale and the Crow,
> The Razor and Hen,
> The Leg and Seven Stars,
> The Axe and The Bottle
> The Tun and The Lute,
> The Eagle and Child,
> The Shovel and Boot."

Often, however, these titles were mere corruptions, as in the case of the "Three Broiled Chickens," the popular name for an old tavern still standing in Woburn, Massachusetts, and kept in Revolutionary days by Lieutenant Joseph Winn who had hung outside his house, with pardonable pride, his coat of arms showing *three spread eagles* on a shield. When the sign was a portrait of some person in public life it generally reflected the political tendencies of the landlord. John Duggan hung out from his house in Corn Court a Hancock presentment remotely after Copley because he admired the patriot and wished to show it.

The "Leg and Seven Stars" of the rhyme just quoted was however merely a deviation from the "League and Seven Stars" or Seven United Provinces. "The Axe and the Bottle" was the Battle Axe differently arranged; the "Goat And The Compass" once read "God Encompasseth us;" the "Bag of Nails," a tavern at Chelsea, England, is a corruption of the word "Bacchanals," — singularly appropriate, surely for a tavern.

In a curious English volume published in 1825 some extraordinary examples of tavern misnomers are given. There is "The Magdalen" for instance, so named because of its proximity to a female asylum which bore this title. "Nothing but being in the neighborhood of such an institution could have rendered such a sign in any way appropriate for a public house," comments our author "for we have never perceived anything in the manner of conducting such concerns as was conducive to virtue, but rather destructive to the morals of youth, and particularly of females." In justice to New England taverns it should, however, be said, that this stricture does not apply to them save in exceptional cases. Apart from other reasons, a landlord was too afraid of losing his sign. For, following the custom

Tavern Signs — and Wonders

in England, Massachusetts, by an act of the General Court in 1710, gave to the sheriff or deputy power, when a taverner had committed any irregularity, " to cause his sign to be taken down."

The Punch Bowl was a favourite tavern-sign. Brookline, Massachusetts, had a very famous house bearing this name and in the Boston *Evening Post* of January 11, 1773 one may find a notice that " a Bear and a Number of Turkeys will be set up as a mark at the Punch Bowl Tavern in Brookline." This introduces us to turkey shoots, a favourite diversion early in the nineteenth century. Captain Basil Hall saw such a " shoot " advertised at a tavern in Tewksbury and asked the landlord about it, whereupon that functionary " laughed at my curiosity but good-humouredly enlightened my ignorance by explaining that these shooting matches were so common in America, that he had no doubt I would fall in with them often. I regretted very much having passed one day too late for this transatlantic battle. It appears that these birds were literal barn door fowls, placed at certain distances, and fired at by anyone who chooses to pay the allotted sum for a shot. If he kills the bird he is allowed to carry it off; otherwise, like a true sportsman, he has the amusement for his money. Cocks and hens, being small birds, are placed at the distance of one hundred and sixty-five feet; and for every shot with ball the sportsman has to pay four cents. Turkeys are placed at twice the distance, or one hundred and ten yards, if a common musket be used; but at one hundred and sixty-five yards if the weapon be a rifle. In both these cases the price per shot is from six to ten cents."

Horses of several colours, white, black and red, were often used for tavern signs here and in England. Addison frequented the White Horse Tavern, Kensington, and there many of his Spectator papers were written, including, very likely, that of April 2, 1710, in which he thus advocates a censorship of signboards: — " Our streets are filled with blue boars, black swans and red lions; not to mention flying pigs and hogs in armour, with many other creatures more extraordinary than any in the deserts of Africa. My first task, therefore, would be like that of Hercules, to clear the city from monsters. In the second place I would forbid that creatures of jarring and incongru-

Tavern Signs — and Wonders

ous names should be joined together in the same sign; such as the bell and the neat's tongue; the dog and the gridiron. The fox and goose may be supposed to have met, but what have the fox and seven stars to do together? And when did the lamb and dolphin ever meet except upon a signpost?" One Massachusetts Inn which still displays the sign of a red lion is that at Stockbridge.

No New Englander, however, seems to have had the hardihood to borrow the Boar's Head sign and name which Shakespeare has immortalized by association with the frolics of Falstaff and Prince Hal. But the Golden Ball, originally set up in honour of royalty, graced the Tory tavern of Colonel Jones at Weston, Massachusetts, as well as many other houses strictly republican in their sympathies. As for the Bell, that was to be seen in every kind of combination, and in England as well as here was so common as a sign that the following rhyme was made upon it:

> "Around the face of blue-ey'd Sue,
>   Did auburn ringlets curl,
>   Her lips seem'd coral dipp'd in dew
>   Her teeth two rows of pearl.
>   Joe, of the Bell, whose wine, they said,
>   Was new in cask, as he in trade,

Among Old New England Inns

Espous'd this nonpareil;
'You keep the bar,' said Joe, ' my dear,
But be obliging, Sue, d'ye hear,
And prove to all who love good cheer
They're welcome to the Bell.'

" A London rider chanc'd to slip
Behind the bar, to dine,
And found sweet Susan's yielding lip
Much mellower than her wine.
As Joe stepped in, he stamped and tore,
And for the London beau he swore
He'd dust his jacket well.
' Heyday!' says Sue, ' What's this, I trow!
You bade me be obliging Joe;
I'm only proving to the beau,
He's welcome to the Bell.' "

Probably the most famous Bell Tavern in New England was that at Danvers, Massachusetts, which is now no longer standing, but which will always be remembered for its connection with Elizabeth Whitman, generally believed to have been the model for Hawthorne's " Hester Prynne." This was a typical inn of the pre-Revolutionary period. Here prices and everyday gossip were discussed; here, on Sundays, the more remote villagers left their horses while attending church, and here, after the two

Tavern Signs — and Wonders

hours' service, they returned to enjoy their dinner in the warmth of a snug corner. This tavern saw mourning for the death of Queen Anne and rejoicing over the accession of the first George. The odious Stamp Act and all Parliament taxes on the colonies were here patriotically denounced and tea was duly proscribed. When one hardy soul disdained the warning concerning this overtaxed beverage, he had to furnish punch for the crowd repeating three times as he drained his cup, the following chaste couplet:

> "I, Isaac Wilson, a boy I be,
> I, Isaac Wilson, I sells tea."

The sign of the house was a wooden bell and the host informed the people of his good cheer by the following strain:

> "Francis Symonds Makes and Sells
> The best of Chocolate also Shells.
> I'll toll you in if you have need,
> And feed you well and bid you speed."

A very spirited sign is that which long hung before the Benjamin Wiggin tavern in Hopkinton, N. H. and which, more lately has been identified with the recently-burned

Among Old New England Inns

Perkins Inn of that same town. Littleton, Massachusetts, displayed before its Lawrence Tavern a sign upon which was painted a soldier and the excellent advice, " Pay Today And Trust Tomorrow."

About the time of the Revolution tavern-signs bearing the head and name of William Pitt became very popular in New England. The landlord of the tavern at York, Maine, put up such a sign and added boldly to it the words, " Entertainment For the Sons of Liberty." In Portsmouth, New Hampshire, as will be seen by reference to the chapter which treats the inns of that town, there was a less spontaneous honouring of William Pitt by a taverner.

Upon pre-Revolutionary tavern-signs General Wolfe was a favourite figure. Boston had a Wolfe tavern near Faneuil Hall and when General Israel Putnam became a landlord at Brooklyn, Connecticut, he hung out over his front door a bravely-painted full-length of this hero. The Wolfe Tavern at Newburyport displays to this day a bold presentment of the English officer's rather comical profile.

Beehives upon tavern signs were by no means uncommon. One such bore the motto,

SIGN OF THE BENJAMIN WIGGIN TAVERN, HOPKINTON

SIGN OF THE WOLFE TAVERN, NEWBURYPORT

Tavern Signs — and Wonders

"By industry we thrive" and another this rhyme:

> "Here in this hive we are all alive,
> Good liquor makes us funny.
> If you are dry step in and try
> The flavor of our honey."

The Worcester Society of Antiquity owns the sign of Walker's Tavern, a famous house in Charlestown, New Hampshire, which displayed dozens of realistic bees hovering around a properly symmetrical hive!

The old sign of the inn at Paxton, Massachusetts shows upon one side Lord Cornwallis and Charles Paxton shaking hands across a well-loaded table at which they appear to be dining. Over the picture are the words: "Our good cheer tends to make enemies friends." But one must not conclude from this that the poltroon marshal of the Admiralty Court of Boston was a favourite among the good citizens of this town. Such, indeed, was far from being the case; they could not forget that Paxton had never fulfilled his promise to give them a bell for the meeting-house if only they would call their settlement after him! Finally, they presented to the General Court of Massachusetts a petition praying that their town "Paxton" be changed "to a name more agreeable." This petition was not granted but it was doubtless a salve to the indignation of Paxtonians that the effigy of this man, described as "an intriguing politician and a despicable sycophant" was hung in effigy upon the Liberty Tree which formerly stood at the corner of Essex and Washington streets.

Signs had their distinct uses, of course, in a time when many streets were without name or number. The amusing story is told of a member of the famous Beef-Steak Club frequented by Johnson and Smollett who, while spending a day in Calais with Lord Sandwich, became so interested in conversation that he strolled along the ramparts far from the Silver Lion Inn at which he was a guest. Then, as he could not speak a word of French, he was at a loss how to find his way back, until he bethought him to clap a silver shilling to his mouth and assume the attitude of a lion rampant. Thereupon, a soldier who supposed him deranged, led him very promptly to the inn where it was believed his keepers would be looking for him. The vigorous lion long

SIGN OF BOLTWOOD'S TAVERN, AMHERST

Tavern Signs — and Wonders

displayed before Boltwood's Tavern in Amherst, Massachusetts, may have similarly served some muddled mind in days gone by.

Moreover, the signs helped people to find the wonders! The [Boston] *Columbian Centinal* of April 28, 1810, announces one of these as follows:

"MONSTROUS SIGHT!

"To be seen at A. Pollard's Tavern, Elm street — A white Greenland sea BEAR, which was taken at sea, weighing 1000 wt. This animal lives either in the sea or on the land. They have been seen several leagues at sea, and floating on cakes of ice. . . ."

Sometimes a "whole caravan of living animals" was advertised to be displayed at one or another of the taverns. The Salem *Gazette* of Jan. 30, 1824, gives a list which reads like a Barnum circus-bill as on exhibition at the Essex Coffee House, — among them "a six-legged heifer" and "the ichneumon, an animal famous for destroying reptiles' eggs, and is worshipped by the Egyptians." A touch which reminds one of the Prologue used by Shakespeare's "horny-handed men of Athens" lurks in a footnote assuring the public that "the room is conveniently fitted, so that Ladies and Gentlemen can view the animals *with perfect safety.*"

Once, at least, a New England tavern appears to have been the scene of a bull-fight. The affair was thus heralded in the Essex *Register* of June, 1809:

"SPORTSMEN, ATTEND!

"The gentlemen SPORTSMEN of this town and its vicinity are informed that a Grand Combat will take place between the URUS, ZEBU, and Spanish BULL, on the 4th of July, if fair weather, if not the next day, at the HALF-WAY HOUSE on the Salem Turnpike. There will also be exposed at the Circus, other Animals which, for courage strength and sagacity are inferior to none." Again the reassuring landlord adds that "No danger need be apprehended during the performance!"

CHAPTER XII

OLD TAVERN DAYS IN NEWBURY

THAT Thomas Hale whose appointment as justice Samuel Sewall opposed in 1721 on the ground that "he hath lately kept an ordinary and sold rum" was the first of a long series of Newbury landlords who ultimately attained distinction in the town's affairs. Described as a man of immense size (he is said to have weighed over five hundred pounds!) with a strong and sonorous voice that could be heard at a great distance, he was long captain of the militia and, in spite of Judge Sewall, became a successful justice of the peace. But he was not by a good deal the first innkeeper in the town. The earliest license was granted almost a century earlier (in 1635) to Francis Plumer. This was the very year of the town's incorporation. Four years later Edmund Greenleaf was ordered to be ensign for Newbury and allowed to keep a house of entertainment; and by 1644 "Tristram Coffyn Sr. is allowed to keep an ordinary, sell wine and keep a ferry on the Newbury Side ... of Carr's island."

Tristram Coffyn possessed a clever wife whose superior intellect had the effect, as not infrequently happens, of getting her husband into trouble. The County records for September 1653 say that "Tristram Coffyn's wife, Dionis, was presented for selling beer," at his ordinary in Newbury, "for 3 pence a qt." Having proved, "upon the testimony of Samuel Moores, that she put 6 bushels of malt into the hogshead she was discharged." The law which she was supposed to have violated had been passed in 1645, and ordained that "every person licensed to keep an ordinary shall always be provided with good wholesome beer of 4 bushels of malt to the hogshead, which he shall not sell above 2 pence the ale qt on penalty of 40 shillings the first offence & for the second he shall lose his license." Goodwife Coffyn had merely worked out a problem in proportion (?) and demanded a higher return for what she represented as better beer.

This progenitor of the Newbury Coffins was also the founder of the Nantucket fam-

COFFIN HOUSE, NEWBURY

Old Tavern Days in Newbury

ily of the same name. He had not long been keeping the ferry and selling beer when he disposed of all his property on the Merrimac to remove to the island town. His son, Tristram Jr., fell heir, by marriage, to another ordinary, the house now known as the Coffin house. (Edmund Greenleaf's license had been transferred in 1650 to Henry Somerby, his son-in-law, and upon Somerby's death in 1652, young Coffin took over the widow and the house.) He was deacon of the first church in Newbury and lived in this house for more than half a century passing the property down, upon his death, to his youngest son, Nathaniel. Nathaniel abode here until he was eighty, discharging meanwhile many offices of trust in the colony. His son, Colonel Joseph Coffin, born December 30, 1702, was the next occupant of the house, and for nearly thirty years acted as the town's clerk. He had eight children, two of whom, the Rev. Paul Coffin D. D. and Charles Coffin M. D. were graduated at Harvard. Another son, Joshua, occupied the half of the house not given over to his father's use. His children — there were finally twelve of them — increased to such an extent that he was obliged to ask for leave to enlarge the old roof-tree and the letter in which he did this gives us a vivid glimpse of a family quarrel. It reads:

" Honored Sir,
" 'Tis in your power to make my life (as to outward circumstances) either Happy or Miserable & I am sure 'twould be with the Greatest Regrett I should do anything to Render your life uneasy. I don't ask you to give me house or land at present, although I don't think in that case I should be unreasonable (considering my family Increases so fast), but at present I only ask Leave to build a Bedroom chimney on my own cost for our present comfort. Which when you have properly weighed the affair & Considered what you have done for Bro. David and Paul, not to mention Boyd, for their convenience, & my present need of what I ask, I Cant suppose you will single me out from the rest of your children as an object of your Displeasure. Since I don't know as either of them have done more to merit your favour, I now Intreat you, Sr, in this Request to treat me only as a son, whose happiness so much depends on your appro-

Old Tavern Days in Newbury

bation & afection. I am Sr, with all Due Reverence & Duty
> "Your Dependent son,
> "JOSHUA COFFIN."

Hard indeed must have been the heart which could have withstood this plea for a chimney! Joshua Coffin, the historian of Newbury, lived and died in this house. He, like all the descendants of the innkeeper Tristram, followed and adorned gentlemanly pursuits.

Another early taverner of Newbury was Hugh March, licensed in 1670 by the court at Ipswich "to keep an ordinary and sell strong drink." For several years previous to March's appointment, there seems to have been considerable difficulty in finding a person well suited to the profession of innkeeper for, two years before, Captain Paul White had undertaken the work rather under protest. White already sold liquor in a wholesale way, and, once introduced to the new occupation, seems to have taken to it very well. At any rate we must so conclude from finding that his wife petitions in 1682, three years after his death, to have the license he had taken out transferred to her.

Meanwhile our friend March, who had begun to keep his famous Blue Anchor Inn because he wanted to, became involved in quite an interesting domestic complication. When his license was granted he had bought an "antient tavern" of Stephen Swett and expended a large sum of money in repairing and enlarging it. Then his good wife Judith died and he married Dorcas, the daughter of Daniel Bowman of Connecticut, whom he believed to be a widow but who, as he was subsequently persuaded, was a deserted wife instead. They had been living together two years when he learned that her first husband was alive and in Virginia! The affidavits, numbering nine in all, in which Hugh and his sons asserted that the woman had all the while had knowledge of her husband's existence, are on file at the office of the clerk of the Supreme Court in Boston and make very interesting reading. The decision of the General Court went against March, however, for it reads " In the case now in Court, touching Hugh March & Dorcas, his wife, the Court, upon what they have heard alledged by them both in the

Old Tavern Days in Newbury

case and duly considered thereof, do judge that the said March ought to take the said Dorcas & retayne hir as a wife, and to observe and & fullfill the marriage Covenant according to his engagement." Mrs. March's statement that the whole story had been built upon the malice and ill-will of March's children had evidently made due impression upon the Court.

But March refused to accept the decision and, rather than support the wife urged upon him by the judge, sold all his real estate, — except just enough for his own uses, — and so was, of course temporarily disqualified from serving as innkeeper. His idea appears to have been to continue the trade through his son John, but as he soon quarrelled with him, also, we finally find him left high and dry, though still keeping up a good fight for what he conceived to be his rights. The petition he sent to the Ipswich court at this stage of the game is most quaint and interesting.

"To the honderd County Court sitting at Ipswich this 26 of September 1682

"The petition of Hugh March of Newbury humbly showeth, That whereas the towne of Newbury being destitute of an ordinary for neer two yeres, being find twise, and likely to be fined the 3rd time, and could find no man that would undertack it, divers of the most considerable men of the towne applyed themselves to mee to keepe the ordinary, at which time i had no need of it or inclination to it, being well sat'ld upon a farme of my owne which was suffitiant to maintaine me; but by the ofton porsuasions and solicitations of those men I was wiling, provided I might have the free consent of the towne and the approbation of the Court, which I had freely and fully in a publick towne meting, by way of voate and by this court's free exceptacion, which moved mee to purchase at a deare rate that place which was the antient place of an ordinary, wch being out of repaire caused me to disburse great sums of mooney in repairing the ould and building new to fit it for the townes and cuntrys benifit, which caused me to sell one good farme and wholy to leave my farm that I lived uppone.

"The ordinary that I bought, tho old and out of repayer, cost me 120 lb besids to the valeu of more than 440 lb I layd out in building barn, stable and housing, with bedding &c to fite myselfe for giving publick conveniant entertainment for the country and towne.

"This ordinary was by me kept about 12 yeres, and no man had just reason to complaine for want of anything that was conveniant, nor did yt ever I heard. Besides the law saith, page 82, that no man shall lose his licance before he be convicted of some broache of law, which i never was:

"Altho I put the ordinary out of my hands for a time, yet it was for my lively hood and that I might live by it as an ordinary.

"It hath bene the uisiall custom of courts and townes to put antiant persons into such places and callings to bee a help to them, rather than to turn them out after all thayr cost to ye undoing and that because the present selectmen do not give ye approbation under thayre hands. I had not only the aprobation of the selectmen, but of the towne also, and of this hondred court for 12 years together, and tharfor hope yt this hondred court will consider my case, and not to suffer any man to be undon by the by and selfe ends of any selectmen; for, if so, the country will scarsly ever be well provided for with an ordinary to content, wch will be a disgrace to the country in other places in the wourld, for who will lay out such an estate to keep an ordinary to be at the mercy of the next new selectman whether he shall hould it above one yeare or no?

"This hondred court hauing in some measure understood how i committed my estate to my sone, and the way that he haue had to deprife mee of my licanse and likewise of my estate, wch i am depely soncable of my afflicttion, being further agrivated by his execution granted from the hondred court. of asistence wch I presume your honors are not unsonsable of: he hauing little mercy on his father, I hope you, the fathers of the land will haufe more mercy upon mee.

"In granting yr poore petioner his licence for the ordinary as formerly, wch (under correction) I conceive is but a rationall request, either to my self or som other yt may be put in, so that I may haue the bonifit of that my estate in that way as formerly, and in so doing you shall oblidg your humbe petioner, to pray.   HUGH MARCH."

The Ipswich court did not grant this request, but the Boston authorities, to whom

Old Tavern Days in Newbury

March then appealed, looked with more favour on his cause, and, in April, 1683, he was again licensed "to keepe a house of publick entertainment in Newbury," — the wife who had precipitated all this to-do having considerately died the month before.

A hundred years later there were at least two very famous taverns in "ould Newbury;" Nathaniel Low's almanac for 1788 gives the names of all the most noted innholders on the road from Boston to Portsmouth and those he mentions in Newbury are Oliver Putnam, who kept what has latterly been known as the Illsley house, and William Davenport, proprietor of the Wolfe Tavern. Oliver Putnam had formerly been a blacksmith and scythe-maker and it is very likely that he preferred his early calling. Certain it is that, after keeping a public house for about fifteen years, he sold out to Isaiah Illsley, who retained possession of the place until May 25, 1802, when he passed the estate over to Stephen Illsley Jr. By this time it had ceased to be an inn and so its history does not properly concern us any longer.

The Wolfe Tavern was much more persistently hospitable. When William Davenport bought the house in 1743 he was a carver, not an innkeeper at all, and he occupied the place as private residence for nearly twenty years. But in 1762 he caused extensive alterations and additions to be made to it and opened it as a house of entertainment for travellers hanging out as a sign a board adorned with the features of General Wolfe, his hero. For William Davenport had been the captain of a company that had gone to help Wolfe at Quebec. There is a tradition that he gave his wife a guinea when he left Newbury in 1759 to join the troops and the story further goes that, by prudence and economy, she was able to return the guinea to him, unused, when he returned home. Very like this guinea helped to buy the extra furnishings necessary to the transformation of his house into an inn. Be this as it may Davenport had been on the Plains of Abraham with his company September 13, 1759, the day when Wolfe gave up his life in the service of his country and it was with a fine sense of loyalty that he displayed the great General's portrait.

This tavern at the corner of Threadneedle Alley and Fish Street (now State Street) soon became a very popular place of resort.

WOLFE TAVERN, NEWBURYPORT

Old Tavern Days in Newbury

John J. Currier, who has written lovingly of "ould Newbury" says that under its roof the hungry and thirsty found comfort, shelter, good suppers and good wine. "Saturday evening, from all parts of the town, men came to the tavern to hear the news and to discuss politics, theology and the state of the crops. During the winter months farmers from the surrounding country brought pork, butter, grain, eggs and poultry to market, and gathered in the capacious bar-room at night, around the cheerful blazing fire, to while away the time with mugs of flip and mulled cider. The land travel from Maine and the eastern part of New Hampshire passed through Newbury on the way to Boston; and Wolfe Tavern or Davenport's inn, as it was often called, soon grew to be famous." In the early days of Masonry St. Peter's Lodge of Free and Accepted Masons often met at Mr. Davenport's inn and the Newburyport Marine Society for many years held its regular monthly assemblies there.

In the days preceding the recall of the Stamp Act the house was a hot-bed of rebellion as may be seen from the following tavern bill which has come down from William

Among Old New England Inns

Davenport to a lineal descendant, George Davenport of Boston:

"Dr. Messrs. Joseph Stanwood & Others of the Town of Newburyport for Sundry expences at My House on Thirsday, Septr. 26th, A.D. 1765. At the Grate Uneasiness and Tumult on Occasion of the Stamp Act.

	Old Tenor
To William Davenport	
To 3 Double Bowls punch by Capt. Robud's Order	£ 3, 7, 6
To 7 Double Bowls of punch	7, 7, 6
To Double Bowl of Egg Toddy	. . 14,
To Double Bowl 22 / 6 Single bowl 11 / 3	1, 13, 9
To Double Bowl Punch 22 / 6 Double bowl toddy 12 /	1, 14, 6
To Bowl Punch 11 / 3 Bowl Toddy 6 /	17, 3
To Double Bowl Toddy 12 / bowl punch 11 / 3	1, 3, 3
To Double Bowl Punch 22 / 6 Nip Toddy 3 /	1, 5, 6
To Mug Flip 5 / To a Thrible Bowl Punch 33 / 9	1, 18, 9
To Double Bowl Punch 22 / 6 To a thrible Bowl Ditto 33 / 9	22, 16, 3
To Double Bowl Punch 22 / 6	1, 2, 6
To a Double Bowl Punch 22 / 6	1, 2, 6
To Thrible Bowl Punch 33 / 9 Double Bowl Ditto 11 / 3	2, 16, 3
To Double Bowl Punch 22 / 6 Bowl Ditto 11 / 3	1, 13, 9

Old Tavern Days in Newbury

To Double Bowl Punch 22 / 6 To Double
Ditto 22 / 6 Bowl   2, 5,
  To 6 Lemons 15 / To Bowl of Punch 11 / 3   1, 6, 3
  To 2 Double Bowls Punch   2, 5,
  To Double Bowle Punch 22 / 6 bowl Punch
11 / 3   1, 13, 9
  To 2 Double Bowls Punch 1 / 5 To bowl
Punch 11 / 3   2, 16, 3
  To Bowl Punch 11 / 3 To Bowl Punch 11 / 3   1, 2, 6
  To the Suppers which were cooked Hot   2, 5,
  To 8 Double Bowls Punch after Supper   9,
  To Double Bowl Toddy 12 / Bowl Punch
11 / 3   1, 2, 6
  To Bowl Egg Toddy 7 /   7,
  To 6 pintes and ½ of Spirits @ 10 / per pint   3, 5,
  To a Breakfast of Coffee for Sd Company   2, 5,
                                              59, 17, 3
                Lawful Money   7, 19, 7½
Newbury Port 28 Sept. 1765
    Errors excepted   WILLIAM DAVENPORT."

On the extreme right of the bill is also a credit account of eleven pounds received in various sums from Captain Robud, Richard Farrow and one Celeby. Five days after this night of revelry at the Wolfe Tavern the effigy of the officer who had accepted the post of stamp distributor in Newburyport was hung from a large elm tree near the inn and, when the tar barrels underneath had been set on fire its rope was cut and the image dropped into the flames. Very likely the idea of this act came during the consumption of those many " Double Bowls punch" Landlord Davenport had brought out in response to clamorous demands.

This good Boniface died September 2, 1773, and was buried on the crest of the Old Hill burying ground, near the Hill Street entrance. His immediate successor at the inn was his son Anthony, but he was soon relieved by Moses Davenport, a brother who had a distinct gift for the calling. Under his management the patrons of the house increased and the business prospered amazingly. Among the notabilities entertained here was the Marquis de Chastellux who with Baron de Talleyrand, M. de Vaudreuil and M. Lynch de Montesquieu, grandson of the famous author, travelled through New England in 1782. The Marquis in the second volume of his Travels (page 240) gives an interesting description of his visit to Newburyport and of his entertainment there:

"The road from Portsmouth to Newbury passes through a barren country. Hampton is the only township you meet with. . . . It

Old Tavern Days in Newbury

was two o'clock when we reached Merimack ferry and from the shore we saw the openings of the harbor, the channel of which passes near the northern extremity of Plum Island, on which is a small fort, with a few cannon and mortars. . . . After passing the ferry in little flat boats which held only five horses each, we went to Mr. Davenport's Inn, where we found a good dinner ready. I had letters from Mr. Wentworth to Mr. John Tracy, the most considerable merchant in the place; but, before I had time to send them, he had heard of my arrival, and as I was rising from table, entered the room, and very politely invited me to pass the evening with him. He was accompanied by a Colonel, whose name is too difficult for me to write, having never been able to catch the manner of pronouncing it; but it was something like Wigsteps " [probably Colonel Edward Wigglesworth]. This Colonel remained with me till Mr. Tracy finished his business, when he came with two handsome carriages well-equipped and conducted me and my Aide de Campe to his country house. This house stands a mile from the town in a very beautiful situation; but of this I could myself form no judgment as it was already night. I went, however, by moonlight to see the garden, which is composed of different terraces. There is likewise a hothouse and a number of young trees. The house is very handsome and well furnished, and everything breathes that air of magnificence, accompanied with simplicity, which is only to be found amongst merchants.

"The evening passed rapidly by the aid of agreeable conversation and a few glasses of punch. The ladies we found assembled were Mrs. Tracy, her two sisters, and their cousin, Miss Lee. Mrs. Tracy has an agreeable and a sensible countenance and her manners correspond with her appearance. At ten o'clock an excellent supper was served; we drank good wine. Miss Lee sung, and prevailed on Messieurs de Vaudreuil and Taleyrand to sing also. Towards midnight the ladies withdrew but we continued drinking Maderia and Xery. Mr. Tracy, according to the custom of the country, offered us pipes, which were accepted by M. de Taleyrand and M. de Montesquieu, the consequence of which was that they became intoxicated and were led home, where they were happy to get to bed. As to myself, I remained perfectly cool, and continued to con-

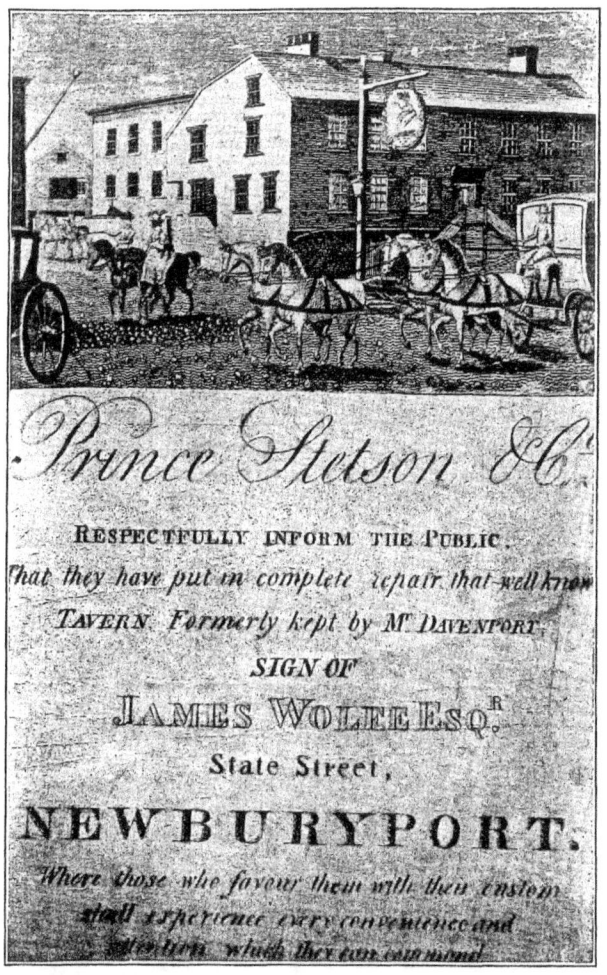

NOTICE OF PRINCE STETSON REGARDING HIS TAKING
CHARGE OF THE WOLFE TAVERN

Old Tavern Days in Newbury

verse on trade and politics with Mr. Tracy who interested me greatly with an account of all the vicissitudes of his fortune since the beginning of the war. . . . I left Newburyport the thirteenth at ten in the morning and often stopped before I lost sight of this pretty little town." Apparently this sprig of the French nobility found the Wolfe Tavern a house to make one regretful at leaving.

In 1804, Thomas Perkins, who had for some years served at the old stand under Moses Davenport, was licensed as an innholder and assumed control of the Tavern on his own account. By 1807, however, Prince Stetson is found to be the landlord, — and during his incumbency it was that the famous old building perished in the great Newburyport fire.

Almost the last public occurrence of importance with which the original Wolfe Tavern may be connected is, therefore, Newburyport's first celebration of Washington's birthday, in the year 1796. The president had many warm friends in the town, and, because they knew that he intended soon to retire from public life they caused the following to be printed in the local paper early in February, "At the desire of several gentlemen it is requested of those who incline to meet in celebration of the Birthday of the President on Monday next the 22nd instant, that they call or send and enter their names by Saturday noon or before with Mr. Richardson at the Union Hall, where it is proposed to dine on that day at 2 o'clock."

This announcement met with a hearty response and in addition to the dinner at Union Hall, — where there were toasts and long speeches in praise of Washington, — a large number of merchants and mechanics sat down to a similar repast in the Wolfe Tavern. Thus, very appropriately, the old building is linked to the present mode of honouring the memory of our most distinguished citizen.

Prince Stetson was not to be daunted by fire, however, in his laudable desire to serve the Newburyport public in a hostelry named the Wolfe Tavern. Only two weeks after the conflagration we find him informing his friends and the public that he shall open his Tavern on Monday next " in the House of Col. Bartlett, State St., where he solicits their favors." Bartlett's house proved to be only a temporary accommodation for the

Old Tavern Days in Newbury

tavern; three years later, Mr. Stetson removed to Salem and Benjamin Hale set up the sign of General Wolfe at the corner of State and Harris streets where it still swings. It is interesting to note that the sign had remained in its place all through the Revolutionary War, notwithstanding the hatred of everything which savoured of royal power. Once, to be sure, the Essex *Journal* declared that this portrait of General Wolfe, displayed in the very centre of the place " is an insult to the inhabitants of this truly republican town." But, fortunately, there were still some older inhabitants who recalled the ardent love which had prompted William Davenport to name his inn after the hero of Quebec and the obnoxious sign was allowed to swing on unmolested. Not long ago it was repainted by a well-known artist and to-day it is a very interesting and stately reminder of old tavern days in Newbury.

Not that the Wolfe Tavern had a monopoly all that time of public entertainment in the town. The Essex *Gazette* of January, 1771, proves the contrary by this notice:

Among Old New England Inns

"INN AT NEWBURY-PORT

"William Lambert, from Yorkshire in England, begs Leave to inform the Publick that he has taken the Inn at Newbury-Port, formerly occupied by Mr. Choate, which is now completely repaired, and new furnished with convenient Furniture, and the greatest variety of excellent LIQUORS. He has also provided commodious Stabling for Horses and every Accommodation for Travellers and others. He humbly intreats Custom and will strive by his good Entertainment to merit the Publick Favour, at the Sign of the Wentworth Arms, near the Ferry, in Newburyport."

Six months later we find that Robert Calder from London, who writes himself down as "late servant to his excellency Governor Wentworth," has purchased William Lambert's lease and offers, in addition to the attractions of his predecessor's advertisement "best Entertainement with diligent attendance." Not for nothing had he bent to the imperious will of Governor Wentworth, it would appear.

Major Ezra Lunt was another of the late eighteenth century innkeepers in Newbury,

Old Tavern Days in Newbury

adding the calling of publican quite easily to that of publisher, stagecoach proprietor and veteran of the Continental army. His inn was on the northwesterly side of Federal street, near the corner of Water street. The splurge *par excellence* in the innkeeping way was made, however, by the enterprising landlord who advertised at the SIGN OF THE AMERICAN EAGLE in the summer of 1799. Under this patriotic headline "Samuel Richardson Informs his friends and the public in general that he has removed from Union Hall into that spacious and convenient building lately occupied by Captain Ebenezer Stocker, East Corner of the Ferryway Wharf, — which he has opened for public Entertainment and will make every exertion to gratify and please those who may visit his House. Every favor will be gratefully acknowledged, Good accommodation for a few Boarders: likewise Stabling for Horses." It is interesting in this connection to note that the Newburyport selectmen had fixed by law the price of these various items of service. So, because the landlords could not underbid in price they overbade in attractions. The law placed " Dinners at taverns, for travellers, of boiled or roast meat, with other articles equivalent, exclusive of wine at 1/.6. Supper and breakfast 1/ each. Lodging 4/. Keeping a horse for one night, or for twenty-four hours, with English hay 2/—."

The Tracy house, which had accommodated Washington, became briefly the Sun Hotel, early in the eighteenth century, its proprietor, Jacob Coburn, informing the public (May 5, 1807), under a sign which quite effectively reflected the features of Old Sol, " that he has opened a spacious HOTEL in State street, Newburyport, the former mansion of the late Honorable Nathaniel Tracy Esq., and where Mr. James Prince last resided. Having at considerable pains and expense put the above in a situation suited to accommodate gentlemen he assures them with confidence that they will find every convenience and an unremitting attention to ensure the favor of the Traveller. Good horses and carriages to be had at all hours."

The dwelling-house of the eccentric " Lord " Timothy Dexter also descended temporarily to tavern uses, heralded by the following genial announcement: " The subscriber of Weare N. H. acquaints the public

Old Tavern Days in Newbury

that he has taken the noted house on High Street, Newburyport, known by the name of Dexter House (where the Lion and the Lamb lie down together in peace and where the first characters in the land are known to make their stay) which he opened on the 20th ult. as a house of Entertainment for the weary traveller who may sojourn thither, and for the conviviality of the jovial citizens of the town who may wish to spend a social hour freed from the cares of busy life; and he respectfully solicits their company, fully persuaded that he shall be enabled to afford them satisfaction. Country people are informed that he will entertain them as reasonably and with as good cheer, both for man and beast, as any regular Innkeeper between M'Gregor's Bridge and Newbury port, having commodious and convenient stables with good attendance. He flatters himself they will call and see . . . . . . William Caldwell." This advertisement might have been written yesterday, so modern is its tone and so little archaic its spelling. Yet its date is April, 1810.

Prince Stetson, formerly of the Wolfe Tavern, returned to Newburyport in 1823 and assumed charge of the Washington hotel on the corner of State and Temple streets. He had the honour of serving Lafayette when the Marquis visited the town in 1824, and took the spacious apartments in the Tracy house which Washington had occupied during his visit in 1789. The landlord's son, Charles, then a lad of thirteen, had the honour of acting as *valet de chambre* to the liberty-lover who had done so much for America in her hour of need.

A tavern which is constantly mentioned in John Quincy Adams's account of his young manhood days in Newburyport is Sawyer's on the Bradford road at or near Brown's springs, and within the present limits of the town of West Newbury. One interesting entry in the diary of this law student is that of May 21, 1788. "I walked," he says, "with Pickman in the evening to Sawyer's where we drank tea and made it almost ten o'clock before we got home. I then went up with my flute to Stacy's lodgings, our general headquarters. About a quarter before twelve Stacy, Thompson, Putnam with a couple of young lads by the name of Greenough and myself sallied forth upon a scheme of serenading. We paraded round town till almost four in the morning."

Old Tavern Days in Newbury

The charming home of Mrs. Harriett Prescott Spofford, near Newburyport's picturesque chain bridge, was once a tavern, also. It was then close to the public highway and its landlord, Ebenezer Pearson, was therefore not exempt from suspicion when Major Elijah P. Goodridge of Bangor, Maine, told, December 19, 1816, of having been assaulted about nine o'clock the previous evening, very near its doors, and robbed of a large sum of money. Pearson proved to be only one of the many who were subsequently accused, however, and, when Daniel Webster took the matter in hand he made Goodridge so contradict himself on the witness-stand that verdicts of "not guilty" were brought in for all the defendants. The whole thing appears to have emanated from the brain of the Major who, in order to escape financial trouble and at the same time account for the loss of his personal property, devised the scheme of a robbery and carried it into effect, firing with his own hand the pistol of the "assailant."

One Newburyport tavern-keeper was a good deal more permanently embarrassed by the cleverness of one of his guests, as we shall see from the following papers on file at the State House in Boston and having to do with the escape of Bridget Phillips, who had been sent to Newburyport for safe keeping during the siege of Boston:

"To the Honorable Provincial Congress at Watertown, June 22, 1775

"The petition of Bridget Philips humbly showeth that she hath lately arrived from Ireland and is desirous of going to her husband now in Boston. She therefore prays the Honorable Congress that they would give her a permit to go into the town of Boston & your petitioners as in duty bound will ever pray.   BRIDGET PHILIPS."

In answer to this petition the following resolution was adopted June 24, 1775: — "Resolved, that General Ward do not suffer or permit Bridget Phillips, wife to an officer under General Gage, to go into Boston, nor any other person whatever, without leave first obtained of this Congress, or some future house of representatives; and that an express be forthwith sent to the committee of safety for the town of Newburyport, to order them to take the most affectual meas-

Old Tavern Days in Newbury

ures to prevent the said Bridget from going out of this province, or to Boston."

The lady got the better of the law-makers, however, as the following letter shows: —

"NEWBURYPORT, 26th July, 1775.

"SIR: —

"We received some time since a Resolve of the late Congress ordering that Bridget Phillips (who called herself the wife of a Captain Phillips in Gen. Gage's Army) should not leave the Province & that the Committee here be desired to attend to her. Upon the receipt of it we applied to the Tavern Keeper, at whose house she was, to keep an eye upon her movements & to inform us should she take any suspicious steps, at the same time informing her that she must not leave the Province. This she judged to be very harsh but appeared for a month past so to acquiesce in it as to elude any suspicion in us that she would take pains for her escape. Upon the arrival of the New General at Cambridge she seemed to flatter herself, her case might be more tenderly considered by them & that upon application they would permit her to go to her husband.

This she mentioned to several of the committee but was told she must not go to Cambridge without consent of a majority of them. However that she never asked & the 18th Inst. she took place in a Chaise with Capt. John Blake (formerly of Boston) from hence to Salem, giving out that she was going to Head Quarters at Cambridge. The Tavern Keeper (Mr. Greenleaf) supposing it not beyond the limits by the Order & from a faulty Inattention never gave the Committee notice. It was not for a day or two known by us that she was gone. Upon enquiry we find that she hired a Chaise & Boy at Salem & in company with Benjn Jenks (who is said to belong to Casco Bay) she went the next day to Haverhill & the next to Portsmouth & by the assistance of this Jenks procured herself to be put on board the Scarborough Man of War there. This Intelligence was bro't us by the said Mr. Greenleaf whom we sent in pursuit of her.

"As she was a Woman & appeared of Some Fashion we did not think it expedient to put her under close Confinement neither did we suppose by the Order it was intended.

Old Tavern Days in Newbury

She left here two Trunks supposed to contain valuable apparrell which might prevent in Mr. Greenleaf the apprehention of her intending to go off. We judged it proper to give you this information & as she wrote for her Trunks to be sent to Boston we beg your Order about the delivery of 'em. Upon this occasion give us leave to remark what we hinted formerly to the Committee of War at Cambridge the ease with which an escape may at any time be made to the stationed ship at Portsmh as things are now ordered.   We are respectfully
"Your obedt servnts
"JONA. TITCOMB.
"p. order of the Committee.
"To the Honb. James Warren, Esq., speaker of the House of Representatives, to be communicated."

The result of all this was that, though Bridget did not get her trunks, Landlord Greenleaf was made pretty uncomfortable, — and what was of far greater importance, — the seaport towns were given leave to do whatever might seem to them wise in the way of preventing other such escapes.

Among Old New England Inns

The privileges of tavern-keeping were so great that often a man with every right to whatever his house might earn was made exceedingly uncomfortable by his rivals. Such was the case with the host of the Boynton Tavern on the road between Newburyport and Rowley. In March, 1811, the other landlords of Byfield protested against Boynton's tavern, stating that while it had been established for some time they doubted whether its continued existence was necessary. "The influence of this tavern is pernicious to the morals, the peace and comfort of some families in the vicinity," declares the protest; after which it goes on to allege that "the undersigned are credibly informed that people are there at very unreasonable hours in the night" and that "even the holy Sabbath is profaned by persons who there pass the Sacred hours in an idle and dissolute manner." Whereupon the petitioners humbly prayed "that the license of Mr. Boynton may not be renewed."

Somehow, though, the tavern lived on, and once it was even able to add to its capacity, thereby bestowing the name of Adding upon the latest scion of the family. Another child of this eccentric landlord had been called

HOME OF MRS. HARRIETT PRESCOTT SPOFFORD,
NEWBURYPORT

BOYNTON TAVERN, ON THE NEWBURYPORT ROAD

Old Tavern Days in Newbury

Tearing because tavern-repairs were in that stage of development at his birth. Verily, some of those old time publicans were men of decided originality!

CHAPTER XIII

THE INNS OF IPSWICH

FEW New England towns of the twentieth century preserve so much of the aspect of "ye olden times" as Ipswich, Massachusetts. Dozens of its houses, still occupied as homes, date back more than a century, and of these a fair number have, happily for us, been at some time in their history a tavern. Our forefathers, it must be remembered in explanation of this, knew nothing of the luxury of hot tea and coffee and so if they would drink anything but water, malt beer and other spirituous drinks had to be supplied and dispensed by somebody. In the records of Ipswich the malster and the tavern-keeper appear very early. The first license to sell was granted Robert Roberts by the Court of Assistants in 1635 and soon many men of high reputation sought like privilege; in 1652 Mr. Robert Payne, Mr. Bartholomew and Jeremy Belcher all re-

The Inns of Ipswich

ceived licenses. Deacon Moses Pengry also kept an ordinary and dispensed spirit!

The manner in which the deacon came to be a taverner is interesting because characteristic of the times. Corporal John Andrews had been his predecessor in the stand on High street known for far and wide as the White Horse. But because the corporal kept his bar open after nine o'clock and *encouraged young men to drink* a petition protesting against the renewal of his license was presented to the Court. The license was accordingly renewed only " until Salem Court" where in June 1658 a second petition was filed in which it was alleged that the recalling of Andrews' privileges " will be an affectual meanes for Ye remooving of much sin and evill and minister cause of joy and thanksgiving to many of gods people, amongst us."

In answer we find a statement that " the Court having considered of the petetion of many of the Inhabitants of Ipswich, together with Ye complaint and information of divers strangers for want of needfull and convenient acomodation and entertaynment at the other ordinarye and the intymation of the selectmen of the need of two in that town, have thought meet to license Corporal Andrews to keepe an ordinary for the entertaynment of strangers only till the next court at Ipswich, and not longer, provided that the Inhabitants doe at the sayd Court present some meet pson to keepe an ordinary wch will accept of the same and the Court shall approve of, only he hath liberty in that tyme to sell wyne and beere to townsmen out of dores." The suitable person fixed upon was Deacon Moses Pengry. He accordingly received his license on September 7, 1658, Andrews being permitted to retain his until the following March.

The Corporal meanwhile appears to have vented his spite upon the innocent Deacon for in the Court Record of April 28, 1658, we find that "Corporal John Andrews stands bound to ye Treserer of this County in the sum of fiftye pound upon condidtion the sayd John Andrews shall appeare at the next Court held at Ipswich to answer to what shall be objected against him about a vehement suspition of severall misdemeanors and facts as pulling down the signe of Moses Pengry and Mr. Browne his gate and dore and Lieut. Sam. Appleton his gate." Mr. Browne and Lieut. Appleton, it is signifi-

The Inns of Ipswich

cant to note, had been among the signers of the petition which recalled the Corporal's license.

Daniel Ringe was licensed in 1661 to keep an ordinary but "not to draw beer above a penny a quart, and to provide meate for men and cattell." The following year John Perkins, Andrew Peters, and John Whipple were licensed, the last to sell not less than a quart at a time and none to be drunk in his house. All were bound "not to sell by retail to any but men of family and of good repute nor sell any after sun sett; and that they shall be ready to give account of what liquors they sell by retail, the quantity, time and to whom." The house of John Whipple is now the home of the Ipswich Historical Society and because it is recognized as the finest existing specimen of colonial architecture it is herewith reproduced even though none of the liquor its proprietor dispensed was "drunk on the premises." Mr. Jonathan Wade, one of the leading citizens, was also licensed to sell at about this time and though there is no record that Wade broke the liquor law he appears to have been an unpleasantly contentious person. In 1645 he had been summoned to trial and fined sixteen shillings for "afronting the Court" and in 1658 he had to pay a fine of five pounds and witness fees for "expensive prices in selling grindstones and other things." These were days, it will be seen, when to set a prohibitive cost upon common necessities was punishable by law.

Innkeepers were restricted along with the rest, 6d a meal being the limit of what they were allowed to charge (1634). In the quality of the comfort provided as well as in the matter of prices the public appears to have been protected, too, at Ipswich. The inventory of Richard Lumpkin, one of the earliest innkeepers of the town, shows that his house was well equipped even so early as 1642, the date under which it is filed in the Ipswich Deeds. For he had

IN THE HALL

One large table, one stoole, two formes	0-15-0
Three chaers and six cushions	4-0
In bookes	2-10-0
One pair of cob-irons, one fire pan, one gridiron, and two paire of trammels and one paire of bellows	10-0
one muskett, one fowling piece	1-10-0

The Inns of Ipswich

IN THE PARLOR

one table with six joined stools	1- 5-0
three chairs and eight cushions	14-0
one bedstead, one trundle bed and curtins	1-10-0
one paire cob-irons one firepan	0- 4-6
one chest	0- 4-0
one fether bed, two bowlsters two pillows, two flock beds, five blanketts one rug one coverlett	8- 0-0
one warming pan with other implements	6-0

IN THE CHAMBER OVER THE PARLOR

one bedstead, one trundlebed	10-0
two flock bedds, one fether bed, one fether bolster, four blanketts, two pillows two coverletts	4- 0-0
four chests, two boxes	1- 5-0
one table	3-0
one corslet	1-10-0
one fetherbed tike	1-10-0

IN THE LEANTO

seven brass kettles, one iron kettle	4-10-0
one small copper	1- 0-0
one iron pott, four posnetts, with other implements	1- 0-0
Ten pewter dishes, etc.	2- 0-0
In plate	4- 0-0

Among Old New England Inns

From this inventory we gain a good idea of the furnishings of an average Ipswich tavern, but we are even more fortunate in possessing a racy picture of actual life in such a house, as it leaped hotly from the pen of the gifted bookseller and publisher, John Dunton.

Dunton was the gay Lothario, immortalized by Pope in the Dunciad, who married (August 3, 1682) one of the sisters of John Wesley's mother and of Defoe's wife. This lady seems to have shared some of her husband's Bohemian tendencies for always they called each other Philaret and Iris, and when their honeymoon days were over they settled down in the Black Raven in Prince's street, London, where they lived for two years without a single care. In 1685, however, following Monmouth's insurrection there came such a depression in the book trade, that Dunton resolved to leave his loving spouse and come to New England to sell his wares. Accordingly he sailed from Gravesend in the October of that year reaching Boston after a four months' voyage. He sold his books, visited Cambridge, and paid his respects to the venerable Eliot in Roxbury. The chief interest of his journeyings

The Inns of Ipswich

for us, however, attaches to his stay with Mr. and Mrs. Stewart at their house in Ipswich, — a visit which he describes thus in a letter he sent home to his wife:

"My Landlady, Mrs. Wilkins, having a sister at Ipswich which she had not seen for a great while, Mrs. Comfort, her daughter (a young gentlewoman equally happy in the perfections both of her body and mind) had a great desire to see her aunt, having never been at her house nor in that part of the country; which Philaret, having a desire to see, and being never backward to accomodate the Fair Sex, profers his service to wait upon her thither, which was readily accepted by the young lady, who felt herself safe under his protection. Nor were her parents less willing to trust her with me.

"All things being ready for our ramble I took my fair one up behind me and rid on our way, I and my Fair Fellow Traveller to Mr. Steward's who wife was Mrs. Comfort's own aunt: whose joy to see her niece at Ipswich was sufficiently Expressed by the Noble Reception we met with and the Treatment we found there; which far outdid whate'er we could have thought. And tho myself was but a stranger to them,

Among Old New England Inns

yet the extraordinary civility and respect they showed me, gave me reason enough to think I was very welcome. It was late when we came thither and we were both very weary, which would not excuse us from the trouble of a very splendid supper, before I was permitted to go to bed; which was got ready in so short a time as would have made us think, had we not known the contrary, that it had been ready provided against we came. Though our supper was extraordinary yet I had so great a desire to go to bed, as made it to me a troublesome piece of kindness. But, this being happily over, I took my leave of my Fellow Traveller, and was conducted to my apartment by Mrs. Stewart herself, whose character I shant attempt tonight being so weary but reserve till tomorrow morning. Only I must let you know that my apartment was so noble and the furniture so suitable to it, that I doubt not that even the King himself has oftentimes been contented with a worser lodging.

"Having reposed myself all night upon a bed of Down, I slept so very soundly that the Sun, who lay not on so soft a bed as I, had got the start of me and risen before me;

The Inns of Ipswich

but was so kind however as to make me one of his first visits, and to give me the BON JOUR; on which I straight got up and dressed myself, having a mind to look about me and see where I was: and having took a view of Ipswich I found it to be situated by a river, whose first rise from a Lake or Pond was twenty miles up, breaking of its course through a hideous swamp for many miles, a harbor for bears; it issueth forth into a large bay, where they fish for whales, due east over against the Island of Sholes, a great place for fishing. The mouth of that river is barred. It is a good haven town. Their Meeting House or church is built very beautifully. There is a store of orchards and gardens about it and good land for Cattel and husbandry.

"But I remember I promised to give you Mrs. Stewart's character &, if I hadn't, yet gratitude and justice would exact it of me. Her stature is of a middle size fit for a woman. Her face is still the magazine of beauty, whence she may fetch artillery enough to Wound a thousand lovers; and when she was about 18 perhaps there was never a face more sweet and charming — nor could it well be otherwise for now at all you call sweet and ravishing is in her Face; which it is as great a pleasure to behold as a perpetual sunshine without any clouds at all; and yet all this sweetness is joined with such attractive vertue as draws all to a certain distance and there detains them with reverence and admiration, none ever daring to approach her nigher or having power to go further off. She's so obliging courteous and civil as if those qualities were only born with her, and rested in her bosom as their centre. Her speech and her Behavior is so gentle sweet and affable, that whatsoever men may talk of magik therein none charms but she. So good a wife she is she frames her nature to her husband's: the hyacinth follows not the sun more willingly than she her husband's pleasure. Her household is her charge. Her care to that makes her but seldom a non-resident. Her pride is to be neat and cleanly, and her thirst not to be Prodigal. And to conclude is both wise and religious which makes her all I have said before.

"In the next place I suppose yourself will think it reasonable that unto Mrs. Steward's I should add her husband's Character: whose worth and goodness do well merit.

WHIPPLE HOUSE, IPSWICH

CALEB LORD HOUSE, IPSWICH

The Inns of Ipswich

As to his stature 'tis inclining to tall: and as to his aspect, if all the lineaments of a sincere and honest-hearted man were lost out of the world, they might be all retrieved by looking on his face. He's one whose bounty is limited by reason, not by ostentation; and to make it last he deals discreetly; as we sowe our land not by the sack but by the handful. He is so sincere and upright that his words and his meaning never shake hands and part but always go together. His mind is always so serene that that thunder but rocks him asleep which breaks other men's slumbers. His thoughts have an aim as high as Heaven tho their residence be in the Valley of a humble heart. He is not much given to talk though he knows how to do it as well as any man. He loves his friend and will do anything for him except it be to wink at his faults of which he is always a severe reprover. He is so good a husband that he is worthy of the wife he enjoys, and would even make a bad wife good by his example."

So much for this model keeper of what is to-day the Caleb Lord house. But not all the literature connected with Ipswich taverns echoes, as do the letters of John

Among Old New England Inns

Dunton, with praise of Ipswich housewives. John Adams, for instance, has only impatient scorn for the hostess of Treadwell's Tavern at Ipswich. "Landlord and landlady are some of the grandest people alive, landlady is the great-grand-daughter of Governor Endicott, and has all the great notions of high family that you find in Winslows, Hutchinsons, Quincys, Saltonstalls, Chandlers, Leonards, Otises, and as you might find them with more propriety in the Winthrops. Yet she is cautious and modest about discovering it. She is a new light; continually canting and whining in a religious strain. The Governor was uncommonly strict and devout, evidently so in his day; and his great-great grand-daughter hopes to keep up the honor of the family in hers and distinguish herself among her contemporaries as much. 'Terrible things sin causes,' sighs and groans the pangs of the new birth. 'The death of Christ shows above all things the heinous nature of Sin! How awfully Mr. Kent talks about death! how lightly and carelessly! I am sure a man of his years, who can talk so about death, must be brought to feel the pangs of the new birth here or made to repent of it forever. How dreadful

The Inns of Ipswich

it seems to me to hear him, I am so afraid of death and so concerned lest I a'nt fit and prepared for it. What a dreadful thing it was that Mr. Gridley died so! — too great, too big, too proud to learn anything; would not let any minister pray with him; said he knew more than they could tell him, asked the news and said he was going where he should hear no news.'

"Thus far landlady. As to landlord, he is happy and as big, as proud, as conceited as any nobleman in England; always calm and good-natured and lazy, but the contemplation of his farm and his sons and his horse and pasture and cows, his sound judgment as he thinks, and his great holiness, as well as that of his wife, keep him as erect in his thoughts as a noble or a prince."

I would rather have been a guest of the red-blooded Stewarts, would not you? The touching story of Lydia Wardwell, who was tied to the fence-post of the Ipswich Tavern where the Court sat, and lashed on the bare back with thirty cruel stripes makes one boil with indignation, even at this distance of time at the ultra-religionists who were so little Christ-like. Of course the act of this " young and tender chaste person " who " as a sign of spiritual nakedness" walked into the Newbury meeting-house, unclothed, during the hour of public worship must have administered a sad shock to the Christians of that day. Whittier's description of another Quaker maiden who similarly distinguished herself makes us feel the horror of the scene:

> " Save the mournful sackcloth about her wound.
>   Unclothed as the primal mother,
> With limbs that trembled and eyes that blazed
>   With a fire that she dare not smother. . . .
>
> " And the minister paused in his sermon's midst
>   And the people held their breath,
> For these were the words the maiden said
>   Through lips as pale as death: . . .
>
> " Repent! repent! ere the Lord shall speak
>   In thunder and breaking seals!
> Let all souls worship him in the way
>   His light within reveals.
>
> " She shook the dust from her naked feet.
>   And her sackcloth closely drew
> And into the porch of the awe-hushed church
>   She passed like a ghost from view."

But fanatical and unfortunate as was this mode of testifying love for the Lord it

The Inns of Ipswich

would not seem to call for brutal treatment before a crowd of tavern-loafers and one does not need to be a Quaker to feel with George Bishop in his "New England Judged" that the punishment much too nearly fitted the crime.

Bishop explains the young woman's act as follows: "Seeing the wickedness of your priests and rulers to her husband [a persecuted Quaker] she was not at all offended with the truth but as your wickedness abounded so she withdrew and separated from your church at Newbury, of which she was sometimes a member and *being given up to the leading of the Lord,* after she had been often sent for to come thither, to give a reason of such a separation, it being at length upon her in the consideration of their miserable condition, who were thus blinded with ignorance and persecution, to go to them, and as a sign to them she went in (though it was exceeding hard to her modest and shamefaced disposition) naked amongst them, which put them into such a rage instead of consideration, they soon laid hands on her, and to the next court at Ipswich had her, where without law they condemned her to be tyed to the fence-post of the tavern where they sat — and there sorely lashed her with twenty or thirty cruel stripes. And this is the discipline of the church of Newbury in New England, and this is their religion and their usage of the handmaid of the Lord, who in a great cross to her natural temper, came thus among them, a sign indeed, significatory enough to them, and suitable to their state, who under the visor of religion, were thus blinded into cruel persecution." Bishop, it is interesting to note, stands alone among the early writers in palliating the offence of Lydia Wardwell and in condemning the men who punished her.

Some of the petitions for inn-keeping privileges in Ipswich are exceedingly quaint. In 1733, for instance, John Stacey, being incapable of labour, reminded the Town "that there is a convenience on the northerly side of the Rock by Ebenezer Smith's for setting an house upon" and prayed that "he might obtain a grant for setting a house for selling cakes, ale etc for his livelihood." His request was granted and the resulting house is still standing upon the site to which it was removed in 1834 from the ledge in front of the old Seminary building. An-

ROSS TAVERN, IPSWICH

The Inns of Ipswich

other old hostelry which may still be easily found is the Ross Tavern built in 1734 and now situated on one of Ipswich's busiest streets under the shadow of a magnificent elm. The town boasts also of an inn at which our first President was entertained, — a famous old place long known as the Swasey house, some account of which will be found in the chapter on the Washington taverns of New England.

CHAPTER XIV

SOME PORTSMOUTH PUBLICANS AND THEIR FAMOUS GUESTS

PORTSMOUTH was exceptionally rich in inn-keepers of unusual personal qualities and they, in turn, had opportunity to entertain many guests of high distinction. For the first regular stagecoach run from any town north of Boston to that centre of New England industries came from Portsmouth, terminating at the inn of Mr. John Stavers. It was the enterprise of his brother Bartholomew who in April, 1761, thus announced his venture:

"For the Encouragement of Trade from Portsmouth to Boston

"A LARGE STAGE CHAIR,

With two good horses well equipped, will be ready by Monday the 20th inst. to start

Portsmouth Publicans and Guests

out from Mr. Stavers, innholder, at the Sign of the Earl of Halifax, in this town to perform once a week; to lodge at Ipswich the same night; from thence through Medford to Charlestown ferry; to tarry at Charlestown till Thursday morning, so as to return to this town the next day; to set out again on the Monday following: It will be contrived to carry four persons besides the driver. In case only two persons go they may be accommodated to carry things of bulk and value to make a third or fourth person. The price will be Thirteen shillings and sixpence sterling for each person from hence to Boston, and at the same rate of conveyance back again; though under no obligation to return in the same week in the same manner.

"Those who would not be disappointed must enter their names at Mr. Stavers on Saturday, any time before nine o'clock in the evening, and pay one half at entrance, the remainder at the end of the journey. Any gentleman may have business transacted at Newbury or Boston with fidelity and despatch, on reasonable terms.

"As gentlemen and ladies are often at a loss for good accommodations for travelling from hence, and can't return in less than three weeks or a month, it is hoped that this undertaking will meet with suitable encouragement, as they will be wholly freed from the care and charge of keeping chairs and horses, or returning them before they had finished their business."

The establishment of regular conveyances between Boston and Portsmouth marked an important step in the history of transportation. To be sure this was not the first stagecoach of the country, for Jonathan Wardwell established on May 13, 1718, a line that ran from his Orange Tree in Boston to Rhode Island, and in 1721 there was a road-wagon over the same route. Moreover, in 1734, two stagecoaches were advertised for this same much-travelled road. But Bartholomew Stavers' line was the first so far north, as has been said, and it prospered from the very beginning. A month after the initial advertisement "several stages having been performed with satisfaction, notice was given that five persons could be carried; that in future the vehicle would leave on Tuesday instead of Monday night and arrive back on Saturday night." In November 1762 it is announced that the "Stage

Portsmouth Publicans and Guests

Chaise will run, except in bad weather, through the winter; fare $3.00."

The distinctive name given this conveyance is interesting. The method of transportation set up in 1767 between Salem and Boston was a "Stage Chaise" while on the shorter routes out of Boston a "Stage Coach" and a "stage wagon" were used. In 1772 Boston was connected with Marblehead by a "stage chariot;" by May 1763 we find Bartholomew Stavers announcing

"The Portsmouth *Flying Stage Coach*

Is now finished, which will carry six persons inside; runs with four or six horses; each person to pay 13s. 6d. to Boston, and 4s. 6d. to Newbury. Sets out from the sign of the Earl of Halifax, every Tuesday morning between 7 and 8 o'clock, goes through Newbury to Boston, and will put up at good inns on the road where good entertainment and attendance are provided for the passengers in the coach. The subscriber, master of the stage coach, is to be spoke with from Saturday night to Monday night, at Mr. John Stavers's, innholder, at the sign of the Earl of Halifax.

"BARTHOLOMEW STAVERS."

Among Old New England Inns

The speed usually attained by a Stavers coach may be judged from the fact that a special express from Boston carrying important news made the journey between eleven o'clock one morning and two the next afternoon. But "on the road good entertainment and attendance were provided for the passengers in this coach;" and at Portsmouth they had the extreme felicity to be dropped at the door of the Earl of Halifax, where the coachman's brother John exercised hospitable sway!

John profited so much from the establishment of the "Stage Chair" that in 1765 he left his first inn on Queen street for the stand which still survives, and which history and romance have combined to make one of the best-known buildings in Portsmouth. The new inn was completed in 1770 and the old sign of the "Earl of Halifax" was transferred to identify the site. In the upper room of this house the Masonic meetings of St. John's lodge were for several years held, and the Grand Lodge of New Hampshire also met here.

But it is with a romantic marriage rather than with Masonry that the house's history is chiefly bound up. For it was in the door-

THE EARL OF HALIFAX (STAVERS INN), PORTSMOUTH

Portsmouth Publicans and Guests

way of this inn that Dame Stavers " in her furbelows " once said " as plain as day "

> " Oh, Martha Hilton! Fie! how dare you go
> About the town half dressed and looking so! "

only to receive from the barefooted girl she had hoped to shame the laughing assurance that she would yet ride in her own chariot. She did, too, for, as I have elsewhere [1] told, she very soon after made an ineradicable impression upon Governor Benning Wentworth, leading personage in the Colony and owner of

> " . . . . A Great House looking out to sea,
> A goodly place, where it was good to be."

But it was also good to be at the Earl of Halifax back in 1774 or thereabouts. At any rate the Tories thought so and used to gather nightly to drink to the King and his continued prosperity. So much indeed was the house a place of resort for " the ruffled and laced government officials " that John Stavers became very unpopular with certain other of his townsfolk. The Sons of Lib-

---

[1] See " Romance of Old New England Roof-Trees."

erty, especially, looked with hostile eye upon the Tory gatherings in the Earl of Halifax, and, one day, when Hopley Yeaton was marching a company of recruits down the street, he threatened to smash the inn's windows if any one looked out. No one looked as it happened and apparently this so disappointed Portsmouth's liberty-lovers that they resolved to *make* an opportunity to affront Landlord Stavers. Accordingly, a few days later, a mob gathered in front of the house and began to chop at the post upon which swung

> "The portrait of the Earl of Halifax
> In scarlet coat and periwig of flax."

In not unnatural irritation Mr. Stavers armed his slave with an axe and bade him tell the invader to desist. Confused in the crowd, the poor black lost his self-command and struck to the ground with the side of his weapon Mark Noble, who was wielding the encroaching axe. Noble survived — but was an insane man for almost all of the forty years he afterwards lived.

Of course this terrible assault still further enraged the crowd, and five minutes later

Portsmouth Publicans and Guests

there was not a pane of glass left in any of the tavern's windows. Meanwhile Mr. Stavers, taking a liberal supply of gold in his pocket, hastened to the stable by the back door, and, bridling his little black mare, rode for his life through Jefferson street. Two men on horseback came hotly pursuing, however, and ere he had gone many miles, drew near enough to hail him and bid him stop. This he had no intention of doing and, adroitly turning into a barn, just after he had passed a curve in the road he gave his followers the slip. Then he took refuge for a fortnight in Stratham with William Pottle Jr., a man who had usually supplied his inn with ale, and who because of his Tory sympathies soon had plenty of troubles of his own.

Portsmouth all this time was in the greatest commotion and there was crying need that someone with a cool head should take the mob in hand. John Langdon, with other leading patriots of the day, went to the inn with all possible speed, therefore. Langdon arrived just in time to put a check upon what had now become wanton destruction. As he entered the northeast parlour one of the mob had just raised a chair to dash in pieces an elegant mirror! Langdon seized the young man's arm. "Stop," he said, "have a dash at me first; you may perhaps be doing more harm than good here."

The affrighted slave had immediately disappeared, and for a long time could nowhere be found. At length he was discovered in a large rain-water tank in the cellar, nearly up to his chin in water! His master, when he was enabled by Captain Langdon's good offices to return to town, was seized by the Committee of Safety and thrust into Exeter jail, where he might have languished much longer than he did had not the victim of the assault sent out the following almost lucid letter in his behalf:

" PORTSMOUTH, February 3, 1777
" To the Committee of Safety the Town of Exeter:

" GENTLEMEN : — As I am informed that Mr. Stivers is in confinement in goal upon my account contrary to my desire, for when I was at Mr. Stivers a fast day I had no ill luck nor ment none against the Gentleman but by bad luck or misfortune I have received a bad blow but it is so well that I hope to go out in a day or two. So by

RICE TAVERN, KITTERY, OPPOSITE PORTSMOUTH

Portsmouth Publicans and Guests

this gentlemen of the Committee I hope you will release the gentleman upon my account. I am yours to serve. MARK NOBLE.
"A friend to my country."

Once released our landlord soon removed all suspicions as to his Toryism. Though he was personally opposed to taking up arms against his brother Englishmen he willingly took the oath of allegiance and loyally kept his promise not to oppose in any way the effort to procure independence. The damage the mob had done his house was not easily forgotten, though, and so slow was he to make the needed repairs in the place that many distinguished officers of the Revolution feasted in rooms that had scarcely a pane of glass in the windows. When the place was finally refitted, he took the hint the mob had so rudely offered and substituted the name and features of William Pitt for those which had offended the patriots of Portsmouth. In 1782 when the French fleet visited Portsmouth all the officers put up at this inn and here to visit them came Lafayette having made the trip from Providence on purpose. Upon this occasion as on many another of state the white uniforms of these brave young men had no doubt been renewed by contact with the large meal chest in Landlord Stavers' attic; it was their habit to complete their morning toilet by rolling over there a few times, thus making up for the lack of the white powder to which they were accustomed.

John Hancock, Elbridge Gerry and General Knox were other distinguished guests at this house and Louis Phillippe and his two brothers failed to be accommodated here only for lack of room. (The future king of France was immediately made welcome, it is interesting to add, in the hospitable home of Governor Langdon and he so enjoyed his stay there that he asked with keen interest years afterward of a Portsmouth lady who had just been presented to him at court, " Is the pleasant mansion of Governor Langdon still standing?")

Washington also once honoured the house with his presence, walking down Pitt street, on foot, to pay his call of ceremony, at the end of his visit in 1789, to General John Sullivan, President of New Hampshire, and his Council here convened.

Concerning the house which was Washington's own headquarters during this visit

Portsmouth Publicans and Guests

to Portsmouth something has been said in another chapter but the grewsome story connected with the place remains to be told. High Sheriff Thomas Packer lived in that house in 1768, and it was in order that he might not be late for his dinner there that he sacrificed the life of Ruth Blay and made his name infamous in history.

This unfortunate young woman was indicted in August, 1768, for concealing the death of an illegitimate child, an omission which made it impossible to determine whether the babe had been murdered or whether it had been dead when born. The English statute prescribed the penalty of death for this offence, so poor Ruth Blay was driven to the gallows in an open cart shrieking in a truly blood-curdling way. Her case had, however, awakened much sympathy, and it was believed that the Governor would grant a reprieve. But when the hour appointed for the execution arrived the papers had not come, and the sheriff, not wishing to be late home for dinner, ordered the execution to proceed.

When the reprieve arrived, only a few moments after the spirit of the young woman had taken flight, the indignation of the crowd was so great that they gathered that evening around Sheriff Packer's house, and erected an effigy bearing this inscription:

"Am I to lose my dinner
   This woman for to hang?
   Come draw away the cart, my boys —
   Don't stop to say amen
DRAW AWAY, DRAW AWAY THE CART!"

Subsequently it was learned that Ruth Blay's child had been still-born and that she was by no means a murderess.

The transition of the Packer house into "Colonel Brewster's Ta'an" as Washington called the place in his Diary, is interesting. Mrs. Packer had a mania for building extensions to her residence, and whenever her husband was absent on his duties of office she improved the opportunity to add a room or two. The house was thus enlarged until it had the proportions of an inn, and Colonel Brewster was glad to take it over as such in 1786.

This was by no means the Colonel's first essay as a landlord, however, for he had long successfully exercised that function at the Bell Tavern, a house which had been built

Portsmouth Publicans and Guests

in 1743 by Paul March and which displayed from a post in front an attractive bell, painted blue. Here the patriots were wont to congregate while the Tories were making merry at the Earl of Halifax, drinking as long if not so deeply as their red-coated rivals. During the period of Col. Brewster's incumbency of the Bell Tavern, the Marquis de Chastellux was here entertained and in the published account of his travels he speaks of Mr. Brewster as "a very respectable man, and much attached to his country."

After Colonel Brewster had transferred his interest to the Packer house Jacob Tilton became the host at the Bell. Tilton seems to have been chiefly known as the father of Johnny Tilton, a town idiot of whom Mr. Charles W. Brewster speaks with regretful tenderness in his delightful book, "Rambles About Portsmouth." Johnny, it seems, had not always been an idiot; his defect of mind was the result of a fall occasioned by a childish attempt to fly. He had been watching the hens flutter out of the loft window in his father's stable, and supposing he could do the same he stood upon the window frame and, flourishing his arms in imitation of the hens' wings, fell to the ground, permanently injuring his brain. Yet his answers, like Hamlet's, had "a happiness that often madness hits on, which reason and sanity could not so prosperously be delivered of," as when, appearing one day at the mill with a sack of corn to be ground, he replied to the miller's query what he knew, "Some things I know, and some things I don't know. I know the miller's hogs grow fat but I don't know whose corn they fat on." After a long and varied career the Bell Tavern was swept away by fire in 1867.

One of the landlords at the Bell had been a Mr. Purcell whose widow afterwards kept the Portsmouth boarding-house with which the career of John Paul Jones is bound up. On June 23, 1779 it was resolved in Congress "that Robert Morris should be authorized to take measures for speedily launching and equipping for sea the *America*, then on the stocks at Portsmouth, N. H.;" on the 26th John Paul Jones was unanimously selected to command her. Jones at once proceeded to Portsmouth, but found the *America* only half built instead of almost ready to be launched. He was under the necessity, therefore, of settling

PURCELL HOUSE, PORTSMOUTH

Portsmouth Publicans and Guests

down for quite a stay, pending the completion of his vessel, and the house in which he took up his quarters is the one on Middle street now known as the Lord house.

There were great doings in this house and out of it while the son of a Scotch gardener superintended the construction of his ship. Some hint of his social activities at this time may be gained from "The Tory Lover" of Sarah Orne Jewett; two years before he had been the hero of that historic quilting-party during which Miss Mary Langdon and her friends made from pieces of their best silk gowns the "first edition" of the stars and stripes that Europe ever saw, and the first to be saluted by the guns of a European naval power. This very flag, indeed, it was which served as the winding sheet for the sixty brave men who gave their lives that the *Bonhomme Richard* should conquer the *Serapis!*

When the birth of the Dauphin of France was officially communicated to Congress in the summer of 1782, Jones testified to the "pleasure and gratitude which he really felt" by a grand fête. At his private expense he had artillery mounted on the *America,* and amid the flags of different nations,

Among Old New England Inns

— with that of France in front, — fired salutes throughout the evening interspersing these festive sounds with a brilliant display of fire-works which Portsmouth folk crowded the river-banks to witness. More romances than could be told in many books the size of this one doubtless had Jones for their hero during these two visits to Portsmouth, for neither man nor woman could resist the wonderful personal magnetism of the little admiral. Even so perfectly balanced and unemotional a character as Dr. Franklin once said of him in a letter to an eminent woman: "No matter what the faults of Commodore Jones may be, I must confess to your ladyship that, when face to face with him, neither man, nor, so far as I can learn woman, can for a moment resist the strange magnetism of his presence, the indescribable charm of his manner, a commingling of the most compliant deference with the most perfect self-esteem that I have ever seen in a man; and above all the sweetness of his voice and the purity of his language. I offer these thoughts to the gracious consideration of your ladyship no less as a warning than as a favourable introduction."

No Portsmouth girl captivated the heart

of this charmer, however, for he seems always to have kept clearly in mind his duty to Aimée de Telison (natural daughter of Louis XV) while worshipping with the purest adoration the Duchess of Chartres, wife of Louis Philippe Joseph, known as the "sailor prince." Jones' friendship with this sweet and lovely woman had developed during the two months that the *Ranger* lay in Brest harbour. Once, at a luncheon she gave for him, his perfect command of seacraft so delighted her that she sent an attendant to bring from her jewel case a Louis XV watch of rare design and great value which her grandfather, the Count de Toulouse (son of Louis XIV by Madame de Montespan), had worn when commanding the French fleet in the great battle with the English and Dutch off Malaga. This mark of favour almost overwhelmed Jones, but he rallied to accept it with the graceful words: "If fortune should favour *me* at sea, I will some day lay an English frigate at your royal highness' feet."

Fortune did favour the gallant soldier and he was soon able to fulfil almost literally his promise by presenting to the Duchess of Chartres the sword of the *Serapis'* captain.

Among Old New England Inns

And when he died, alone in his French apartments at the early age of forty-five, the pretty token with this lady's miniature on its dial was found clasped in one hand. All through his career, punctuated as it was by more or less serious friendships with women on two sides of the Atlantic, he had evidently worshipped with a holy love this most pure and adorable of duchesses.

CHAPTER XV

ON THE ROAD

AFTER Levi Pease had proved that money was to be made by conducting stage lines, a good many people went into the business, and taverns prospered proportionately. As we have already seen, however, riding in the early conveyances was not an unmitigated joy, for, even after the roads improved, the vehicles were for a long time crude in the extreme. Thomas Twining, a young Englishman who visited the United States in 1795, has left us a vivid picture of the kind of "stage-waggon" in which he travelled. It was "a long car with four benches. Three of these in the interior held nine passengers. A tenth passenger was seated by the side of the driver on the front bench. A light roof was supported by eight slender pillars, four on each side. Three large leather curtains suspended to the roof, one at each side and the third behind, were rolled up or lowered at the pleasure of the passengers. There was no place nor space for luggage, each person being expected to stow his things as he could under his seat or legs. The entrance was in front over the driver's bench. Of course the three passengers on the back seat were obliged to crawl across all the other benches to get to their places. There were no backs to the benches to support and relieve us during a rough and fatiguing journey over a newly and ill-made road."

Not until twenty years later, when the Concord coach, — so-called because it was first built in Concord, New Hampshire, — came into use, was there anything like comfort to be had while on the road. One of these original coaches which has seen years of service in old tavern days is herewith reproduced, loaded with a group of merry young people costumed to celebrate an Old Home Day in Hopkinton, New Hampshire.

The condition of early eighteenth century roads and the structure of the primitive stage being taken into consideration, it seems as if the time made by the drivers was often surprisingly good. When Israel Hatch put on daily stages from Boston to Providence

OLD CONCORD COACH

WADSWORTH INN, HARTFORD

On the Road

about 1793 he covered the distance between five o'clock in the morning and two in the afternoon, changing horses once at the halfway house in Walpole. And every rival did the thing a little better than those who preceded him. Hatch's line had been running only ten years, when the *Columbian Centinal* and *Massachusetts Federalist* advertised as follows:

"PROVIDENCE STAGE

"A New line of Stages will commence running on Monday, the 2d day of January next, and will start from the Bunch of Grapes Tavern, State Street, in Boston, every morning, precisely at 8 o'clock, and arrive at Providence the same afternoon; and also will start from Barker's Tavern, in Providence (formerly Thomas Seahen's), head of Packet-Wharf, and arrive at Boston the same afternoon.

"The Proprietors of these Stages have been particularly attentive to the neatness, elegance and convenience of their Carriages, the goodness and strength of their horses, the carefulness and civility of their Drivers;

and have, and will use exertion for the accommodation of their Passengers.

"The Proprietors take this method to inform the public, to prevent impositions, that they are not accountable for any baggage unless receipted for from this date.

"Asa Foot.
"Abel Wheelock.
"Isaac Trask.
"Gragg & Easte.

"N. B. — The Stage Books will be kept at the Bunch of Grapes Tavern, and at Asa Foot's Tavern (formerly kept by Mr. Forbes), Brattle-Square, and at Mr. J. Wheelock's Marlborough-Street No. 37, sign of the Indian Queen, in Boston; and at Barker's Tavern, in Providence (formerly Thomas Seahen's), head of Packet-Wharf.

"Extra Carriages, of all kinds, may be had at either of the Stables of the above Subscribers, at the shortest notice.

"Also, Intelligence carried by express.
"Boston, Dec. 30, 1803."

By 1831 the famous Telegraph Line from Boston to Albany was binding its drivers by contract to make seven miles an hour on the

On the Road

average, including stops! This was in the high tide of our staging days, however, and the reign of the railroad was then not far off. To accommodate the most aristocratic of the Albany passengers the famous Wadsworth Inn, Hartford, which still survives, — tap-room and all, — was built.

The development of stage travel may be interestingly traced by comparing the "timetables" published in the almanacs of the day. In the first year of the nineteenth century the Old Farmer gave a list made up of twenty-five different entries and telling with exactness the conditions of travel between Boston and Albany, Providence, New York, Leominster, Portsmouth, Amherst, Plymouth, Salem, Marblehead, Taunton, New Bedford, Dorchester, Milton, Cape Ann, Medford, Newburyport, Haverhill, Groton, Cambridge, Roxbury, Brookline, Watertown, Dedham, Quincy and Canton. This modest list covers all the lines running out of Boston in 1801. By 1819, however, business had so increased that the following from the "List of Stages that start from Tavern in Boston" published in the *Massachusetts Register* of that year represents only a few of the lines quoted.

"Albany mail by Northampton from Earl's, Hanover street, Monday, Wednesday and Friday at 2 A. M. By Springfield from Earl's, Tuesday, Thursday and Saturday at 2 A. M.

"Albany accommodation by Framingham and Northampton from Boyden's, Bromfield's lane, Monday, Wednesday and Friday at 1 A. M.

"Burlington (Walpole, Burlington, Windsor, Hanover and Montreal Mail) from Boyden's, Monday, Wednesday and Friday at 2 A. M.

"Concord, N. H., and Hanover over Londonderry turnpike from Barnard's, Elm street, Monday, Wednesday and Friday at 5 A. M.

"Duxbury every Monday, Wednesday and Friday 3.30 A. M. and evening, Tuesday, Thursday and Saturday at 5 A. M. from Davenport's.

"Framingham, from Patterson's Wednesday and Saturday at 2 P. M.

"Gloucester, from Miller's Elm street, every day at 11 A. M.

"Haverhill, from Wild's, Tuesday, Thursday and Saturday at 10 A. M.

"Newport and New Bedford from Boy-

On the Road

den's Tuesday, Thursday and Saturday at 4 A. M.

"New York commercial mail by Worcester, Stafford and Hartford from Earl's daily at 1 A. M.

"New York middle line from Earl's, in summer to Norwich, Conn., Tuesday, Thursday, Saturday and Sunday, 5 A. M. In winter on middle road to Hartford Monday, Wednesday and Friday at 5 A. M.

"Providence mail from Davenport's every day except Sunday at 9 A. M.

"Salem from Davenport's daily except Sunday at 9 A. M. and 4 P. M.

"Lunenburg and Groton from Boyden's Tuesday and Thursday at 8 A. M., and Saturday at 4 A. M.

"Plymouth and Sandwich to Falmouth from Davenport's Tuesday, Thursday and Saturday at 5 A. M."

From Badger & Porter's Stage Register, 1836, I note the following:

"Boston and Albany mail stage via Northampton leaves 7 Elm street, Boston, Monday, Wednesday and Friday at 2 A. M. Distance to Albany 165 miles. Fare from Boston to Northampton $4.50, to Albany $8.75.

"Boston and Montreal L. C. stage, new line, via Haverhill, N. H., leaves Boston every Monday, Wednesday and Friday mornings.

"Boston, Concord, Hanover, Burlington, Montreal and Quebec mail stage, leaves Wilde's, No. 11 Elm street, Boston, every morning except Sunday at seven o'clock.

"Boston and Worcester accommodation stage leaves 7 Elm street, Boston, Monday, Wednesday and Friday at 10 A. M. and arrives in Worcester at 4 P. M. Distance 42 miles. Fare $2.

"Boston and Providence mail coaches, leave Marlboro Hotel, Boston, every morning, Sundays excepted, at 5 A. M. to meet the steamers for New York, and leave Providence every morning at 7 A. M., and arrive in Boston at 1 P. M. Also the steamboat mail coach leaves Providence on the arrival of the boats from New York. An accommodation coach leaves as above daily at 11 A. M. for Providence. Fare $2.

"Boston, Haverhill and Concord, N. H. Mail stage leaves No. 11 Elm street, Boston, Tuesday, Thursday and Saturday, at

On the Road

7 A. M., and arrives in Concord at 6 P. M. Distance sixty-eight miles. Fare $3.

" Boston and Keene, N. H. North Star line via Lowell leaves Nos. 7 and 9 Elm street, Boston, Tuesday, Thursday and Saturday at 5 A. M., and arrives in Keene same evening.

" Boston Forrest Line stages for Saratoga, Albany, Troy and Lake George, leave stage office, No. 9 Elm street, Boston, Monday, Wednesday and Friday, at 2 P. M., via Lowell, Nashua and Charlestown.

" Boston and New Bedford mail stage via Taunton leaves Marlboro Hotel, Boston, Tuesday, Thursday and Saturday, at 7 A. M. Arrives at Taunton at 1 P. M., and in New Bedford the same evening. Fare $3.

" Boston, Plymouth, Sandwich, Falmouth and Barnstable, mail stage, leave Stone's City Tavern, Boston, every morning except Sunday, at 4 A. M., and arrives in Falmouth and Barnstable same evening connecting with the boat for Nantucket.

" Boston, Fitchburg, Fitzwilliam and Brattleboro, Vt., mail stage leaves Wilde's, No. 11 Elm street, Boston, every day, at 5 A. M. Fare $3.75.

" Boston, Portsmouth, N. H., and Portland, Me., accommodation stage, leaves Eastern Stage House, 84 Ann street, Boston, every morning, except Sundays, at 8, and arrives in Portland, at 5 P. M. Distance to Newburyport, 38 miles, fare $2; to Portsmouth, 60 miles, fare $3; to Portland, 110 miles, $6.

"Boston, Concord, N. H., and Burlington, Vt., Mail Pilot Line, leaves the stage office, No. 9 Elm street, Boston, every day for Burlington. Distance 210 miles.

"Beverly and Boston stage leaves Stone's City Tavern, Boston, every day, except Sunday, at 4 P. M., and arrives in Beverly at 6. Distance 16 miles. Fare $1.

"Gloucester and Boston, mail stage, leaves City Tavern, Brattle street, Boston, every day, except Sunday, at 11 A. M., and arrives in Gloucester at 4 P. M. Fare from Boston to Lynn $62\frac{1}{2}$ cents; to Salem, $1; to Manchester, $1.50; to Gloucester, $1.75; to Sandy Bay, $2.

"Newton Upper Falls and Brighton stage, leaves Wilde's, No. 11 Elm street, Boston, every day at 4 P. M., for Newton Upper Falls; and Tuesday and Saturday continues through to Dover and Taunton.

On the Road

"Omnibuses and Coaches

"Charlestown and Boston hourly coaches. A coach leaves Simond's Hotel (late Jackman's), Charlestown, at 7 A. M., and 5 Brattle street, Boston, at 9 A. M., and continues to leave each place every hour until 8 P. M. every day except Sunday. The coach stops at each of the intermediate hotels in Charlestown. A room is provided at each of the public houses for the convenience of passengers.

"New line of half-hourly coaches between Cambridgeport and Boston leave as follows, viz.: Half-past 7 A. M., and continue to leave each office every half-hour through the day, until 8 P. M. Passengers taken and left at any place in Cambridge, Cambridgeport and Boston. Office in Boston at 51 Brattle street. Fare to Cambridge 25 cents. Cambridgeport 12½ cents.

"Roxbury and Boston hourly omnibuses (old line) leave Roxbury Hill every morning except Sunday at 7 Norfolk ave., Washington st., Boston, at 7, and continue to leave each place every half-hour through the day until 8 P. M. from Roxbury and 8.30 from Boston. Fare 12½ cents.

Among Old New England Inns

"Jamaica Plains. The old line runs an omnibus to Jamaica Plains, leaving Norfolk avenue and Washington street at 10 A. M., 4 and 6 P. M. Fare 25 cents.

"East Boston. An omnibus called the 'Maverick' and connected with the ferry-boat is in constant requisition for passengers going to or coming from East Boston."

Later on in the forties two fine omnibuses called the "Governor Dudley" and "General Washington" were run between Boston and Grove Hall. They were long and had very high wheels and a steep flight of steps in the rear, with iron railings on each side. The guard stood on the steps and collected the fares, while the driver held the reins over four and sometimes six horses. These omnibuses were highly decorated and were embellished with portraits of their namesakes painted on each side.

The Dock square and Canton street line was soon after established by Hobbs & Prescott, who afterwards sold out to J. H. Hathorne, who in turn sold out to the West End Road at the time of the consolidation. Hobbs & Prescott also had a line running to the Norfolk House.

On the Road

Some of us who are still in the early thirties remember well these old Hathorne coaches, lumbering yellow things which plied between Salem street, Charlestown, and Northampton street, Boston, and never ran on Sundays because Mrs. Hathorne wished the horses to have one day in seven for rest. Groton, which is several times mentioned in these lists, was a famous coaching centre.

The earliest line of stage coaches between Boston and Groton thus advertised itself in the *Columbian Centinal* of April 6, 1793.

"NEW LINE OF STAGES

" A Stage-Carriage drives from Robbins' tavern at Charles River Bridge on Monday and Friday in each week, and passing through Concord and Groton, arrives at Wyman's tavern in Ashley in the evening of the same days; and after exchanging passengers there with the Stage-Carriage from Walpole it returns on Tuesdays and Saturdays, by the same route to Robbins's. . . . The Charlestown Carriage drives also from Robbins' on Wednesday in each week, and passing through Concord arrives at Richardson's tavern in Groton, on the evening of the same day, and from thence returns on Thursday to Robbins. . . . Another Carriage drives from Richardson's tavern in Groton, on Monday in each week, at six in the morning, and passing by Richardson's tavern in Concord, at ten o'clock in the forenoon, arrives at Charlestown at three o'clock in the afternoon. . . ."

Very likely it was from one of these " Carriages " that the hero of the following graphic little sketch descended: " At early dusk on some October or November evening, in the year 1794, a fresh, vigorous, bright-eyed lad, just turned of fifteen, might have been seen alighting from a stage-coach near Quaker Lane [now Congress St.] as it was then called in the old town of Boston. He had been two days on the road from his home in the town of New Ipswich, in the State of New Hampshire. On the last of the two days the stage-coach had brought him all the way from Groton in Massachusetts; starting for that purpose early in the morning, stopping at Concord for the passengers to dine, trundling them through Charlestown about the time the evening lamps were lighted, and finishing the whole

On the Road

distance of rather more than thirty miles in season for supper. For his first day's journey there had been no such eligible and expeditious conveyance. The Boston stage-coach, in those days, went no farther than Groton in that direction."[1]

The first public conveyance between Boston and Groton was a covered wagon hung on chains for thoroughbraces. The transportation price was two dollars for each passenger. By 1807 there was a tri-weekly line of coaches to Boston and as early as 1820 a daily line, which connnected at Groton with others extending into New Hampshire and Vermont. Not long after this there were two lines to Boston running in competition. One of these, the Telegraph and Despatch line had a driver named Phineas Harrington, familiarly called "Phin" by the tavern-keepers and by his passengers of whom he never took more than eight. "Phin" was a very little man and it was said of him that on cold and stormy nights he used to get inside one of the lamps fixed to the box in order to use the lighted wick as a foot-warmer!

[[1] Memoir of Hon. Nathan Appleton in the Proceedings of the Massachusetts Historical Society v. 249, 250."]

Among Old New England Inns

Besides the stagecoaches the carrier wagons added greatly to the business of Groton and helped largely to support the taverns. For, in those days, the town was on one of the main thoroughfares leading from Boston to Canada via New Hampshire and Vermont. Often as many as forty huge wagons drawn by four or six horses each would pass through the village in a single day, laden on the down-trip with country produce and, on the return, with the hundred and one articles found in the village stores of the northern states.

The list of those who have been tavern-keepers at Groton is a very long one. In the early days no great preparations appear to have been necessary here for the entertainment of strangers, the result being that many farmers took in casual travellers whom they treated quite as members of the family. By 1752, however, Groton had so developed as a stopping-place that Caleb Trowbridge, Jr. declared that he "lives upon a publick Road leading from Dunstable to Harvard, which is frequented by many Travellers; that the publick Houses on said road are fifteen Miles distant from each other;" that he "has only Liberty to Retail, yet is often

On the Road

crowded with people who want necessary Refreshment, but is not allowed to sell it to them; he therefore prays he may now obtain a Licence as an Innholder." His prayer was graciously granted.

Isaiah Thomas's Almanack for 1785 prints a list of Groton innholders for that year, and among them appears the name of Captain Jephthah Richardson, who for many years kept a tavern on the site of what is now the Baptist Church. During the war of 1812, this house was locally famous as a recruiting station. It was also well known to wayfarers as an important staging centre.

Groton is so fortunate as to possess to-day a well-preserved Revolutionary tavern, in which guests are still entertained. Originally a dwelling-house and occupied before our struggle with England by Rev. Samuel Dana, — who had the hardihood to preach a warm defence of George III and his methods to a congregation notably patriotic in their sentiments and so to earn his dismissal from church and town, — it was kept during the latter part of the war by Captain Jonathan Keep. Capt. Keep was succeeded by his brothers, Isaiah and Joseph, who were landlords as early as 1798. In 1825, Joseph

Hoar, who had just sold the Emerson Tavern at the other end of the village street, became the incumbent. Excepting the year 1836, when Moses Gill and his brother-in-law, Henry Lewis Lawrence, were the landlords, Mr. Hoar continued in charge until the spring of 1843 when he sold out to Thomas Treadwell Farnsworth. At this period the house was a temperance one. Daniel Hunt, James Minot Colburn and Joseph Nelson Hoar (a son of the former landlord) have since been proprietors here. For a time in recent years the place was managed by three daughters of Mr. Hoar under the name of Central House, but its present owner is Charles H. Dodge and its present title the Groton Inn.

Twining's description of stagecoach travel having been quoted, some pages back, it seems only fair to give one or two other persons' views on this interesting subject. John Mellish, who travelled in 1806 did not seem to find it bad:

"Having taken my leave of a number of kind friends with whom I had associated during my stay in Boston, I engaged a passage by the mail stage for New York, and was called to take my place on the 4th of

GROTON INN, GROTON

On the Road

September at two o'clock in the morning. It is the practice here for the driver to call on the passengers before setting out, and it is attended with a considerable degree of convenience to them, particularly when they set out early in the morning. The mail stages here are altogether different in construction from the mail coaches in Britain. They are long machines hung upon leather braces with three seats across, of a sufficient length to accommodate three persons each, who all sit with their faces towards the horses. The driver sits under cover without any division between him and the passengers; and there is room for a person to sit on each side of him. The driver, by the post-office regulations, must be a white man, and he has charge of the mail which is placed in a box below his seat. There is no guard. The passengers' luggage is put below the seats, or tied on behind the stage. They put nothing on the top and they take no outside passengers. The stages are slightly built and the roof suspended on pillars; with a curtain to be let down or folded up at pleasure. The conveyance is easy and in summer very agreeable."

Then as now, no doubt, impressions of

travel depended very much upon the temperament of the traveller. John Lambert, who toured Vermont and lower Canada at just about this same time, gives a most melancholy account of his trip from Burlington to St. Albans: "I had an uncomfortable seat in the hind part of the wagon upon the mail bag and other goods. I might, indeed, have sat in front along with the driver, but my legs would have been cramped between a large chest and the fore part of the wagon. Of two evils I chose the least: but I shall never forget the shaking, jolting, jumbling and tossing, which I experienced over this disagreeable road, up and down steep hills, which obliged me to alight, (for we had only two poor jaded horses to drag us) and fag through the sand and dust exposed to a burning sun. When we got into our delectable vehicle again, our situation was just as bad; for the road in many parts was continually obstructed by large stone; stumps of trees, and fallen timber; deep ruts and holes, over which, to use an American phrase, we were 'waggon'd' most unmercifully." Perhaps the nature of the country, as well as temperament, had, after all, something to do with these differing accounts.

EAGLE TAVERN, EAST POULTNEY

On the Road

It would be interesting to know whether Lambert rested his weary bones, on that journey to Canada, at the Eagle Tavern, East Poultney, Vermont. It was there in his time as it is to-day, right across the road from the village green and exceedingly hospitable in aspect, though it now takes in only an occasional guest for whom provision cannot elsewhere be found. In Revolutionary days the house was a famous rallying centre, and it was here that Captain William Watson delivered that famous toast: " The enemies of our country, — may they have cobweb breeches, porcupine saddle, a hard trotting horse and an eternal journey." It was this doughty captain, too, who, upon the death of his good dog, Comus, placed the remains in a wooden box and buried them beside the road back of the tavern, erecting, to mark the spot, a stone with this inscription:

"Comus is dead! Good dog, well bred;
Here he lies — enough said.''

Within a stone's throw of the Eagle Tavern, Horace Greeley learned the printing trade and very often, no doubt, he spent an evening in its public room talking politics to the other lads of the little town.

And now, just to take out of our mouths the taste of Lambert's grumbling, let us enjoy the description supplied by Abdy, the Oxonian, of stage travel as he found it in the New England of 1835:

"I left Northampton on the 16th at three, A. M., for Boston, and arrived at that place about eight in the evening. The road was good and if we had not changed our vehicle three times during the journey, and stopped at the various post-offices for the bags, and at the hotels for refreshment, we should have got in much sooner. The first fifteen miles were performed in an hour and forty minutes. The distance is ninety-four miles. The passengers were inclined to be sociable and as it was a fine day and the country not uninteresting, the journey passed off pleasantly enough. An English coachman would have been somewhat amused with the appearance of the stage and the costume of the driver. The former was similar to some that are common enough in France though not known on our side of the channel. It was on leathern springs; the boot and the hind part being appropriated to the luggage,

On the Road

while the box was occupied by two passengers in addition to the 'conducteur' and as many on the roof. On the top, secured by an iron rail, were some of the trunks and boxes, and inside were places for nine; two seats being affixed to the ends, and one, parallel to them across the middle of the carriage. Our driver sat between two of the outsides, and, when there was but one, on the box over the near wheeler; and holding the reins, or lines, as he called them, in such a manner as to separate his team into couples, not a-breast, but in a line or tandem fashion, drove along with considerable skill and dexterity. When he got down, he fastened the 'ribbons' to a ring or a post in front of the house where he had occasion to pull up."

A pleasant picture surely, this of the genial driver fastening his ribbons before the hospitable New England inn where his stage-load of sociably inclined travellers are to stop for their noonday meal. Shall we not leave them at the door, enveloped in the welcoming smile of the landlord, who in anticipation of their coming has prepared for them the choicest viands of which his larder can boast?

CHAPTER XVI

SOME TAVERNS OF ROMANCE

THE alluring adjective "romantic" is conferred upon taverns for widely different reasons. This old house in Westfield, Massachusetts, for instance, has for years been thus distinguished because it was supposed to be the scene of an ardent salute bestowed upon Landlord Fowler's wife, one Revolutionary morning, by no less a person than the British General Burgoyne, who was then returning, a prisoner, to the Continental camp at Cambridge. But, a few years ago, an enterprising student of local history arrived at the conclusion that the kisser was not Burgoyne at all, but the German General Riedesel; evidence further went to show that the kissee was in all probability the landlord's daughter instead of his wife. At this point, however, our naïve lady gave up research for she could not see why Riedesel should have kissed any strange young

FOWLER TAVERN, WESTFIELD

Some Taverns of Romance

woman when his own charming wife was near at hand! To-day, therefore, the Fowler Tavern may be said to memorialize a KISS, the parties thereto being undetermined.

Some other New England taverns no longer standing have more clearly defined reasons for reverence at the hands of those who love romance. The old Fountain Inn at Marblehead was the opening scene of the most romantic story in all American history. For it was here, as she was scrubbing the tavern floor, that Sir Harry Frankland first caught sight of Agnes Surriage!

The gallant Sir Harry was at this time (1742) collector of the port of Boston, and he had come riding down to Marblehead's picturesque coast to transact some business connected with old Fort Sewall, then just a-building. At the Fountain Inn he stopped for a long draught of cooling ale. And, there before him in the tap-room, vigorously wielding the Colonial substitute for a mop, was a beautiful girl-child of sixteen, with black curling hair, dark eyes and a voice which proved to be of exceeding sweetness, as the maiden, glancing up, shyly gave her good-day to the gallant's greeting. The girl's feet were bare, and this so moved

Frankland's compassion that he gently gave her a piece of gold with which to buy shoes and stockings. And then he rode slowly away, wondering why his heart was beating so much more quickly than was its wont.

Shortly afterwards Frankland was again in Marblehead on business, and he was not slow, we may be sure, in finding his way to the tavern for another mug of ale and another sight of the charming child, just budding into womanhood, whom he had seen performing with patience and grace the duties that fell to her lot as the daughter of humble fisherfolk. He was surprised to find her feet still bare and he asked her, a bit teasingly, what she had done with the money he gave her. Quite frankly she replied, blushing the while, that she had bought the shoes and stockings, but was keeping them to wear to meeting. This reply argued hitherto unsuspected depths of poverty on the part of Agnes's parents, and Frankland was not long in looking them up; nor was he so long as one feels he ought to have been in obtaining from them permission to remove their daughter to Boston to be educated as his ward.

Some Taverns of Romance

For several years, however, the relation between these two was exactly what Frankland had said it would be, and Agnes was in close touch with her Marblehead pastor as well as with her mother. Meanwhile, she was being taught reading, writing, grammar, music and embroidery by the best tutors Boston-town could provide and she grew daily, we are told, in beauty and maidenly charm.

So the inevitable end was helped to come. At first, one is forced to believe, Frankland had not meant to wrong the child so trustingly given into his care. But the death of Agnes's father threw the girl permanently on his hands just at the very time when his sudden elevation to the baronetcy made marriage to her appear an impossibility. So there came about a situation which caused Agnes to be dropped by the ladies who had formerly been kind to her, and that made the baronet decide to set up a new home in Hopkinton, Massachusetts, instead of remaining in censorious Boston.

I have elsewhere [1] told the story of the idyllic life led by these two at Frankland Hall, of their visit in 1754 to Frankland's

[[1] See " Romance of Old New England Churches."]

home in England, of Sir Harry's surprise and Agnes's chagrin at the coolness of their reception there, and of the tragedy of the Lisbon earthquake, which gave the maiden a superb opportunity for heroism and the man the very fright he needed. For, while pinned down by a weight of stone and suffering untold agonies from the pain of a wound in his arm, our young gallant vowed to amend his life and atone to Agnes, if God in his mercy should see fit to deliver him. When the deliverance came through the self-forgetful devotion of the woman he had so grievously wronged he wasted not a moment, we may be sure, in summoning a priest to tie the knot too long ignored. That his spirit had been effectually chastened, one reads between the lines of this entry in his diary, which may still be seen in the rooms of the Massachusetts Historical Society in Boston: "Hope My providential escape will have a lasting good effect upon my mind." Sir Harry Frankland was no libertine. All his life he passed in fasting, humiliation and prayer the anniversary of that Lisbon earthquake.

With the old Bell Tavern in Danvers, Massachusetts, is connected the sad death of

Some Taverns of Romance

Elizabeth Whitman, from whose touching story Hawthorne is believed to have drawn the inspiration for his "Scarlet Letter." Elizabeth Whitman was the daughter of the Reverend Elnathan Whitman, pastor of the Second Church, Hartford, Connecticut, and one of the Fellows of the Corporation of Yale College, — a man distinguished for scholarly traits, the love of rare manuscripts and forgotten books, and whose library at the time of its destruction in 1831 had been for years the envy of our large universities. His daughter, however, cared less for literature than for life and though engaged, first to the Reverend Joseph Howe of Church Green in Boston, and after his death to the Reverend Joseph Buckminster, whose name and memory is an illuminated page in the history of New England Congregationalism, died alone at a Danvers tavern with no husband at hand to acknowledge himself the father of her dead child. Though I shall not repeat here this girl's sad story which I have told in another place,[1] I am glad to reproduce an advertisement, new to me, which I have recently found in the *Salem Mercury* of July 29, 1788 and which is in-

[[1] See "Romance of Old New England Roof-Trees."]

teresting because inserted by the keeper of the Bell Tavern in the hope of identifying his mysterious guest:

"Last Friday, a female stranger died at the Bell Tavern, in Danvers; and on Sunday her remains were decently interred. The circumstances relative to this young woman are such as to excite curiosity and interest our feelings. She was brought to the Bell in a chaise from Watertown, as she said, by a young man whom she had engaged for that purpose. After she had alighted and taken a trunk with her into the house, the chaise immediately drove off. She remained at this inn until her death, in expectation of the arrival of her husband whom she expected to come for her, and appeared anxious at his delay. She was averse to being interrogated concerning herself or connections; and kept much retired to her chamber employed in writing needle-work &c. She said, however, that she came from Westfield, in Connecticut; that her parents lived in that State; that she had been married only a few months; and that her husband's name was Thomas Walker; — but always carefully concealed her family name. Her linen was all marked E. W. About a

Some Taverns of Romance

fortnight before her death she was brought to bed of a lifeless child. When those who attended her apprehended her fate they asked her, whether she did not wish to see her friends: She answered that she was very desirous of seeing them. It was proposed that she should send for them; to which she objected hoping in a short time to be able to go to them. From what she said and from other circumstances, it appeared probable to those who attended her, that she belonged to some country town in Connecticut: Her conversation, her writings and her manners, bespoke the advantage of a respectable family & good education. Her person was agreeable; her deportment amiable & engaging; and, though in a state of anxiety and suspense, she preserved a cheerfulness, which seemed to be, not the effect of insensibility, but of a firm and patient temper. She was supposed to be about 35 years old. Copies of letters, of her writing, dated at Hartford, Springfield, and other places, were left among her things. — This account is given by the family in which she resided; and it is hoped the publication of it will be a means of her friends' ascertaining her fate."

I, personally, believe that Elizabeth Whit-

Among Old New England Inns

man *was* waiting for her husband in the old Bell Tavern. But diverse points of view are always stimulating, and some readers may like to compare with my story of her life the following extract from the history of Danvers: "She was possessed of an ardent poetical temperament, an inordinate love of praise, and was gifted with the natural endowment of beauty and perfect grace, while she was accomplished with those refinements which education can bestow. She was lovely beyond words. But her natural amiabilities were warped and perverted by reading great numbers of romances, to the exclusion of almost all other reading. She formed her idea of men by the exaggerated standards she saw in the books to which she resorted; and thus when she looked around her she saw no one who realized her ideal. She subsequently became intimate . . . with Judge Pierpont Edwards." Evidently Mr. Hanson himself gave too much weight to the statements in that meretricious volume "Eliza Wharton," whose treatment of the dead woman's story he proceeds indignantly to condemn.

Danvers still has one picturesque old hostelry, the Berry Tavern, which has enter-

BERRY TAVERN, DANVERS

Some Taverns of Romance

tained the public for over seventy years and upon whose site stood yet another inn more than one hundred years back of that. Nearly opposite the Berry Tavern there long flourished, too, the house of Deacon Gideon Putnam, which was run by John Piemont at the time John Adams went to the Court in Ipswich before he was President.

Lancaster, Massachusetts, has a number of romantic taverns, among them the Old Brick Inn used by William Dean Howells in "The Undiscovered Country" as the shelter for his heroine when she and her spiritualistic father have lost their purse and their way.

"'We will stop at that tavern,' said Egeria."

"They had been passing through a long reach of woodland that stretched away on either side of the road, when they came to a wide, open plateau, high and bare. It looked old and like a place where there had once been houses, though none were now in sight; from time to time in fact the ruinous traces of former habitations showed themselves by the wayside. A black fringe of pines and hemlocks bordered the plain where it softly rounded away to the eastward; a vast forest of oak and chestnut formed its western boundary. At its highest point they came in sight of a house on the northern slope, a large square mansion built of brick; an enormous elm almost swept the ground with its boughs on its eastern side; before it stood an old-fashioned sign-post, and westward, almost in the edge of its forest lay its stabling.

" 'That must be the tavern,' said Boynton, instinctively making haste towards it."

This Brick Inn, which Howells with true artistic feeling prefers to call the Elm Tavern, was built in 1804 for the traders of the Union Turnpike Company. Lancaster was then getting to be an important staging town and several houses had sprung up in answer to demand. To-day, however, these are either private residences, abandoned houses or places of doubtful repute,— such as Egeria and her father soon discovered their " Elm Tavern " to be. During the years between the incorporation of Lancaster and its destruction by the Indians in 1676, there is no record of any public hostelry within its borders. But in 1681, the year of the resettlement of the town, the Great and General Court ordered " that for the future the

Some Taverns of Romance

selectmen of all Towns shall approve of all Persons to be Licenced before Licence be granted to any of them by the County Courts to keep such Publique House or be Retailer of Strong Liquors in any of said Towns, and all Persons shall annually renew thare License at the Spring Court in thare respective Countys." All innkeepers were further required to have " some inoffensive sign, obvious, for direction to strangers, and such as have no such sign after three months so Licenced shall lose thare Licence and others be allowed in thare stead." The first man to profit by this requirement was Nathaniel Wilder whose license was granted in 1690 and whose place of doing business was a garrisoned house on the southeast slope of George Hill.

A highly romantic figure was this first Lancaster landlord. In 1673, he had married Mary Sawyer, grand-daughter of John Prescott, and in 1676 had fled with this young wife and an infant son from an Indian massacre in the course of which most of his near neighbours were slain. The revolting tragedies of this day so burned into his mind that, the following August, he and three other men murdered on Hurtleberry Hill,

Concord, some Indian women and children whom he there encountered.

Now, as it fell out, these were *not* "bad Indians" but the wives of two Christians and when their bodies were found "not far from another, some shot through, others their brains beat out with hatchets," the perpetrators of the assault were immediately arrested, tried and condemned to death. Upon trial, however, it was found that Wilder had not actually participated in the act of killing, and he escaped by paying a heavy fine. But the blood shed on Hurtleberry Hill was paid for all the same by the Wilder family, for he himself was shot down by an Indian at the outset of the morning assault made upon Lancaster July 31, 1704, by the French and Indians led by Chevalier Beaucour, — and two of his sons later paid with *their* lives for their father's crime against the redmen.

In 1717, Capt. John White, also famous as an Indian fighter, kept a licensed ordinary in Lancaster for a single year. By trade Capt. White was a smith, but he became renowned as an associate of Captain Lovewell in his campaigning against the Indians. He was the hero of the day,

Some Taverns of Romance

March 10, 1775 when he marched through Boston at the head of his sixty rangers, mostly from Lancaster, Groton and that vicinity, displaying ten bloody scalps, worth a thousand pounds bounty, won by the night surprise of a war party near the source of the Salmon river in New Hampshire.

When Still River was a part of Lancaster, Captain Samuel Willard held a license and kept an inn in an admirably preserved specimen of the better class of farmhouses of the period. He was afterwards an innkeeper in the Mrs. Charles Nichols house, and it was while here that he led some Indian attacks. His charge for an ordination dinner, which included wine, has come down to us as 3s 6d though the usual price of a meal was less than half that. Casual lodging for a person was four pence per night in Lancaster, for a horse six pence for twenty-four hours, and for a yoke of oxen a penny or two more.

Many romantic traditions cling about the South Lancaster house formerly known as the Bowers Inn. Built in Revolutionary days by Dr. Josiah Wilder, it was for many years one of the most stately and commodious mansions in the whole country side. In

1778, Dr. Wilder lost three children by death within six weeks, and his wife, also, apparently died of the same dread fever that had stricken down the little ones. When placed in her coffin she was so wondrously fair, however, that her husband could not believe the spirit to have left her body and, with the faint hope that she might still breathe to spur him on, he worked and worked over her until, at last, she smiled into his eyes and LIVED, literally raised from the dead. From 1800 to 1805 the house was kept as an inn by Captain Josiah Bowers, who fought at Bunker Hill, but did nothing else for a lifetime which was to his credit. After leaving the inn he took up his residence in another Lancaster house, and there he and his sharp-tongued wife lived a cat and dog life until, one day when her gibes were too bitter to be borne, — he walked around to the well and threw himself headlong into it. Happily, he left a considerable sum for the benefit of worthy Lancaster widows, so that his name is to-day identified with what means comfort and solace to many care-worn women.

John Ayers of Brookfield, — known in early days as Quawbawg, — was another

Some Taverns of Romance

calculating landlord who finally came out a hero. In 1674 history shows us this landlord refusing to pay his share of the parson's support on the ground "that he keeps the ordinary and has for time past and should be free from it." (The tavern keeper usually furnished the sacrament wine, and repeatedly was given hints "to accommodate the church occasion.") But, though he would not contribute to the parson's salary, John Ayers proved himself every inch a man when King Philip's war broke out the following year. Things were looking pretty black just then for Quawbawg. The redmen had made a sudden rush upon the little settlement, and the men had been forced to hurry their terror-stricken families to the shelter of Ayers' Tavern. Eighty-two persons were shut up within the walls of the house, and to this number were soon added four more for two women gave birth to twins. At the beginning of the fray many of the men were killed and wounded, but when the Indians, "like so many wild bulls," piled up hay and wood against the walls and set it on fire, the few who had survived sallied out and intrepidly quenched the flames. "The next night," says a witness, "the savages renewed their attack. They used several stratagems to fire us, namely by wildfire on cotton and linen rags with brimstone in them, which rags they tied to the piles of their arrows sharp for the purpose and shot them to the roof of our house after they had set them on fire, which would have much endangered in the burning thereof, had we not used means by cutting holes through the roof and otherwise to beat said arrows down, and God being pleased to prosper our endeavors therein." Thanks, however, to the rain "sent by the Lord for the salvation of His people" and to relief brought from neighbouring towns Sergt. Ayers's ordinary as well as its host of involuntary guests were saved from conflagration and from worse than death at the hands of the Indians. The old house survived for many years, but it has now long since fallen into decay.

CHAPTER XVII

WHEN LAFAYETTE CAME BACK

MANY of the public houses at which Lafayette stopped during his visits to this country in 1824 and 1825 have already been described in the chapter on the Washington taverns, but it seems worth while to speak of the Lafayette inns in a group because of the opportunity thus afforded to rehearse one of the most interesting episodes in our social history. Few Americans under fifty, I dare say, have read the story of Lafayette's triumphal tours through New England, but it is a tale well worth hearing, not only because one of the greatest men associated with our country's history is its hero, but also because it spreads before us, as in a panorama, the habits and customs of a time now gone for ever.

Free punch as well as bread and cheese were furnished at the city's expense to the men waiting to escort Lafayette into Boston on that occasion, and Josiah Quincy, who tells this incident in his "Figures of the Past," remarks that though there would have been the greatest indignation had someone proposed to provide free books at the expense of the taxpayers, there seemed no reason whatever why municipal punch should not flow on this and similar occasions!

When all is said, however, there *was* no occasion similar to that 1824 tour of Lafayette. Congress had offered to send a ship expressly to convey to our shores him who had once ventured his all in our defence, but the noble Republican preferred to come over as a private citizen and so sailed quietly from Havre. But, once within our borders, he was the guest of the nation, and the salute which welcomed him just before he landed at Staten Island was, by direction of the President, that due to the highest military rank in our service. In New York every kind of public honour was paid him and, — what must have touched him most, — the citizens generally mounted the revolutionary cockade (black and white) in compliment to him who had languished in an Austrian dungeon out of desire that the French people should be free.

When Lafayette Came Back

The first spot in New England which it pleased Lafayette to visit during this tour was Putnam's Hill at Greenwich, or Horseneck, as the place is generally called, in allusion to the doughty general's hazardous ride. Lafayette chose to walk down this hill, and, as he made his way along the steps cut in the precipice, a salute of twenty-four guns was fired in his honour. From Greenwich to Stamford and from Stamford to Bridgeport and New Haven the aged soldier travelled rapidly, every bridge and toll-gate along the way being thrown open freely to him and his escort. The enthusiasm which pervaded all classes in these Connecticut towns is worth noting. The story is told of an old lady in charge of a turnpike gate to whom a facetious traveller observed: "Well, madam, I suppose you are very glad General Lafayette has come, as you must have made oceans of money to-day at the gates?" The old lady felt very indignant at the remark. "Sir," she replied, "you must know that the General and his friends go through this gate free of toll; and I should like to have him pass a thousand times!" "Oho, then your gates are free now?" "Yes," replied the Connecticut dame, without a moment's hesitation, "for such men as Lafayette, but not for those who come so far behind him."

Even the horses were exhorted to make the most of this extraordinary occasion. "Behave pretty now, Charley," the driver of Lafayette's coach was heard to say to one of his pair, "behave pretty, you are going to carry the greatest man in the world."

Morse's Hotel was the General's New Haven headquarters and here he was met by the veterans of the Revolution and many friends and associates of other days. In front of the house passed a procession of military corps and of Yale students and, after reviewing these, Lafayette enjoyed a breakfast "with the mayor, aldermen and about one hundred invited guests which was handsomely served up by Mr. Morse at the expense of the city." While the feast was in progress word was brought in that the wives and daughters of the honoured guests were overflowing the parlours and begging the honour of being presented to the great man. Such a call was, of course, not to be refused by a gallant Frenchman, and, the duties of the table being ended, the Marquis hastened to put himself at the service of the ladies.

GOLDEN BALL TAVERN, PROVIDENCE

When Lafayette Came Back

A visit to the public green, some private calls, and an inspection of the College, occupied the rest of the forenoon, and about three o'clock the General took his departure on the lower road by East Haven, Guilford, Saybrook and Lyme to New London. Morse's Hotel was afterwards the Franklin Hotel but the place as a public house disappeared many years ago.

In Norwich the crowd from the wharf bridge to the hotel of the great general was so dense that it was only with difficulty that Lafayette and his escort could make their way through, and during the supper which followed reiterated cheers were repeatedly sent up from outside; at each of these bursts of enthusiasm the hero of the occasion presented himself at the window and bowed his appreciation.

The Providence inn honoured by Lafayette's presence was the Golden Ball of which we have already heard in connection with Washington's visit to New England in 1789. Thither the people's guest rode uncovered in a barouche drawn by four white horses and followed by an imposing procession. Upon his visit to the State House, crowds of ladies strewed flowers in his path, and afterwards, at the hotel, he received for nearly two hours in his apartment and appeared at intervals on the piazza in response to the tumultuous applause outside. Then, about half past four, he set off for Massachusetts, being met just beyond Pawtucket by the aides of His Excellency, Governor Eustis, who escorted him to the mansion which still stands, though sadly degenerate, and which is variously known as the Shirley or Eustis House, Roxbury. Lafayette, it is interesting to note, availed himself more of private hospitality than Washington had done. There was not the danger there would have been in the President's case of offending certain citizens by accepting the entertainment offered by certain others.

It had been two o'clock in the morning when Lafayette reached Roxbury, and he was an old man. Consequently, it was not until the following afternoon (Tuesday, August 22, 1824) that he made his entry into Boston and was presented by Governor Eustis to Mayor Josiah Quincy (the elder). Every possible arrangement had been made for the entertainment of the city's distinguished guest, with the result that all the buildings along the line of march were taste-

When Lafayette Came Back

fully hung with bunting and the French and American flags were everywhere shown appropriately entwined.

On the site of the Old Liberty Tree Mr. S. Haskell had just erected a four-story brick building, which he had named Lafayette Hotel, in honour of the expected guest. At this point, therefore, the decorations were especially effective. A civic arch had been reared twenty-five feet high, decorated with French and American flags and displaying in the centre a large scroll with the words "WASHINGTON AND LAFAYETTE: A REPUBLIC NOT UNGRATEFUL." Upon tablets at either side in golden letters was the following:

"The fathers in glory shall sleep
That gathered with thee in the fight,
But the sons will eternally keep
The tablet of gratitude bright;
We bow not the neck and we bend not the knee,
But our hearts, Lafayette, we surrender to thee."

On the east side of the arch were two interesting verses on the Liberty Tree

"Of high renown, here grew the tree
Of elm, so dear to Liberty;

Among Old New England Inns

    Your sires, beneath its sacred shade,
      To Freedom early homage paid.

"This day with filial awe surround
    Its root that sanctifies the ground
And by your father's spirits swear
    The rights they left you'll not impair."

Upon reading these verses, Lafayette, to whom liberty had meant so much of sorrow and service, was deeply affected. So was the crowd on either side, and the ovation they then gave the aged general was such that the procession had to come to a halt. Whereupon a most pleasing incident occurred. For from the door of the hotel emerged a beautiful young girl with a silk sash of red, white and blue draped across her shoulders, and bearing upon a silver salver glasses and a bottle of the red claret wine of France. Stepping to the side of the barouche she invited the General to partake, which he did with his usual graceful courtesy. Thus it came about that the first refreshment taken by Lafayette in the new city of Boston was furnished him from the hotel bearing his name, now Brigham's Hotel.

When Lafayette Came Back

After this incident another and remarkable one took place. As Lafayette rode up Tremont street, receiving on all hands the homage and congratulations of the immense throngs that greeted him, he perceived, seated on a balcony of a house then called " Colonnade Row," Mme. Scott, the sometime wife of the sturdy old Governor John Hancock. She had been his hostess in the old Hancock mansion on Beacon street as far back as the year 1781, and now, after a lapse of forty-three years, was instantly recognized by the general. With the inborn courtesy of a Frenchman, Lafayette directed his conveyance to stop in front of the house, and rising, with his hand placed over his heart, made a graceful obeisance, which was gracefully returned. Then the lady burst into tears and exclaimed, " I have lived long enough!"

The procession had now come to Boylston street, and was ordered to halt. The pupils of the public schools, under the direction of their teachers, had been arranged in a double line on the Tremont-street mall, and were protected by peace officers. The children had been instructed during the past month to sing the national hymn of France, " The

Marseillaise." They were all provided with bouquets of bright flowers; the girls were all dressed in white, wearing red sash ribbons and blue ribbons on their summer hats; the boys were also attired in red, white and blue, white pants, blue jackets and a red ribbon on their hats. The moment Lafayette entered the mall, the children struck up, in good voice and time, that glorious anthem "Marseillaise." The effect was electrical.

The third incident of the day now took place, and, as was each of the others, was entirely unexpected by the committee! A young girl threw her bouquet in front of Lafayette. Her patriotic act was instantly taken up and every child all along the line threw bouquets upon the mall, and Lafayette literally passed over a bed of natural flowers, strewn at his feet, and in his honour. It was the most affecting incident of the day.

A battalion of light infantry was formed on Park-street mall, and passed in review by the general. As he entered the State House grounds a salute was fired by artillery posted on the high ground south of the Frog Pond. He paid a short visit of courtesy to the governor and council, after which he was escorted to his lodgings in the stately

When Lafayette Came Back

old-time residence of Thomas Amory, Esq., now standing at the corner of Park and Beacon streets. Shortly after reaching his lodgings, he appeared on the balcony, having on either side of him Governor Eustis and ex-Governor John Brooks, both of whom wore their old Continental uniforms.

The dinner of that festal day was served at the Exchange Coffee House on State and Congress streets, — not the magnificent building erected by Charles Bulfinch in 1808, but the less pretentious structure which succeeded that elegant edifice on the same site and which continued until 1853 to be a popular tavern and the starting-place of most of the stages. Among the toasts of the occasion was this neat one by General Lafayette: " The City of Boston, the CRADLE OF LIBERTY. May Faneuil Hall ever stand a monument to teach the world that resistance to oppression is a duty, and will, under true republican institutions become a blessing."

On Phi Beta Kappa day Lafayette was in Cambridge to hear the great oratorical triumph of Edward Everett, a speech so inspired, so overpowering, that at its close every man in the assembly was in tears.

Among Old New England Inns

Josiah Quincy, who was present as a recent Harvard graduate, wrote, twenty years afterward, that he could conceive of nothing more magnificent in the way of speech-making. And certainly the effort must have been magnificent if it, as a whole, lived up to this paragraph in it:

"Welcome, friend of our fathers, to our shores! Happy are our eyes that behold these venerable features! Enjoy a triumph such as never conqueror or monarch enjoyed, — the assurance that throughout America there is not a bosom which does not beat with joy and gratitude at the sound of your name. You have already met and saluted, or will soon meet, the few that remain of the ardent patriots, prudent counsellors and brave warriors with whom you were associated in achieving our liberty. But you have looked round in vain for the faces of many who would have lived years of pleasure on a day like this, with their old companion in arms and brother in peril. Lincoln and Greene, Knox and Hamilton, are gone; the heroes of Saratoga and Yorktown have fallen before the only foe they could not meet. Above all, the first of heroes and of men, the friend of your youth, the

When Lafayette Came Back

more than friend of his country, rests in the bosom of the soil he redeemed. On the banks of his Potomac he lies in glory and in peace. You will revisit the hospitable shades of Mt. Vernon; but him whom you venerated as we did you will not meet at its door. His voice of consolation, which reached you in the Austrian dungeons, cannot now break its silence, to bid you welcome to his own roof. But the grateful children of America will bid you welcome in his name. Welcome! thrice welcome to our shores! And whithersoever throughout the limits of the continent your course shall take you, the ear that hears you shall bless you, the eye that sees you shall bear witness to you, and every tongue exclaim with heartfelt joy, Welcome! Welcome! Lafayette!"

Charlestown, Medford, Dorchester and Quincy were also visited by the General, but in each instance he returned to Boston to sleep. On the day before his departure from the city he dined in a marquee on Boston Common with twelve hundred people, probably the largest number ever seated at a single dinner-table in New England. Then on Tuesday morning he left the city, escorted by a troop of cavalry, to visit Portsmouth. Lynn, Marblehead and Salem did him honour on the way, the Lafayette Coffee House in the last-named city being the scene of his entertainment. Beverly, too, saluted him as he passed through to Ipswich, in which town he partook of a collation at the public house of Mr. Treadwell. Through Rowley to Newburyport went the distinguished Frenchman, and in the latter place he was entertained, as Washington had been before him, in what was formerly Nathaniel Tracy's mansion house and is now the Public Library.

Wednesday found him in Portsmouth, a guest at the elegant mansion house of Governor Langdon. Then he returned to Boston and prepared for a fresh start; New York, Washington and Philadelphia were still awaiting him! Thursday morning, accordingly, found the General passing through West Cambridge and Lexington on his way to Worcester and beyond. On the spot where the first blood of the Revolution was shed a marquee had been pitched, and here the guest of honour partook of refreshment. A similar entertainment was enjoyed at Concord, and that night the hero lodged with Mr. Wilder in Bolton, with whom he had

When Lafayette Came Back

a previous acquaintance. Friday morning he journeyed to Lancaster, where he greeted the surviving soldiers of the Revolution, as usual, and listened to an address delivered by the Rev. Dr. Thayer. Thence he pressed on to Worcester through Sterling and West Boylston. Judge Lincoln was his host in the shire town and the addresses, given and received, were most touching and sincere.

Bennett's Hotel, Hartford, now no longer a public house, honoured itself by honouring him, but because he had been detained overnight at Stafford by an accident to his carriage he could not stop in Connecticut's capital so long as he had intended to do, and about half past three set sail on the steamboat *Olliver Ellsworth* towards New York. At Middletown he left the steamer to salute the townspeople gathered in his honour, but by the time Saybrook, further down the river was reached, the General was fast asleep, worn out with the fatigue of his fortnight of festivity, and in spite of the disappointment of thousands he was not awakened. So, wrapped in needed slumber, he passed out of New England.

The following June, however, he was back again laying the corner-stone of Bunker

Among Old New England Inns

Hill monument to the accompaniment of Webster's matchless oration. And on this occasion he journeyed up into New Hampshire and was entertained at Dunbarton by the son of General Stark. In nearby Hopkinton (N. H.) he held a public reception in front of the Wiggin Tavern and was greeted, no doubt, by a large number of the town's citizens. Yet the only data that has come down to us about the day comes from an entry made by Miss Betsey P. Eaton, afterwards Mrs. Brockway, in her school dictionary: " June 22, 1825. Keeping school in this village this summer, and Esquire Chase called at the door saying LAFAYETTE was here, and wished me to dismiss the school that we might all have the pleasure of shaking hands with so distinguished a personage. His aids were Ignatius Sargent and Peter C. Brooks, citizens of Boston."

. . . . . .

To this time in our history, though in no way connected with Lafayette, belong several well-preserved Maine taverns of historic and staging interest. First place among these will undoubtedly be accorded to the house in Freeport, in which were

WIGGIN TAVERN, HOPKINTON

When Lafayette Came Back

signed the final papers separating Maine from Massachusetts. Built about a century and a quarter ago for Dr. John Hyde, a successful physician of that day, the house was afterwards sold to a landlord who made it famous as the Jameson Tavern. It was one of the principal stopping-places between Boston and Bangor, and many well-known men timed their journeys " down-east " so that they might enjoy the comfortable beds, good cuisine and excellent liquor this inn offered. For in those days Maine was not a prohibition district and the Jameson Tavern displayed a roomy bar in what is now the kitchen of Mrs. Charles Cushing's private residence.

The thing that chiefly distinguishes this house, however, is the fact that in its front northeast room there met in 1820 the commissioners who were empowered to make Maine a state. The representatives of both Maine and Massachusetts worked more than a fortnight here on the matter and in the end it was settled that Maine should give Massachusetts $180,000 for her part of the public lands in that state. Of this sum $30,000 was in Indian claims which Maine assumed, and the remaining $150,000 was to be paid in forty years with interest at five per cent. The commissioners which made this bargain included Timothy Bigelow of Groton, Massachusetts, Levi Lincoln of Worcester, Benjamin Porter of Topsham and James Bridge of Augusta, Maine. These four chose Silas Holman of Bolton, Massachusetts, and Lathrop Lewis of Gorham, Maine to complete the board. Negotiations had been begun, some time previous, by the three commissioners from Maine joined by Daniel Rose of the Senate and Nicholas Emery of the House and proceeding to Boston they had been met by the Massachusetts commissioners. It was only after a long session, during which the board sat at several towns and cities in Massachusetts that they met at Jameson Tavern in Freeport and signed the final papers.

Machias, Maine, has an old Burnham Tavern which has recently been purchased by the Daughters of the American Revolution, who will use it as a museum; and in the town of Durham, Maine, there stands a well-preserved house, now owned by Mr. Wesley Day, which is an excellent specimen of the better class of early public houses in that state.

JAMESON TAVERN, FREEPORT

When Lafayette Came Back

Bath, Maine's shipping city, is able to point with pride to the Shepard Inn, an old mansion which is still in the family of those who made it famous a century ago as a staging-house. The first sight that met the traveller who entered here early in the nineteenth century was a little window in the front hall which served as a bar, and over which were handed hot toddies, gin fizzes and many another delectable drink. Upstairs in those bygone days was a big room provided with a swinging partition. When a big banquet or a dance was being prepared for, this could be hooked up out of the way, but on ordinary occasions it divided the upper part of the house into two rooms, where as many temporary beds as might be needed could be set up for the accommodation of the travellers (mostly men) whom the big yellow coaches had brought to the door. The greatest treasure in the house, then as to-day, was the wallpaper of the north parlour. This was brought from Italy more than a century ago by Captain James Hall, a relative of the inn's original proprietor and is in coloured sheets about a yard square. One of the scenes depicted is the vatican of Rome.

Among Old New England Inns

With the passing of the stagecoach, however, this and hundreds of other old taverns closed their doors to the public for ever. They had served their time, and they quietly made way for a more bustling generation.

"No longer the host hobbles down from his rest
In the porches cool shadows to welcome his guest
With a smile of delight and a grasp of the hand
And a glance of the eye that no heart could withstand.

"When the long rains of Autumn set in from the west
The mirth of the landlord was broadest and best;
And the stranger who paused over night never knew
If the clock on the mantel struck ten or struck two.

"Oh the songs they would sing and the tales they would spin
As they lounged in the light of the old-fashioned inn;
But the day came at last when the stage brought no load
To the gate as it rolled up the long dusty road."

But though the age of the stagecoach has passed, the reign of the motor-car is now on, and dozens of vehicles draw up at the inn door in place of the single rumbling coach. Other times, other manners and not worse manners either, from the landlord's point of

SHEPARD INN, BATH

When Lafayette Came Back

view; for these merry loads of automobilists have good appetites and pay well for what is served them. Moreover, if they are graciously and hospitably received, they come again and again. There is, indeed, nothing they like better than journeying in twentieth century touring-cars among the old New England inns, whose proprietors have adapted their houses to meet modern demands.

THE END.

INDEX

Abbott, Miss Priscilla, 183.
Abbotts's Tavern, Andover, Mass., 182.
Adams, John, 37, 91, 93, 96, 154, 158, 209, 226, 286, 343.
Adams, John Quincy, 190, 266.
Adams, Helen Reddington, 120.
Adams, Colonel Herschel, 120.
Adams, Samuel, 98, 161.
Addison, 232.
Allen, Ethan, 70, 71.
Ames, Hon. Fisher, 212.
Ames, Nathaniel, tavern-keeper, 23, 209.
Amherst College, 53.
Amherst House, 52, 53.
Amory, Thomas, 361.
Anchor Tavern, Lynn, 67.
Andrews, John, tavern-keeper, 276.
Andros, Sir Edmund, 114.
Aplin, Joseph, 130.
Appleton, Hon. Nathan, 325.
Appleton, Samuel, 276.
Armitage, Joseph, tavern-keeper, 65, 66, 67.
Arms, David, 64.
Arnold, Eleazer, tavern-keeper, 140, 142.
Arnold, Peleg, tavern-keeper, 139, 140.
Arnold, Thomas, tavern-keeper, 139.
Arnold Tavern, Old Warwick, R. I., 132, 138.

Arnold's Tavern, Union Village, R. I., 139.
Arnold's Tavern, Weymouth, Mass., 113.
Austin, Samuel, tavern-keeper, 10.
Ayers, John, tavern-keeper, 348.
Baker, C. Alice, 63, 65.
Baker, Erastus, 65.
Baldwin Tavern, Shrewsbury, Mass., 37, 39, 40, 45.
Barker, Joshua, 85.
Barrett, James, 200.
Barnard's, 316.
Barnard, Salah, 64.
Barrington, Major, 137.
Barton, Major William, 132, 134, 135, 136, 139.
Beaucour, Chevalier, 346.
Beers, Isaac, tavern-keeper, 154.
Belcher, Gov. Jonathan, 55, 62.
Belchertown, 62.
Bell Tavern, Danvers, Mass., 234, 338, 340.
Bell Tavern, Portsmouth, N. H., 304, 306.
Bennett, John, tavern-keeper, 157.
Bennett's Hotel, Hartford, Conn., 365.
Bernard, Governor, 93.
Berry Tavern, Danvers Mass., 342.
Bigelow, Timothy, 200.

373

Index

Bishop, George, 289.
Black Horse Tavern, Concord, Mass., 110.
Black Horse Tavern, Marlborough, Mass., 195.
Blake, Capt. John, 270.
Blake, Henry T., 152.
Blay, Ruth, 303.
"Blew Anchor Tavern," Boston, 73, 74.
Blue Anchor Tavern, Cambridge, 223.
Blue Anchor Inn, Newburyport, 246.
Bliss's "Colonial Times on Buzzard's Bay," 72.
Blunt, Capt. John, 175.
Boltwood, Elijah, 52.
Boltwood, Solomon, 52.
Boltwood Tavern, 53.
Bonaparte, Jerome, 158.
Bourne, Garrett, 83.
Bowen, Col. Ephraim, 125, 128.
Bowen Inn, Barrington, R. I., 220.
Bowers Inn, 347.
Bowers, Capt. Josiah, tavern-keeper, 348.
Bowman, Daniel, 246.
Boyden's, 316.
Boynton Tavern, 272.
Brackett, Anthony, 99, 100.
Bradish's Tavern, Cambridge, 70.
Brewster, Charles W., 305.
Brewster, Col., 304.
Brick Inn, Lancaster, Mass., 344.
Bridge, James, 368.
Briggs, Sam., 213.
Brigham's Hotel, 358.
Brigham's Tavern, Westborough, 224.
British Coffee House, 91, 92.
Brookfield, 56, 60, 62.
Brooklyn, Conn., 236.
Brooks, Peter C., 366.

Brown, Jacob, tavern-keeper, 152.
Brown, John, 125.
Browne, Rev. Edmund, 191.
Bucklin, Joseph, 127.
Buckman Tavern, The, 107.
Buckminster, Rev. Joseph, 339.
Bulfinch, Charles, 361.
Bull, Ole, 204.
Bulkeley, Rev. Peter, 109.
Bunch of Grapes Tavern, 75, 85, 88, 89, 91, 313.
Burdick, Benjamin, 96.
Burgoyne, Gen., 334.
Burnett, Governor William, 86.
Buss, Sergeant William, 108.

Carr, Sir Robert, 77.
Calder, Robert, 262.
Caldwell, William, tavern-keeper, 265.
Catamount Tavern, Bennington, Vt., 71.
Chapin, Erastus, 157.
Chartres, Duchess de, 309, 310.
Chase, George Wingate, 178.
Chastellux, Marquis de, 99, 156, 256.
Christophers, Christopher, 35.
Church, Doctor, 97.
Clark, Andrew, tavern-keeper, 150.
Clark's Hotel, 185.
Clauson, John, 4.
Clifford's Tavern, Dunbarton, N. H., 71.
Clinton, Sir Henry, 132.
Coburn, Jacob, tavern-keeper, 264.
Coffin, Dr. Charles, 243.
Coffin, Col. Joseph, 243.
Coffin, Joshua, 243, 245.
Coffin, Nathaniel, 243.
Coffin, Rev. Paul, D. D., 243.

374

Index

Coffin, Tristram, Jr., 243.
Coffin, William, tavern-keeper, 85.
Coffyn, Dionis, 242.
Coffyn, Tristram, Sr., tavern-keeper, 242.
Cold Spring, 56, 62.
Cole, Samuel, tavern-keeper, 74.
Coles, Robert, 10.
Colonial Inn, Concord, Mass., 108.
Concord, N. H., 312.
Conkey's Tavern, Pelham, Mass., 43.
Cooper's Tavern, Arlington, 112.
Cordis's, 91.
Cornwallis, Lord, 237.
Cory, Samuel, 138.
Craft, Colonel, 89.
Craven, Lady, 100.
Cromwell, Oliver, 68, 76, 78, 100.
Cromwell's Head Tavern, Boston, 99.
Currier, John J., 253.
Cushing, Zenas, 170.

Dalton, Hon. Tristram, 171.
Dana, Rev. Samuel, 327.
Danvers, Mass., 234.
Davenport, Anthony, tavern-keeper, 256.
Davenport, George, 254.
Davenport, Moses, tavern-keeper, 256.
Davenport, William, tavern-keeper, 251, 255, 256.
Davenport's, 316.
Day, Wesley, 368.
Deerfield, 55, 57, 58, 65.
Dexter, Timothy, 264.
Dickinson, Joel, 52.
Dinwiddie, Governor, 100.
Drake, Samuel Adams, 87.
Drown, Solomon, Jr., 131.
Dudingston, Lieut. William, 122, 123, 124, 126, 127, 128, 129.
Duggan, John, tavern-keeper, 229.
Dunbarton, N. H., 71, 366.
Dunton, John, 68, 69, 73, 280.
Durham, Maine, 368.
Duxbury, Tavern at, 11.
Dwight's, Col., Brookfield, 56.
Dwight, Theodore, 35.

Eagle Tavern, 331.
Earl of Halifax Tavern, 295, 298.
Earle, Alice Morse, 72, 224.
Earl's, 316.
Eastern Stage House, 320.
East Poultney, Vt., 331.
Eaton, Betsey P., 366.
Edwards, Jonathan, 62, 153.
Edwards, Judge Pierpont, 342.
Ellery Tavern, Gloucester, 222.
Emery, Nicholas, 368.
Endicott, Gov., 65, 66, 286.
Essex Coffee House, 239.
Eustis, Gov., 361.
Everett, Edward, 361.
Exchange Coffee House, Boston, 361.
Exchange Hotel, Worcester, 51.

Fairbanks, Mrs. S. A., 45.
Faneuil Hall, 361.
Farnsworth, Thomas Tread-well, tavern-keeper, 328.
Farrar, Major John, 37.
Farrar's Tavern, Shrews-bury, Mass., 37, 50.
Fearing, Benjamin, tavern-keeper, 71, 72.
Felt, J. B., 169.
Field, Edward, 130, 143, 214.
Fields, James T., 203.
Fisher, Joshua, tavern-keeper, 210.

Index

Fisher's Tavern, Dedham, 211.
Flagg, John, tavern-keeper, 160.
Foot, Asa, tavern-keeper, 314.
Fort Sewall, Marblehead, 335.
Foster, William, 85.
Fowler, Landlord, 334.
Fowler, Henry, 6.
Frankland, Sir Harry, 225, 335, 338.
Franklin, Benjamin, 308.
Frary, House, 63.
Freeport, Me., 366.

Gage, General, 106.
Gaspee, 122, 125, 126, 127, 129.
Gerry, Elbridge, 186, 302.
Golden Ball Inn, Providence, R. I., 188, 189.
Golden Ball Tavern, Weston, Mass., 104, 106, 233.
Goodman, Richard, tavern-keeper, 218.
Goodrich, Elijah P., 267.
Greeley, Horace, 331.
Green Dragon Tavern, 96, 97, 99.
Greenleaf, Edmund, tavern-keeper, 241, 243.
Greenwich, Conn., 114.
Greyhound Tavern, 19.
Grimes, Old, 40.
Groton Inn, 328.
Gunnison, Hugh, tavern-keeper, 13, 75, 76.

Hadley, 56, 60.
Hale, Thomas, 19, 241.
Hall, Capt. Basil, 220, 231.
Hall, Capt. James, 369.
Hall, Henry F., 185.
Hancock, Governor, 98, 159, 162, 164, 166, 167, 229, 302.
Hancock, Madame, 165.

Hancock Tavern, Boston, 102.
Harrington, Phineas, 325.
Hatch, Israel, 312.
Hatfield, 57, 59.
Hathorne, J. H., 322.
Haven's Tavern, North Kingston, R. I., 29.
Hawthorne, Nathaniel, 207, 234.
Hayward, John, tavern-keeper, 110.
Heard, Augustine, 170.
Heard, John, 170.
Hernton, John, 5.
"Hester Prynne," 234.
Hilton, Martha, 175, 297.
Hitchcock, David, 158.
Hoar, Judge E. Rockwell, 111.
Hoar, Joseph, tavern-keeper, 328.
Hodgson, Adam, 221.
Holman, Silas, 368.
Holmes, Francis, tavern-keeper, 85.
Homan, Capt. Richard, 170.
Hopkins, Capt. John B., 126.
Hopkins, Chief Justice, 123.
Hopkinton, Mass., 237.
Hopkinton, N. H., 235, 312, 366.
Houghton, John, tavern-keeper, 215, 216.
How, Adam, tavern-keeper, 202.
How, David, tavern-keeper, 194.
How, Ezekial, tavern-keeper, 195.
How, John, 104, 108.
How, John, tavern-keeper, 192, 193.
How, Increase, tavern-keeper, 170.
Howe, Rev. Joseph, 339.
Howe, Lyman, tavern-keeper, 203.

Index

Howells, William Dean, 343.
Hudson, William, Sr., tavern-keeper, 75.
Hudson, William, Jr., tavern-keeper, 76, 77.
Hunt, John, 136.
Hurtleberry Hill, Concord, Mass., 345.
Hutchinson, Governor, 84.
Hutchinson, Thomas, 77.
Hyde, Dr. John, 367.

Illsley House, 251.
Illsley, Stephen, Jr., 251.
Ingersoll, Colonel, 85.
Ingersoll's, 165.
Ipswich, 169, 208, 247, 274-291, 343.

Jackson, Hon. Jonathan, 173.
Jacob's Inn, 184.
Jameson Tavern, 367.
Jewett, Sarah Orne, 307.
Joel Smith Tavern, Weston, Mass., 105.
Jones, Captain, tavern-keeper, 104, 107.
Jones, Col. Elisha, 107.
Jones, Ephraim, tavern-keeper, 110.
Jones, John Paul, 99, 306, 307, 308, 309, 310.
Josselyn, John, 8.

Kellogg's, Hadley Ferry, 59, 218.
Kemble, Captain, 22.
Keep, Capt. Jonathan, tavern-keeper, 327.
King's Arms, Boston, 13, 75.
Knapp Tavern, 114, 118, 119.
Knapp, Timothy, 115.
Knight, Sarah, 21 et seq., 219.

Lafayette, 42, 51, 85, 90, 158, 189, 197, 266, 301, 351-366.

Lafayette Coffee Houses, Salem, Mass., 364.
Lafayette Hotel, Boston, 358.
Lambert, John, 330.
Lambert, William, tavern-keeper, 262.
Lancaster, Mass., 343.
Langdon, Mary, 307.
Larned's Tavern, Watertown, 56.
Lawrence Tavern, 236.
La Tour, 9.
Lear, Tobias, 176, 177, 178.
Leary, Robert, tavern-keeper, 7.
Lee, Gen. Charles, 132, 133, 139.
Leicester, 56, 60.
Leverett, Governor, 78.
Lewis, Lathrop, 368.
Liberty Tree Tavern, 83.
Lincoln, Levi, 368.
Lincoln's "History of Worcester," 44.
Lindsay, Benjamin, 124.
Littleton, Mass., 236.
Livingston, Elizabeth, 34, 35.
Livingston, Madam, 33.
Locke, Samuel, 183.
Longfellow, Henry Wadsworth, 191, 192, 194, 203, 205, 206.
Lord, Caleb, 285.
Lord House, Portsmouth, N. H., 307.
Lovewell, Capt., 346.
Low, Nathaniel, 251.
Lumpkin, Richard, tavern-keeper, 278.
Lunt, Major Ezra, tavern-keeper, 262.

Machias, Me., 368.
Marblehead, 335.
March, Hugh, tavern-keeper, 245, 247, 250.
March, Paul, tavern-keeper, 305.

Index

Marlboro Hotel, Boston, 318, 319.
Marlborough, Earl of, 75.
Marlborough, Mass., 56, 61.
Marshall, Thomas, tavern-keeper, 68, 69.
Marston, John, tavern-keeper, 85, 90.
Mather, Cotton, 15.
Mather, Samuel, 22, 225.
Mawney, John, 127, 129.
Mead, Jonathan, 117.
Mellish, John, 328.
Milford, Conn., 150.
Miller's, 316.
Molesworth, Captain Ponsonby, 81.
Molyneux, William, 93.
Monk, George, tavern-keeper, 73.
Montague, Admiral, 124.
Montesquieu, M. Lynch de, 256.
Monti, Luigi, 204.
Moores, Samuel, 241.
Morris, Robert, 306.
Morse's Hotel, New Haven, 354.
Mowry Tavern, 121.
Mowry, Landlord, 3, 5, 6.
Munroe, President, 190.
Munroe, Thomas, 111.
Munroe Tavern, Lexington, 112.

Newburyport, 170, 172, 236, 241-273.
Newburyport Marine Society, 253.
New Ipswich, N. H., 324.
Nichols, Mrs. Charles, 347.
Noble, Mark, 298, 301.
Norcross, Frederic Walter, 87.
Northampton, 57, 60, 62.
Northey, Abijah, 168.
Northfield, 59.

Oliver, Andrew, 84.
Otis, James, 91, 93, 94, 95, 96.
Overing House, 133, 135.

Packer, Thomas, 303.
Paine, General, 107.
Parker, Captain, 107.
Parsons, David, 52.
Parsons, Gideon, 52.
Parsons, Joseph, 64.
Parsons, T. W., 204.
Parsons, Zenas, tavern-keeper, 157.
Patterson's, 316.
Paxton, Gen. Charles, 209, 237.
Paxton, Mass., 237, 238.
Pearson, Ebenezer, tavern-keeper, 267.
Pease, Levi, tavern-keeper, 36, 48, 50, 51, 160, 209, 311.
Pease Tavern, Shrewsbury, Mass., 37.
Pecker, Bart, 181.
Pengry, Deacon Moses, tavern-keeper, 275, 276.
Perkins Inn, Hopkinton, N. H., 236.
Perkins Tavern, Ashford, Conn., 185.
Perkins, Thomas, tavern-keeper, 259.
Phillippe, Louis, 302.
Phillips, Bridget, 268.
Phillips, Henry, 80.
Phips, Sir William, 86.
Pickman, 266.
Pitcairn, Major, 107, 110.
Pitt, William, 236, 301.
Plumer, Francis, tavern-keeper, 241.
Pollard's Tavern, Boston, 239.
Porter, Benjamin, 368.
Porter's Tavern, Cambridge, 69.

Index

Portsmouth, N. H., 174, 236, 292-310.
Pottle, William, Jr., 299.
Pownall, Governor, 86.
Prentice, Rev. John, 218.
Prescott, Gen., 132, 133, 137, 138.
Preston, Captain, 82.
Price, Henry, 88.
Price, Ezekial, 214.
Prince, James, 264.
Prudence Island, 135.
Pullin, Richard, tavern-keeper, 96.
Punch Bowl Tavern, Brookline, Mass., 231.
Purcell, Landlord, 306.
Putnam Cottage, 114.
Putnam, Deacon Gideon, tavern-keeper, 343.
Putnam, Gen. Israel, 114, 236.
Putnam, Gen. Rufus, 90.
Putnam, Oliver, 251.
Putnam's Hill, Greenwich, Conn., 353.
Pynchon, Capt. John, 219.

Quincy, Josiah, 47, 352, 362.

Red Horse Tavern, Sudbury, 191.
Revere, Paul, 96, 100, 107.
Rice, Reuben, 111.
Rice, Henry, 188.
Richardson, Captain Jephthah, tavern-keeper, 327.
Richardson's Tavern, Groton, Mass., 324.
Riedesel, Gen., 334.
Ringe, Daniel, tavern-keeper, 277.
Robbins's, 323.
Roberts, Robert, tavern-keeper, 274.
Robinson, Commissioner, 92, 96.

Rochefoucault, Duke de la, 160.
Rockwood, Harvey, 53.
Rogers, Homer, 195.
"Romance of Old New England Churches," 20, 62, 339.
"Romance of Old New England Roof-Trees," 197, 297.
Rose, Daniel, 368.
Ross Tavern, Ipswich, 291.
Royal Exchange, 79, 81, 83.
Rutan's Hotel, 72.

Scott, Madame, 359.
St. George Tavern, Boston, 101.
Sabin Tavern, 122, 124, 126.
Salem, 167.
Saltonstall, Rev. Gurdon, 30.
Saltonstall, Nathaniel, 15.
Sawtell's Tavern, Shirley, Mass., 113.
Sawtell, Obadiah, tavern-keeper, 113.
Scot's Tavern, 60, 158.
Sessions, Darius, 123.
Salter, Aeneas, 18.
Sargent, Ignatius, 366.
Sawyer's, 266.
Sewall, Samuel, 17, 19, 20.
Sewall's Diary, 17, 208.
Shays, Captain Daniel, 43, 45.
Shays Rebellion, The, 42, 45.
Sheaffe, Susanna, 81.
Shepard Inn, Bath, Me., 369.
Sherman, Roger, 151, 154.
Ship Tavern, Boston, 77, 78.
Shirley, Governor, 101.
Shrewsbury, Mass., 36, 50, 56, 61.
Simond's Hotel, Charlestown, 321.
Smith, Aaron, 42, 52.
Smith, Sarah, 64.
Somerby, Henry, 243.
Southworth, Constant, tavern-keeper, 11.
Spencer, 159.

Index

Spencer, General, 139.
Spofford, Mrs. Harriett Prescott, 267.
Springfield, 60.
Stacey, John, tavern-keeper, 290.
Stanton, Col. Joseph, 132, 134.
Stanwood, Joseph, 254.
Stark, Gen. John, 89, 366.
Stavers, Bartholomew, 292, 295.
Stavers, John, tavern-keeper, 292, 295, 297.
Stetson, Prince, tavern-keeper, 259, 265.
Stevens, James, tavern-keeper, 223.
Stewart, Landlord, 281.
Stiles, Rev. Ezra, 70.
Stockbridge, 233.
Stocker, Captain Ebenezer, 263.
Stone's City Tavern, Boston, 319.
Stratford Ferry, 49.
Sudbury, 56, 61.
Sunderland, 59.
Sun Hotel, Newburyport, 264.
Surriage, Agnes, 225, 335.
Swasey House, Ipswich, 291.
Swasey, Major Joseph, 170.
Swasey, Susanna, tavern-keeper, 170.
Sykes, Colonel Reuben, 46, 51.
Symonds, Francis, tavern-keeper, 235.

Taft's Inn, 183.
Talleyrand, Baron de, 256.
Talleyrand, 102.
Tilton, Jacob, tavern-keeper, 305.
Titcomb, Jonathan, 271.
Tracy, John, 257.
Tracy, Nathaniel, 172, 264.

Tripp, John, 220.
Trowbridge, Caleb, Jr., 326.
Tucker, William E., 170.
Turner, Robert, 74.
Twining, Thomas, 311.

Upshall, Nicholas, 79.
United States Arms, 51.
Upton Tavern, 45.

Vane, Governor, 75.
Vardy, Luke, tavern-keeper, 79, 81.
Vaudereuil, M. de, 256.
Vila, James, 85.
Vyall, John, 1, 77.

Wade, Jonathan, 277.
Wadsworth Inn, Hartford, Conn., 315.
Wales, Henry Ware, 204.
Walker, Thomas, 340.
Walker's Tavern, Charlestown, N. H., 237.
Wallace, tavern-keeper, 18.
Walpole, 313.
Wanton, Governor, 123.
Ward, General Artemas, 39, 44.
Ward's "Old Times in Shrewsbury," 50.
Wardwell, Jonathan, 294.
Wardwell, Lydia, 287, 290.
Warren, James, 271.
Warwick Neck, R. I., 135, 138.
Washington, George, 37, 51, 100, 101, 148-190, 201, 260, 302.
Washington Hotel, Newburyport, 265.
Watertown, 56, 61.
Watson, Capt. William, tavern-keeper, 331.
Waumanitt, 5, 6.
Wayside Inn, Sudbury, Mass., 116.
Webster, Daniel, 96, 267, 366.

Index

Wells, Me., Tavern at, 11.
Wentworth Arms, Newburyport, 262.
Wentworth, Gov. Benning, 297.
Wentworth, Col. Michael, 175.
West Brookfield Tavern, 117, 158.
Westcarr, Dr. John, 219.
Westfield, Mass., 334.
Weston, 56.
Whipple, Capt. Abraham, 126, 127.
Whipple, John, tavern-keeper, 12.
Whipple, John, 277.
White, Capt. John, tavern-keeper, 346.
White, John, 179.
Whitman, Elizabeth, 234, 339.
Whitman, Rev. Elnathan, 339.
Whitman, Valentine, 6.
Whittier, John Greenleaf, 288.
Wigglesworth, Edward, 257.
Wiggin Tavern, 235, 366.
Wilder, Nathaniel, tavern-keeper, 215, 345.
Wilder, Dr. Josiah, 347.
Wild's, 316.
Wilde's, 319.

Willard, Major Simon, 109.
Willey, Zebulon, 175.
Williams, Abraham, tavern-keeper, 160.
Williams, Eleazer, tavern-keeper, 157.
Williams, Job, 85.
Williams, Rev. John, 64.
Williams, Roger, 4, 6.
Williams Tavern, Marlboro, Mass., 116, 160.
Winn, Lieut. Joseph, tavern-keeper, 209, 229.
Winship, Jason, 112.
Winthrop, Gov., 7, 9, 75.
Wolfe, General, 236, 252.
Wolfe Tavern, Newburyport, 236, 251, 253, 255, 265.
Woodbridge, Benjamin, 80.
Woodward, Richard, tavern-keeper, 212.
Worcester, 56, 61.
Worcester Society of Antiquity, 237.
Wright, Amos, tavern-keeper, 111.
Wright Tavern, The, Concord, Mass., 110.
Wyman, Jabez, 112.

Yeaton, Hopley, 298.
York, Maine, 236.

www.ingramcontent.com/pod-product-compliance
Lightning Source LLC
Chambersburg PA
CBHW050245230426
43664CB00012B/1835